FORGED IN
Faith

W9-BRM-942

How Faith Shaped *the* Birth *of the* Nation 1607–1776

FORGED IN Faith

ROD GRAGG

HOWARD BOOKS
A Division of Simon & Schuster, Inc.

NEW YORK NASHVILLE LONDON TORONTO SYDNEY

For my wife, Cindy,
with love

Published by Howard Books, a division of Simon & Schuster, Inc.
1230 Avenue of the Americas, New York, NY 10020

Copyright © 2010 by Rod Gragg

All rights reserved, including the right to reproduce this book or portions thereof in any form whatsoever. For information, address Howard Subsidiary Rights Department, 1230 Avenue of the Americas, New York, NY 10020.

In association with Lee Hough and the literary agency of Alive Communications

First Howard Books trade paperback edition May 2011

HOWARD and colophon are registered trademarks of Simon & Schuster, Inc.

For information regarding special discounts for bulk purchases,
please contact Simon & Schuster Special Sales at 1-866-506-1949
or business@simonandschuster.com.

The Simon & Schuster Speakers Bureau can bring authors to
your live event. For more information or to book an event,
contact the Simon & Schuster Speakers Bureau at 1-866-248-3049
or visit our website at www.simonspeakers.com.

Edited by Between the Lines
Cover design by Faceout Studio
Interior design by Jaime Putorti

Manufactured in the United States of America

10 9 8 7 6 5 4 3 2 1

Library of Congress Cataloging-in-Publication Data

ISBN 978-1-4165-9629-5
ISBN 978-1-4516-2350-5 (pbk)
ISBN 978-1-4391-6692-5 (ebook)

All Scripture quoted in this work is from the King James Version of the Bible.

O! Lord our heavenly Father, King of kings and Lord of lords . . . look down in mercy, we beseech thee; on these our American States who have fled to thee from the rod of the oppressor and thrown themselves upon thy gracious protection, desiring henceforth to be dependent only on thee. . . .

—Official Prayer of the First Continental Congress, September 7, 1774

Blessed is the nation whose God is the LORD *and the people whom he hath chosen for his own inheritance.*

—Psalm 33:12

CONTENTS

INTRODUCTION

He was old now—white-headed and weather-faced—but his memories were rich. He had been present at creation—at the birth of the nation. What scenes he had witnessed: Stamp Act protests, rousing debates in the Massachusetts legislature, ministers passionately preaching freedom from the pulpit, crowds crying, "No taxation without representation!"—and tons of tea spreading like brown ink in Boston Harbor. He had almost been captured by British troops at Lexington in 1775, when the shots were fired that changed the world. He had served as a delegate to the Continental Congress—as the most famous man there, by some estimates. He could remember the faces, the voices, the votes for independence—and the fresh, new appearance of the Declaration of Independence, which bore his signature.[1]

He was Samuel Adams, and in March 1797 he was seventy-four years old. He had served God and the people almost his entire life, and he was not finished yet. Not quite. He had been a political writer, an agitator, a legislator, a signer of the Declaration of Independence, a principal founding father, a member of the Massachusetts convention that ratified the U.S. Constitution, the lieutenant governor of Massachusetts—and now, in his final years, he was the state's governor. He had seen so much—a grand, sweeping survey of America-in-the-making—and yet, he still had important duties to perform.[2]

One of them was before him now. It was his responsibility as governor to issue an official proclamation for the commonwealth of Massachusetts. This was no frivolous public statement. It did not resemble future proclamations issued by governors to promote tourism, celebrate sports victories, or recognize beauty queens, state fairs, and cooking festivals. On March 20, 1797, founding father Samuel Adams, now governor of Massachusetts, issued an official state proclamation calling for a "Day of Solemn Fasting and Prayer" in Massachusetts.[3]

It was not an unusual government action in eighteenth-century America: legislatures, governors, and the American Congress had officially called for days of thanksgiving and had set aside official days for prayer and fasting. On the designated days, normal activities ceased in most places. Businesses closed. Traffic disappeared. Countless Americans assembled in their churches. Ministers of the Gospel, the most respected professionals in America, led them in worship, confessing sins, giving thanks, and respectfully imploring the blessings of Almighty God.[4]

Adams now did so again. With the "advice and consent" of the state legislature, he officially proclaimed that a day in May would be set aside throughout Massachusetts "for the purpose of public fasting and prayer." On that day, "Ministers of the Gospel, with their respected congregations" were asked to "assemble together and seriously consider, and with one united voice confess our past sins and transgressions, with holy resolutions, by the Grace of God, to turn our feet into the path of His Law—Humbly beseeching Him to endue us with all the Christian spirit of Piety, Benevolence and the Love of our Country; and that in all our public deliberations we may be possessed of a sacred regard to the fundamental principles of our free elective civil Constitutions. . . ."[5]

As governor, Adams also called on the people of Massachusetts to pray for the state's businesses, its industry, its education system, for the other American states, and for the national government. "And I do hereby recommend," he added, "that all unnecessary labour and recreation may be suspended on the said day." The proclamation concluded with an official request that would undoubtedly seem startling to many in a distant, future America:

> *I concede that we cannot better express ourselves than by humbly supplicating the Supreme Ruler of the World—That the rod of tyrants may be broken into pieces, and the oppressed made Free—That wars may cease in all the Earth, and that the confusions that are and have been among the Nations may be overruled for the promoting and speedily bringing on that holy and happy period, when the Kingdom of our Lord and Saviour Jesus Christ may be everywhere established, and all the people willingly bow to the Sceptre of Him who is the Prince of Peace.*[6]

By issuing such an official proclamation, were the governor and legislature of Massachusetts violating the United States Constitution? Not to their thinking. Samuel Adams had signed the Declaration of Independence and had voted to ratify the U.S. Constitution. Therefore, he not only understood the original intent of America's founding documents—he had helped *make* them. So had many others in his day, and they too had crafted, assisted, or observed Fast Day proclamations such as the one Samuel Adams issued in 1797. For them, America's foundation of faith was common knowledge, and they viewed American liberty as a legacy of the Judeo-Christian worldview. In their day, it was an accepted fact that American and English law were based on the Higher Law of the Bible—and so were America's founding documents.[7]

"The general principles on which the fathers achieved independence, were the only principles in which that beautiful assembly of young gentlemen could unite," wrote founding father John Adams. "And what were these general principles? I answer, the general principles of Christianity. . . ." America's founding fathers, however, did not act alone: their decisive, deliberate actions reflected the common values of the people they represented. *They* were the real founding fathers—the people of Colonial America whose values forged the nation. Today, they are largely forgotten. So too are many of the key events that motivated them, such as the Great Awakening, and many of the leaders who inspired them, such as Jonathan Edwards, Samuel Davies, George Whitefield, even Samuel Adams. Fading too among the American public is awareness of the nation's founding values, such as Higher Law and inalienable rights.[8]

Some modern historians, such as the Jewish scholar Abraham Katsh, have labored mightily to preserve a record of America's faith-based founding. Of the Declaration of Independence and the United States Constitution, Katsh wrote: "there runs through these two prime instruments of American government the deeper meaning and higher purpose of a constant regard for principles and religious ideas, based on a profound sympathy with the Scriptures. . . ." The historical record is clear: America was forged on faith. But is that foundational fact common knowledge in contemporary America? Or has it been cast aside amid the clutter of modern distractions? Or perhaps lost by the neglect of the disinterested?[9]

In a contemporary classroom survey of upper-level American university students, all demonstrated extensive knowledge of popular culture—music and musicians, actors and actresses, star performers of the NBA, NFL, and NASCAR. They correctly identified the leading contestants in a televised talent show and the titles of contemporary motion pictures. When queried on topics from American history, all demonstrated a general knowledge that was decidedly superior to the random on-the-street interviews frequently cited in the modern news media. Fewer than 10 percent, however, correctly identified Jonathan Edwards. One percent knew of George Whitefield. Twice as many thought Samuel Adams was an alcoholic beverage rather than a founding father. One percent recognized the Great Awakening. None—not one—was able to correctly identify John Calvin's *Institutes* or apparently had ever heard of Higher Law.[10]

A century after his death, New England theologian Jonathan Edwards, whose 1741 sermon launched the Great Awakening, was deemed so important that Harvard historian George Bancroft devoted numerous pages to him in his epic *History of the United States of America*. Fifty years later, in the early twentieth century, Pulitzer Prize–winning historian Edward Channing depicted Edwards as a "keen intellect" who "united wonderful skill in the use of language and remarkable power of expression." In the same era, *Encyclopaedia Britannica* described Edwards as "an earnest, devout Christian and a man of blameless life," who had achieved a "great work" of scholarship. When New York University established the nationally acclaimed Hall of Fame for Great Americans in 1901, Edwards was honored as one of its first inductees, and was enshrined alongside George Washington, John Adams, and Thomas Jefferson.[11]

By the twenty-first century, however, Americans and their heroes had changed. Jonathan Edwards was now unknown to most and discredited by others. In contrast to the respectful treatment Edwards had received from biographers a century earlier, he was now denounced for "high-handedness and bigotry" by a leading online student encyclopedia. The famous sermon that sparked the Great Awakening was dismissed as an "appeal to religious fear," and the faith in Christ inspired by his preaching was belittled as emotional "convulsions and hysteria." As for the Great Awakening—the unprecedented revival that inspired American independence? It was merely an odd "religious frenzy," the encyclopedia's student readers were informed, which spun "out of control" and stifled "liberal interpretation of doctrine."[12]

As the American national consensus shifts from a traditional, God-centered worldview to a secular, man-centered philosophy, perspectives and priorities change. History, however, does not. It may be ignored, reinterpreted, revised, or even concealed, but the historical evidence remains unchanged: America was forged in faith. Those extraordinary people who forged it—the people of Colonial America—hoped that cornerstone foundation and its history would always be preserved. Some, however, feared that someday America's historic faith might be diminished—along with the freedom it inspired. "While the People are virtuous they cannot be subdued," Samuel Adams wrote, "but when once they lose their Virtue, they will be ready to surrender their Liberties. . . ."[13]

CHAPTER 1

"Plead Our Cause, O Lord"

Already they were bickering. It was day two of the First Continental Congress—Tuesday, September 6, 1774. Delegates from twelve of America's thirteen colonies had assembled at Carpenters' Hall in Philadelphia to officially react to deteriorating relations between Great Britain and its American colonies. Decades of disagreement had led to a tense crisis between the colonies and the Mother Country. In an attempt to resolve the issues, the colonies had dispatched delegations to Philadelphia's grand assembly, which was the first of its kind in America. Opening deliberations had been cordial and productive. The delegates had voted to call their assembly the "Continental Congress," had appointed Virginia delegate Peyton Randolph as its president, and had agreed to meet in Philadelphia's Carpenters' Hall. Then came day two—and the opening display of cooperation sank into a mire of argument.[1]

At issue was the question of how to count votes. Large colonies wanted their large populations to count for more. Small colonies wanted equal representation. Amid the debate, Philadelphia's church bells began tolling at the news that British forces were bombarding the city of Boston. It was a false alarm, but it added to an atmosphere of anxiety in Congress. The dark mood may have been heightened by the deadly risk each delegate faced by simply being there. The unprecedented assembly was unauthorized by Britain's King George III or the British Parliament. Among the delegates in attendance were men who believed the British government's treatment of the American colonies amounted to tyranny. Such politics were deemed treasonous by some, and the delegates undoubtedly knew what grisly fate sometimes befell traitors to the Crown.[2]

If arrested and convicted of high treason, a delegate might find himself in Great Britain's notorious Tower of London, waiting to be "drawn and quartered." If so sentenced, he would first be hanged until almost dead, then cut down and disemboweled. While still alive, he would be forced to watch his intestines burned. Then, one by one, other bodily organs would be torturously removed until death finally occurred. Afterward, his corpse would be beheaded and his torso cut into quarters. Finally, his head would be publicly mounted on a post. "Let us prepare for the worst," New Jersey delegate Abraham Clark at one point advised a colleague; "we can Die here but once." Debate on how to count votes concluded with a consensus—a single vote for each delegation—but the tension among delegates led some to fear that the Continental Congress might dissolve in disunity.[3]

Then Massachusetts delegate Thomas Cushing made a motion. Cushing was a forty-nine-year-old Boston lawyer, a Harvard alumnus, and a successful merchant. A member of the Massachusetts Committee of Safety, he was a prominent champion of Colonial political rights—always "busy in the interest of liberty," according to a colleague. He observed the second day's tense deliberations with the savvy of a seasoned statesman—then he acted. From now on, Cushing formally proposed, Congress should officially open its day with prayer. The motion reflected Cushing's personal faith—he was a deacon at Boston's Old South Congregational Church—and it also reflected the common faith of most delegates. Even so, Cushing's motion for prayer provoked an immediate challenge.[4]

Concerns were voiced by John Rutledge of South Carolina and John Jay of New York. A thirty-five-year-old London-educated attorney, Rutledge was renowned for his eloquence and political acumen. The older of two brothers in the South Carolina delegation, he would eventually become his state's governor and later the chief justice of the U.S. Supreme Court. He was anything but a critic of Christianity: tutored by clergymen as a child, he was an Anglican who worshipped at Charleston's St. Michael's Church.[5]

John Jay was also a believer. At twenty-eight, the New York attorney was a prominent member of New York City's Trinity Church. Descended from French Huguenots who had been driven from Europe for their Protestant faith, he would eventually become president of the American Bible Society. Like Rutledge, he too would someday become a governor and a U.S. chief justice, and—like Rutledge—he made no argument for separation of church and state. They were merely concerned that a congressional prayer might increase disunity because so many Christian denominations were represented in Congress. Could the delegates unite in a congressional act of worship?[6]

Massachusetts delegate Samuel Adams believed so—and he quickly rose to support Cushing's prayer motion. By almost any measure, Sam Adams was the most famous advocate of Colonial rights in America—and the most controversial. Politics was his passion, and he was a master of the craft. An instrumental leader in the Massachusetts legislature, he was viewed by many as Colonial America's leading defender, but Britain's leaders called him an "angel of darkness." He too was devout. Raised in a family of committed Christians, he had considered the ministry in his youth. Now, as a middle-aged Calvinist, he took his faith seriously, and was said to possess "the dogmatism of a priest."[7]

He was "no Bigot," Sam Adams told his fellow delegates. He "could hear a Prayer from a Gentleman of Piety and Virtue, who was at the same Time a Friend to his Country"—and he heartily endorsed the call to congressional prayer. Congress agreed—and promptly passed Cushing's motion. Beginning the next day, the Continental Congress would officially open every day's session with prayer. But who would be the first to pray? In an obvious display of congressional unity, Samuel Adams, a Puritan Congregationalist, nominated an Anglican clergyman to offer the first official prayer. Congress approved his nomination and promptly sent an invitation to the selected minister.[8]

His name was Jacob Duché, and at age thirty-seven, he may have been the most popular preacher in Philadelphia. The Anglican pastor of Philadelphia's prestigious Christ Church, Duché was the son of a former Philadelphia mayor and brother-in-law to congressional delegate Francis Hopkinson. A graduate of Cambridge University, he was well educated, served as professor of oratory at the College of Philadelphia, and was renowned for his eloquence in the pulpit. The invitation to open Congress with prayer was a measure of his prominence, but carried genuine risk: Duché was a minister in the Church of England, Britain's official state church, and accepting the invitation could have put him in harm's way with the British government. He accepted anyway.[9]

The next morning—Wednesday, September 7, 1774—the pastor appeared before the delegates attired in Anglican clergyman's robes. When the Congress was called to order, he opened the day's session with a formal prayer, then followed it by reading from the Bible. The Bible passage Duché read was the Anglican "collect" for the day—the scripture scheduled for that day in the Anglican Book of Common Prayer—Psalm 35:

> *Plead my cause, O LORD, with them that strive with me: fight against them that fight against me. Take hold of shield and buckler, and stand up for mine help. Draw out also the spear,*

and stop the way against them that persecute me: say unto my soul, I am thy salvation.

Let them be confounded and put to shame that seek after my soul: let them be turned back and brought to confusion that devise my hurt. Let them be as chaff before the wind: and let the angel of the LORD *chase them. Let their way be dark and slippery: and let the angel of the* LORD *persecute them.*

For without cause have they hid for me their net in a pit, which without cause they have digged for my soul. Let destruction come upon him at unawares; and let his net that he hath hid catch himself: into that very destruction let him fall. And my soul shall be joyful in the LORD*: it shall rejoice in his salvation. . . . Let them be ashamed and brought to confusion together that rejoice at mine hurt: let them be clothed with shame and dishonour that magnify themselves against me.*

Let them shout for joy, and be glad, that favour my righteous cause: yea, let them say continually, Let the LORD *be magnified, which hath pleasure in the prosperity of his servant. And my tongue shall speak of thy righteousness and of thy praise all the day long.*[10]

Assembled in the intimidating shadow of Royal power, the delegates found the relevance of Psalm 35 to be extraordinary. It was all the more striking for those who realized that particular Psalm had been placed in the prayer book as the reading for September seventh many years earlier. "It seemed as if Heaven had ordained that Psalm to be read on that morning," Massachusetts' John Adams wrote his wife. Duché's prayers were apparently equally moving. The Secretary of the Continental Congress, Charles Thompson, managed to record one of them as it echoed in the stillness of Carpenters' Hall.

O! Lord, our heavenly father, King of Kings and Lord of lords: who dost from thy throne behold all the dwellers upon earth and reignest with power supreme & uncontrouled over all kingdoms, empires and governments, look down in mercy, we beseech thee, upon these our American states who have fled to thee from the road of the oppressor and thrown themselves upon thy gracious protection, desiring henceforth to be dependent only on thee.

To thee they have appealed for the righteousness of their Cause; to Thee do they look up, for that countenance & support which Thou alone canst give. Take them, therefore, Heavenly Father, under thy nurturing care: give them wisdom in council, valour in the field. Defeat the malicious designs of our cruel adversaries. Convince them of the unrighteousness of their cause. And if they persist in their sanguinary purposes, O! let the voice of thy unerring justice sounding in their hearts constrain them to drop the weapons of war from their enerved hands in the day of battle.

Be thou present, O God of Wisdom and direct the counsels of this honourable Assembly. Enable them to settle things upon the best and surest foundation, that the scene of blood may be speedily closed; that harmony and peace may effectually be restored, and truth and justice, religion and piety prevail and flourish amongst thy people. Preserve the health of their bodies and the vigour of their minds; shower down upon them and the millions they represent such temporal blessings as Thou seest expedient for them in this world, and crown them with everlasting glory in the world to come. All this we ask in the name and through the merits of Jesus Christ thy son, Our Saviour, Amen. [11]

Some delegates were moved to tears. Duché's prayer, marveled John Adams, was "as pertinent, as affectionate, as sublime, as devout, as I ever heard offered up to Heaven. He filled every Bosom present." Connecticut's Silas Deane said the congressional devotion was "worth riding One Hundred Mile to hear." On a motion by New York's James Duane, the delegates unanimously voted to award Duché the official thanks of Congress. After the prayer and Bible-reading, some said, Congress had a renewed sense of purpose and unity.

Their decision to find their way by faith was typical of Colonial America.[12] In eighteenth-century America, observed Colonial scholar Patricia Bonomi, "the idiom of religion penetrated all discourse, underlay all thought, marked all observances [and] gave meaning to every public and private crisis." The philosophical foundation of Colonial American culture, law, and government was the Judeo-Christian worldview. It was also the flame of inspiration that fired the American quest for freedom. The common people of Colonial America and their leaders would soon establish a new nation, and it would be founded on an old Book—the Bible.[13]

CHAPTER 2

"New Jerusalem"

From the overhanging limbs of a riverside tree, Robert Hunt rigged a canopy from an unwanted sail, declared the crude shelter a "church," and called his congregation to worship. It was 1607, and Hunt was the chaplain of what would be the first successful English colony in America—the newly founded Jamestown settlement on the forested coast of Virginia. An Anglican minister who had been educated at Cambridge University, he had answered a call to leave his parish church and accompany three shiploads of English colonists to the foreboding wilds of the New World. No English colony had yet survived in North America, and only males were allowed on the maiden voyage to Jamestown. So taking the post of chaplain or vicar meant assuming grave risks, and saying good-bye to his wife and two children for an unknown period. Even so, Hunt had felt led to accept the call. On December 19, 1606, he and 104 other colonists had left England aboard the *Susan Constant*, the *Discovery*, and the *Godspeed*—bound for the distant, mysterious New World.[1]

Calamity befell Hunt almost immediately. Stormy weather forced the ships to hug the English coast for two weeks, and the chaplain became seriously ill with an unidentified shipboard malady while still a mere twenty miles from home. The other passengers expected him to die, but Hunt surprised them and recovered. He then set about winning their trust. That was no small achievement: they were a boisterous, bickering lot, and, according to one of their number, a few were "little better than Atheists." By the time they made landfall in Virginia's Cape Henry in April 1607, however, they were willing to join Hunt in their first collective action in the New World: they erected a cross at Cape Henry, and thanked God for safe passage. The chaplain's love for the Lord and his pastor's heart for the people reportedly won their respect. So too, perhaps, did his pluck—he was described as "courageous" as well as "honest [and] religious."[2]

Whether by patience, pluck, or providence—or all three—the determined chaplain brought light into the "darkness" of the New World wilderness. Sobered by an Indian attack that killed two of their number, the settlers moved inland from Cape Henry and established a crude settlement on the James River, which they named Jamestown in honor of the king. Immediately, the Reverend Hunt took an active role. As Jamestown's chaplain and vicar, he dedicated the selected site "in the name of God" and shouldered a share of the physical labor—"We are all laborers in a common vineyard," he told the colonists. In his ministry, he summoned the settlers to public prayer mornings and evenings, preached two sermons every Sunday, oversaw regular communion, and tended to the colonists like a shepherd to his flock. Eventually, he moved worship services to a church that boasted four walls, even though one worshipper called it a "homely thing like a barne."[3]

Hacking out a life in the North American forest was far more grueling than Jamestown's colonists had imagined. Amid the harsh, hardscrabble conditions, morale teetered, but Hunt remained faithful and uncomplaining—even when a fire consumed his church, clothes, and precious books. As conditions turned deadly and the colonists were struck down by New World illness and hardship, Hunt nursed the ill and ministered to the dying. He also eased the colonists' contentious ways. "Many were the mischiefs that daily sprung from their ignorant (yet ambitious) spirits," a Jamestown leader would report, "but the good Doctrine and exhortation of our preacher Mr. Hunt reconciled them. . . ." According to Jamestown's Captain John Smith, the courageous chaplain "quenched those flames of envie, and dissention." After more than a year of God's work in the wilderness, Robert Hunt was stricken by illness and died. His ministry had been brief, but the faith he followed would prove critical to the colony's survival.[4]

Along with its capitalist mission, the colony of Virginia was also faith-based from the beginning. Named for Queen Elizabeth I, the "Virgin Queen," it had been chartered in 1606 to the London Company by King James I. The company intended to employ colonists to harvest gold and other natural resources, and find a water passage through the New World to expand the lucrative trade with the faraway East Indies. Critical support for colonization of Virginia was fueled by the preaching of the Reverend William Crashaw, a prominent Puritan pastor and scholar in early-seventeenth-century England. From 1605 to 1613, Crashaw was rector of London's renowned Temple Church. There, in 1609, he preached a sermon that compared English colonization of the New World with the call of the Israelites into the Promised Land. "I say, many greater States than this is likely to prove hath as little or less beginning," he predicted. Printed and distributed throughout England, Crashaw's call to colonize the New World for Christ proved instrumental to the struggling colony, helping infuse it with financial support and new settlers.[5]

The original charter for the Virginia colony officially cited the "propagating of Christian Religion" as a goal for colonization and called it a "noble" work. Jamestown's early days were more desperate than "noble," but the Judeo-Christian worldview was central to the colony's creation and its survival. An Anglican minister named Richard Hakluyt was the colony's chief visionary in the beginning. A member of an influential family of merchants and investors, Hakluyt was an English authority on overseas navigation, exploration, and colonial development. A principal in the London Company, he believed New World colonization would enrich England, give it world dominance, reward its investors—and enable Englishmen to carry the Gospel to untold scores of Native American people. Although noble efforts to Christianize Virginia's Indians were indeed made by some—including an attempt to establish an Indian "college"—Anglo-Indian relations were marked more by conflict than conversions. Even so, Jamestown's settlers came to America equipped with the biblical worldview, and, eventually, the application of biblical principles gave the colonists the discipline necessary to survive.[6]

They sorely needed assistance. Most were former city dwellers untrained in farming, hunting, and other survival skills. They managed to survive an early Indian attack, but most were soon struck down by fatal diseases. They had built their settlement on low, swampy land up the James River from Chesapeake Bay, and dysentery, scurvy, and malaria killed scores of them. So did starvation, which was encouraged by indolence and attitude. The Old World artisans and gentry among them refused to do the hard work that was necessary for survival—clearing trees, uprooting stumps, planting, weeding, construction. Even so, a socialistic form of government—the common store system—entitled everyone to equal rations from a common storehouse regardless of how much they worked. Amid constant squabbling and demoralizing dissension, the colonists began starving to death. When they had consumed all their livestock, they turned to dogs, cats, rats, and mice. Eventually, some reportedly resorted to cannibalism. Almost two-thirds of them died.[7]

Finally, Captain Smith, a professional soldier and explorer, saved the colony by obtaining food from neighboring Indians—and by enforcing a compulsory work program based on a New Testament admonition: "if any would not work, neither should he eat." Discarding the common-store system, Smith insisted that settlers had to work in order to draw rations. So they held on—barely: when Smith returned to England in 1609, the starving resumed and within months, the colony was again in peril. A relief expedition arrived in 1610, however, and Virginia's new governor, Lord De La Warr, secured the colony with fresh supplies and several hundred more colonists. Captain Smith considered the timing of the rescue to be providential. "God inclineth all casual events to worke the necessary helpe of his Saints," he proclaimed. Two and a half centuries later, Pulitzer Prize–winning historian Samuel Eliot Morison would conclude: "The only thing that kept Virginia alive in these difficult years was the patriotism and deep religious faith of some of the leaders."[8]

Two of those leaders who "kept Virginia alive" were Sir Thomas Gates and Sir Thomas Dale, both knighted English military officers appointed by the London Company to preserve the Virginia colony during its desperate early years. Destruction seemed imminent on several occasions, and Jamestown's severe conditions reduced some colonists to personal savagery—described by one of their number as "disordered persons, so prophane, so rioutous, so full of treasonable Intendments." In 1609, Governor Gates established a code of laws for the colony, which Governor Dale expanded two years later during his administration. Both governors oversaw harsh, military-style law enforcement, which embittered many Virginia settlers—but the laws produced the discipline necessary for the colony's survival.[9]

Gates and Dale believed that biblical principles were the cure for frontier savagery, and that Christianity was the proper foundation for an orderly society. To Dale, wilderness Virginia offered the opportunity to establish what he envisioned as a "new Jerusalem." Building on statutes implemented earlier by Gates, he established a code of laws for Virginia—the *Laws Divine, Moral and Martial*. It was the first formal criminal and civil code in America. Like English law, it was based on the Bible. "First," stated the introduction to the *Laws*,

> *since we owe our highest and supreme duty, our greatest, and all our allegeance to him, from whom all power and authoritie is derived . . . the King of kings, the commaunder of commanunders, and Lord of Hosts, I do strictly commaund and charge all Captaines and Officers . . . to have a care that the Almightie God bee duly and daily served, and that thy call upon their people to heare Sermons, as that also they diligently frequent Morning and Evening praier themselves by their owne exemplar and daily life, and dutie herein, encouraging others thereunto. . . .*[10]

Governor Dale returned to England in 1616. His successor eased the harsh military penalties for wrongdoing in Virginia, but kept Dale's laws in place. Virginia was hardly the "new Jerusalem" Dale had envisioned, but his Bible-based code of laws eventually transformed the colony from a desperate state of rebellion, starvation, disease, and desperation to a "tranquil and prosperous" colony. It was a long and arduous transformation, marked at times by disasters and disillusionment, but also by a determination, perseverance, and faith that were indeed "noble" at times. Jamestown evolved into the first successful English colony in America and established a precedent for American law and culture, both of which began at Jamestown with a faith-based foundation—the Judeo-Christian worldview.[11]

That worldview helped establish another important American precedent in Virginia—self-government. By 1619, the colony was relatively stable and was expanding inland. Gone were the slovenly ways of the common-store system, which had been replaced by free enterprise and biblically inspired accountability. "When our people were fed out of the common store," observed a colonial leader, "glad was he who could slip from his labour, or slumber over his taske . . . the most honest among them would hardly take so much true paines in a week as now for themselves they will doe in a day." The Virginia colonists learned to grow tobacco, which gave the colony an expanding economy. To provide wives for the Virginia settlers, the London Company recruited English women—"young and incorrupt maids," they were called—and the colony was infused with the stability of family life. Within a dozen years, Virginia had been transformed from desperation to development, thanks to rule of law, family life, and free enterprise—all of which were faith-based. So too was the dramatic jump forward in political freedom that occurred in 1619.[12]

That year, Virginia governor George Yeardley convened the first legislative assembly in America. Known as the House of Burgesses, it was composed of twenty-two elected representatives, or burgesses, chosen by the Virginia colonists. Governor Yeardley was acting at the direction of Sir Edwin Sandys, the London Company's new treasurer and chief officer. The son of an Anglican archbishop who had helped translate the Bible into English, Sandys was the author of a popular and respected book on the state of Christianity in Europe and a book of hymns. He was also a principal leader in the English Parliament, who believed the Virginia Colony would prosper if its colonists could own land and exercise self-government.[13]

Under Sandys's direction, the London Company restructured the colony under what was called the Great Charter, which allowed private land ownership, implemented a strategy to Christianize Virginia's Indian tribes, and established the House of Burgesses, which was also called the General Assembly. Company officials in London initially held veto power, and the legislature was under nominal oversight of the king—but England's monarchs took little interest in distant Virginia's fledgling General Assembly. Gradually, the law of the land in Virginia was determined by the House of Burgesses—which grew into a bicameral legislature elected by the people. It became the cornerstone of American government and established two fundamental precedents for the future American nation: America's political tradition would be self-government, and it would be based on the biblical worldview.[14]

The English common law that inspired American law and government was also based largely on the Bible. The English constitution was not a single document, but was a collection of legal traditions, judicial rulings, and historic statutes that developed from Anglo-Saxon culture, Christianity's canon law, and milestone legal statutes—especially the Magna Carta. In 1215, a group of English barons forced England's King John to sign a document that guaranteed basic God-given or inalienable freedoms to his subjects, and officially proclaimed that even the English monarchy was under rule of law. The Magna Carta, as King John's concession would be known, was the legal cornerstone of Britain's constitutional monarchy. It was drafted by a leading Christian theologian and authority on canon law—Stephen Langton, the archbishop of Canterbury—and was rooted in the Higher Law of Scripture.[15]

The unique, biblical foundation of English law was clearly reflected in the initial actions taken by the House of Burgesses. It first convened on Friday, July 30, 1619, in a church—Jamestown's newly built fifty-foot-long meeting house. Its opening act as America's first legislative assembly was a prayer. Opening with prayer was a deliberate action, executed, according to a Jamestown official, because "mens affaires doe little prosper where Gods service is neglected." Jamestown's Anglican minister, the Reverend Richard Bucke, delivered it while the lawmakers respectfully stood at their seats. Bucke prayed that "it would please

God to guide and sanctifie all our proceedings to his owne glory and to the good of the Plantation."[16]

The legislators enacted dozens of statutes. Among them were laws mandating church attendance on the Lord's Day, a measure requiring that Sundays be kept "in holy and religious order," a provision to financially support Virginia's Anglican clergymen, and regulations outlawing drunkenness and "Gaming with Dice & Cardes." Two years later, in 1621, a new constitution for Virginia dedicated the colony anew to "the Advancement of the Honour and Service of God, and the Enlargement of His Kingdom." The enlargement of the colony faced a severe setback in 1622, when a devastating Indian attack claimed the lives of hundreds of colonists. The attack and mismanagement of the colony by the London Company led King James to revoke the colony's charter and make Virginia a royal colony. In 1698, the colony's capital was shifted from Jamestown to nearby Williamsburg. The Jamestown settlement eventually disappeared, but the colony of Virginia survived and prospered—and its heritage of Bible-based self-government became a model for the future American nation. Meanwhile, some 450 miles up the forested coast of America, another model was emerging—and it too was founded on faith.[17]

CHAPTER 3

"One Small Candle"

On November 9, 1620, the passengers and crew of the *Mayflower* looked across the gray waters of the Atlantic at the forested shore of New England—and realized they had come to the wrong place. They were supposed to be offshore a site near modern New York—land claimed by the colony of Virginia. Like the Jamestown colonists, they too had a charter from the London Company to establish a colony on Virginia's northern rim. Following a fierce Atlantic storm, however, they wound up off the coast of what would become Massachusetts. Realizing their error, they headed down the coast for their intended destination, but off Cape Cod's eastern shore they were stopped by dangerous shoals and rough seas. They had already endured a grueling two-month voyage and a storm so ferocious that it cracked the *Mayflower*'s main beam. Had they not rigged a makeshift repair they might have been doomed.[1]

They had survived, they believed, only by the grace of God. "In sundrie of these storms the winds were so fierce & the seas so high," one of them would later recall, "[and] they comited themselves to the will of God. . . ." Faced now with more rough seas, they abandoned attempts to reach their intended destination in Virginia. Although outside the jurisdiction of their charter, they decided to establish their colony where they had made landfall—on the coast of Massachusetts. After anchoring in Cape Cod Bay, off the site of modern Provincetown, they moved across the bay to the place where they would make their home. They would call it Plymouth Colony, and they would eventually become known as the Pilgrims. Plymouth Colony would prove to be the second successful English colony in America—and it too would be faith-based.[2]

"Being thus arrived in a good harbor and brought safe to land," Pilgrim leader William Bradford would report, "they fell upon their knees & blessed the God of heaven, who had brought them over the vast & furious ocean, and delivered them from all the periles & miseries therof, againe to set their feet on the firme and stable earth. . . ." Bradford and about a third of the *Mayflower*'s 102 passengers belonged to a Puritan sect known as Separatists—and they were the driving force behind the expedition and its vision for a colony in America. The tumultuous Atlantic waves were not the only "periles & miseries" the Plymouth Separatists had faced: they had come to the New World wilderness to establish a Christian safe haven from forces they feared in Europe.[3]

English Separatists were so named because they had separated from the official state denomination—the Church of England—and no longer considered themselves Anglicans. Theologically, the Church of England held to the fundamental doctrines of the Protestant Reformation, but it had retained distinctive elements of Catholic worship. Mainstream Puritans wanted the Anglican Church to purify itself of all remnants of Catholicism, but they kept their church membership. Separatists, however, believed every local church should be independent and self-governing. That position was illegal under England's Uniformity Act of 1559, and was punishable by fines and imprisonment—or worse.

Early Separatist leaders had been executed in England, and sect members had suffered ridicule, threats, and persecution.[4]

Scores of Separatists had fled to the Netherlands, where religious freedom was allowed. After years in a foreign land, however, some had begun to worry that their children were losing their English heritage. They had also begun to fear that political changes between the Netherlands and Spain might land them under control of Catholic Spain, which had executed thousands of Protestants a generation earlier. In 1617, members of a Separatist congregation in the Dutch city of Leiden prayerfully decided to seek a new life in the New World—where they could live their faith without persecution. Encouraged by their pastor, the Reverend John Robinson, the group contacted the London Company's Sir Edwin Sandys, who had helped the Jamestown colonists achieve self-government, and Sandys arranged a charter for them to establish a colony on what was then Virginia's far northern rim. Upon awarding the charter, Sandys wrote the congregation: "I betake you with this design, which I hope verily is the work of God, to the greatest protection and blessings of the Highest."[5]

The Leiden congregation decided that one group of colonists would go first, led by church leaders William Brewster and William Bradford, and another group under Pastor Robinson would follow later. Robinson had a reputation for sound judgment, solid integrity, and sincere faith—"a worthy Instrument of the Gospel," a contemporary called him. He had inspired the Pilgrims' New World venture, but he would not live to see it: he would die of illness before he could rejoin the Pilgrims. Even so, they would be accompanied to America by his parting words. In July 1620, after the Leiden congregation observed a day of solemn prayer and fasting, Robinson preached a farewell sermon.[6]

"Brethren," he told them, "we are now quickly to part from one another, whether I may ever live to see your face on earth any more, the God of Heaven only knows, but whether the Lord hath appointed that or not, I charge you before God and his blessed angels that you . . . follow the Lord Jesus Christ." Then he preached on a text from the book of Ezra: "I proclaimed a fast there, at the river of Ahava, that we might afflict ourselves before our God, to seek of him a right way for us, and for our little ones, and for all our substance." The application was obvious: the tiny band of Separatists was bound for the New World "to seek of him a right way . . . for our little ones, and for all. . . ."[7]

After a false start from Southampton, about one hundred men, women, and children left Plymouth, England, in September 1620, bound for wilderness America aboard the *Mayflower*. Twenty-seven of the adult passengers were Separatists; the rest were non-Separatists recruited to bolster the colony's numbers. The majority—called "Strangers" by the Separatists—mainly sought a new start in a new land. Most, however, shared the Separatists' Judeo-Christian worldview, and the two groups were compatible enough that they would collectively become known as the Pilgrims. "Being thus passed the vast ocean," William Bradford would note, "they had now no friends to wellcome them, nor inns to entertaine or refresh their weatherbeaten bodys, no houses or much less townes to repaire too . . . and the whole countrie, full of woods & thickets [was] wild & savage."[8]

Like the Jamestown settlers, the Pilgrims were unprepared for the challenges of the North American wilderness—it was so radically different from Europe. "They lacked everything but virtue," observed Pilgrim scholar Roland G. Usher. "They . . . brought really nothing but good constitutions, loyalty to each other, good sense, patience, forbearance and devotion to a high religious ideal." That "high religious ideal" was Christianity, and it proved to be the crucial foundation for building a lasting colony amid the perils of the New World. They had landed outside the boundary of their charter and the jurisdiction of the London Company—which allowed them to build a faith-based colony with almost unrestricted freedom. Some type of civil government was necessary for law and order, however: a few "Strangers" were already muttering that once ashore "none had power to command them."[9]

Before boarding ship in England, the Pilgrims had received a good-bye letter from Pastor Robinson, which had been read aloud to them at dockside. In it, he had encouraged them "daily to renew our repentances with our God" and to treat each other with respect—and "not easily take offence." He had predicted that some kind of civil government would be needed for the colony, and he advised them to establish a form of self-government based on "God's ordinances" with carefully chosen leaders who would govern "in the image of the Lords power and authoritie." Establish a Bible-based government, administered by "virtuous" leaders, he counseled them. "Lastly, wheras you are become a body politik, using amongst your selves civil government . . . let your wisdome & godliness appeare, not only in chusing shuch persons as do entirely love and will promote the common good, but also in yielding unto them all due honour & obedience in their lawful administrations. . . ."[10]

When they reached America, the Pilgrims promptly followed the pastor's advice about organizing a "body politik." Before leaving the *Mayflower*, forty-one Pilgrim men—Separatists and Strangers alike—assembled in the ship's main cabin. There, led by William Brewster, William Bradford, and John Carver—the colony's first governor—they signed a constitution or compact for governing the new colony. It would become known as the Mayflower Compact, and, like Virginia's milestone legislative assembly, it would establish a precedent for constitutional law in America. It stated in full:

> *In the Name of God, Amen. We, whose names are underwritten, the Loyal Subjects of our dread Sovereign Lord King James, by the Grace of God, of Great Britain, France, and Ireland, King, Defender of the Faith, &c.*

Having undertaken for the Glory of God, and Advancement of the Christian Faith, and the Honour of our King and Country, a Voyage to plant the first Colony in the northern Parts of Virginia; Do by these Presents, solemnly and mutually, in the Presence of God and one another, covenant and combine ourselves together into a civil Body Politick, for our better Ordering and Preservation, and Furtherance of the Ends aforesaid: And by Virtue hereof do enact, constitute, and frame, such just and equal Laws, Ordinances, Acts, Constitutions, and Officers, from time to time, as shall be thought most meet and convenient for the general Good of the Colony; unto which we promise all due Submission and Obedience.

In Witness whereof we have hereunto subscribed our names at Cape-Cod the eleventh of November, in the Reign of our Sovereign Lord King James, of England, France, and Ireland, the eighteenth, and of Scotland the fifty-fourth, Anno Domini; 1620.[11]

The Mayflower Compact reflected the Bible-based self-government the Pilgrims practiced in their Leiden congregation, and its drafters cited their source of authority—"In the name of God, Amen." It also reflected the historic Judeo-Christian tradition that government should be modeled on the "covenants" that God established with His people in the Bible. In keeping with this belief, the Compact's signers vowed to "covenant and combine ourselves together into a civil Body Politick" in order to establish "just and equal laws . . . for the general Good of the Colony." It clearly recognized that all law and authority—even that of a king—was by the "Grace of God," and its signers emphasized that they were acting "solemnly and mutually in the presence of God." The main purpose of the Plymouth Colony and its government, the Compact stated, was to promote "the glory of God, and the advancement of the Christian faith." This extraordinary cornerstone precedent for American law and government—the first

American constitution—was thus founded not on the whims of man, but on the Higher Law of the Bible.[12]

In the wilderness of New England, the Pilgrims also followed Pastor Robinson's advice to treat each other with biblical charity. When winter illnesses spread through their village of crude huts, the healthy sacrificially served those who were ill or dying—even when the "healthy" was reduced to seven adults. The few served the many, recalled one of them, and "spared no pains, night nor day, but with abundance of toyle and hazard of their owne health, fetched them woode, made them fires, drest them meat, made their beds, washed their loathsome cloaths . . . shewing herein their true love unto their friends & bretheren."[13]

Plymouth Colony lost half its population that first winter. In the spring, the survivors befriended a Native American man named Squanto, who taught them how to grow corn and catch fish, and who came to be valued by the grateful Pilgrims as a treasured "instrument sent of God for their good." When the *Mayflower* left for England, no Pilgrims were aboard: all had chosen to remain in America. Historians would attribute their survival and success to their aptitude, fidelity, wisdom, and practicality, but Pilgrim leader William Bradford placed the credit elsewhere: "it was the Lord which upheld them," he said simply.[14]

In 1621, the Council for New England, which held the charter to the land where the Pilgrims landed, granted them a patent for the colony. That year they also celebrated a fruitful harvest. "We set the last spring some twenty acres of Indian corn, and sowed some six acres of barley and pease," reported colonist Edward Winslow. "God be praised, we had a good increase of Indian corn, and our barley indifferent good. . . . And although it be not always so plentiful as it was at this time with us, yet by the goodness of God we are so far from want. . . ." The plentiful harvest of 1621 also led to the enduring American tradition—Thanksgiving. Catholic colonists in New Spain had assembled to give thanks to God for their survival, and so had the Jamestown Anglicans. It was the Pilgrims of Plymouth, however, who would be credited for establishing America's distinctive Thanksgiving holiday with a joyous observance in the autumn of 1621.[15]

Days of thanksgiving were a Christian tradition that was modeled on the Jewish feast days recorded in the Old Testament. The Feast of Harvest (or Firstfruits) and the Feast of Tabernacles (or Ingathering) celebrated God's grace and provision at harvesttime. It was a time of rejoicing when all work ceased, Sabbath-style, and the people gathered in worship, offered the firstfruits of their labors to the Lord, extended mercy to the poor, and gave thanks to God. The New Testament called on believers to personally maintain an attitude of thanksgiving, and the early Church observed times of thanksgiving. Later, in Medieval England, churchmen brought a lamb or a loaf of bread to mass on Lammas Day in thanksgiving for harvesttime.[16]

Following the Reformation, Protestants discarded the annual Catholic festivals, observing instead days of prayer, fasting, and thanksgiving. In his influential work, *A Christian Dictionairie*, seventeenth-century Puritan theologian Thomas Wilson, an English pastor at Canterbury, described a Christian thanksgiving in his day. His book was published just eight years before the Pilgrims left for the New World, and recorded the meaning of a thanksgiving observance in the early 1600s. A biblically authentic thanksgiving, Wilson wrote, included an "acknowledging and confessing, with gladness, of the benefits and deliverances of God, both toward ourselves and others to the praise of his Name." It included "Remembrance of the good done to us . . . Confessing God to be the Author and giver of it . . . being glad of an occasion to praise him, and doing it gladly, with joy."[17]

The famous 1621 celebration at Plymouth was the first of its kind for the Pilgrims in America, but it was not their first thanksgiving observance. During their years in Holland, the Separatist

Pilgrims had repeatedly witnessed Leiden's annual day of thanksgiving, when the city's Protestants gave thanks to God for Leiden's deliverance from a brutal 1574 siege by the Spanish army. The future Pilgrims also celebrated their own thanksgiving observances in Holland, beginning soon after their arrival with an event designed to thank God for their escape from English persecution. The Separatist Pilgrims carried the practice to the New World, where they held thanksgiving observances in obedience to scripture such as Psalm 107:

> *O give thanks unto the LORD, for he is good: for his mercy endureth for ever. Let the redeemed of the LORD say so, whom he hath redeemed from the hand of the enemy; and gathered them out of the lands. . . . They wandered in the wilderness in a solitary way; they found no city to dwell in. Hungry and thirsty, their soul fainted in them. Then they cried unto the LORD in their trouble, and he delivered them out of their distresses. And he led them forth by the right way, that they might go to a city of habitation. Oh that men would praise the LORD for his goodness, and for his wonderful works to the children of men!*[18]

The celebrated 1621 thanksgiving event at Plymouth was apparently commissioned by Pilgrim leader William Bradford, who had become Plymouth's second governor. The colony's first governor, John Carver, had died during the colonists' first winter. So had Bradford's wife, Dorothy, who tragically fell overboard and drowned soon after the *Mayflower* reached Cape Cod. Despite the heartbreaking losses and severe hardships, the colony had survived the winter—a feat that Bradford attributed to the grace of God. After a good harvest the following autumn, the governor made certain that the survivors "might after a speciall manner rejoice together." Pilgrim Edward Winslow, who also became a Plymouth governor, recorded a description of the event in a letter to a friend in England. Additional insight into the celebration was preserved in a memoir that Bradford later recorded. After "we had gathered the fruits of our labours," as Winslow put it, Governor Bradford dispatched a four-man hunting party to obtain game for a celebration.[19]

The hunters returned with a week's supply of "fowle"—presumably the "waterfoule" and "wild Turkeys" that Bradford reported as plentiful at the time. Added to the event's menu was a supply of venison, which was contributed by Pokanoket Indians. Ninety members of the tribe and their leader, Massasoit, attended the celebration and were "entertained and feasted" as guests. The Pilgrims may have invited them as "strangers" in fulfillment of an admonition in the book of Deuteronomy: "And thou shalt rejoice in thy feast, thou, and thy son, and thy daughter, and thy servant, and thy maid, and the Levite and the stranger. . . ." If the celebration featured other foods normally consumed by the Plymouth Pilgrims, it would have also included beaver, baked clams, lobster, cod, bass and other fish, Indian corn, peas, beans, cabbage, onions, parsnips, English cheese, porridge, biscuits, and corn-based hasty pudding. Typical beverages would have been ale and spring water.[20]

The event lasted three days, and featured sports activities—"Recreations" in Winslow's words—which, if they were the usual Puritan fare, included footraces, jumping competition and wrestling. The festival's entertainment also included the use of firearms. Winslow reported that "we exercised our Armes," which may have referred to target shooting or a firing demonstration for Massasoit and his Pokanoket. The event's three-day length was unique: the usual Puritan thanksgiving observance lasted either a day or an entire week. Typically, it was preceded by a worship service, which Winslow did not mention in his letter. Did that mean the devout Pilgrims failed to worship? Or did Winslow simply assume the letter's recipient understood Separatist practices? The faith-based nature of the Pilgrims' 1621 event was clearly demonstrated by the pattern they established with numerous other thanksgiving observances at Plymouth Colony.[21]

In 1623, for instance, when a prolonged drought threatened the colony's crops and survival, Plymouth's magistrates called for a day of prayer and fasting. Edward Winslow would record that event, too:

> *To that end a day was set apart by public authority, and set apart from all other employments, hoping that the same God who had stirred us up hereunto, would be moved hereby in mercy to look down upon us, and grant the request of our dejected souls. . . . For though in the morning when we assembled together, the heavens were as clear and the drought as like to continue as ever it was; yet (our exercise continuing some eight or nine hours) before our departure the weather was over-cast, the clouds gathered together on all sides, and on the next morning distilled such soft, sweet, and mild showers of rain, continuing some fourteen days, and mixed with such seasonable weather as it was hard to say whither our weathered corn or drooping affections were most quickened or revived. Such was the bounty and goodness of our God.*

The lifesaving rain "gave them cause of rejoicing and blessing God," Governor Bradford would report, and Plymouth's leaders declared an official day of thanksgiving to God for his "gracious and speedy answer." With similar sentiment, Edward Winslow concluded his account of the original thanksgiving: "And although it be not always so plentifull as it was at this time with us, yet by the goodness of God, we are so farre from want. . . ."[22]

In 1623, the Plymouth Pilgrims survived another serious but less obvious threat—the same common-store socialism that had plagued Jamestown. According to William Bradford, some colonists liked the common-store system and believed "that the taking away of property, and bringing community into a common wealth, would make them happy and flourishing." Instead, it bred "confusion & discontent, and retarded much employment that would have been to their benefit and comfort," according to Bradford. "God in his wisdom," he concluded, "saw another course fitter for them."[23]

The "fitter" course was the same biblical principle that Captain John Smith had adopted at Jamestown—"if any does not work, neither should he eat." Bradford replaced the common-store with the free enterprise system, which allowed the private ownership of land. "This had very good success," he would later report, "for it made all hands very industrious, so as much more corne was planted then other waise would have bene by any means the Government or any other could use. . . ." This was more than a mere shift in economic policy: it was a faith-based decision to trust God and embrace individual initiative rather than looking to the government as provider.[24]

It set a precedent for the future American nation, which would thrive on personal freedom and individual initiative—the free enterprise system. Another precedent was set in 1636, when the Pilgrims established Plymouth's General Court, composed of the colony's governor and seven deputies chosen "to rule and govern the plantation within the limits of this corporation." It was a smaller Plymouth equivalent of Virginia's House of Burgesses. The deputies were chosen by the colonists to represent them, and therefore were authorized to govern by the consent of the governed. Like Virginia's legislature, it was a form of representative government grounded on the Higher Law of the Bible. The Pilgrims of Plymouth, observed nineteenth-century historian James Thatcher, "held the bible in estimation as the basis of all laws; and the precepts of the gospel [to be] the rules of their lives and the fountains of their dearest hopes. It was the interwoven sentiment of their hearts that the sovereign power resides with the people, and this was the fundamental axiom upon which their government was reared."[25]

Plymouth Colony grew slowly. Its people were poor, and their hardscrabble struggle discouraged new colonists for years to come. Even so, they remained true to their vision that God had called them to America as New World pioneers with a purpose. They were confident that they had been providentially placed in "New England" to craft a culture that honored and reflected biblical truth. They identified themselves with the Hebrew people of the Old Testament, who were led by God from Egyptian slavery into nationhood within the Promised Land. "Thou hast brought a vine out of Egypt," wrote the psalmist. "Thou preparedst room before it and didst cause it to take deep root, and it filled the land."[26]

The Pilgrims knew that Bible passage and fervently believed it applied to them. "God brought a vine into *this* wilderness," one proclaimed; "he made room for it and caused it to take deep root, and it filled the land." Plymouth's Separatists, like Jamestown's Anglicans, would mold the future of America in a mighty way, and at the root of their influence was a common faith. "Virginia as a Church of England colony and Plymouth as a separatist colony were products of the Reformation as it affected England," observed twentieth-century Colonial scholar Clarence Ver Steeg. "These transplanted ideas were eventually to be modified and molded into institutions."[27]

William Bradford predicted such an impact. "Thus, out of small beginnings, greater things have been produced by his hand that made all things of nothing," he wrote; "and as one small candle may light a thousand, so the light here kindled hath shone to many . . . [L]et the glorious name of Jehovah have all the praise." At Plymouth and Jamestown, this "one small candle"—the Judeo-Christian worldview—kindled the flames of freedom for the future American republic. And soon, thousands more would fuel the blaze.[28]

CHAPTER 4

"Farewell, Dear England"

Francis Higginson gathered his wife and eight children on the deck of their departing ship to watch the English coastline disappear over the distant horizon. "Farewell, dear England," he cried, "and all the Christian friends there!" Higginson and his family were among the first of a colossal wave of Puritan emigrants who followed the Pilgrims from England to distant America in the 1630s. "Our heads and hearts," wrote one to those left behind, "shall be fountains of tears for your everlasting welfare, when we shall be in our poor cottages in the wilderness." In extraordinary numbers, England's Puritans abandoned the familiar surroundings of the Old World and set their faces toward the New. An initial surge brought two hundred emigrants to New England's Massachusetts Bay in 1630. It was followed by eight hundred more. Then another seven hundred arrived. Then three thousand in a single year—as ship after ship spilled these devout people of the Book onto the wilderness shores of New England.[1]

Never had England recorded such an exodus of its people. They did not come in a single weather-beaten vessel, as did the Pilgrims aboard the *Mayflower.* Instead, they were ferried across the Atlantic in *fleets*—seventeen ships transported one thousand passengers at one point. In a single decade, from 1630 to 1640, more than twenty thousand English Puritans immigrated to Massachusetts Bay Colony. So massive was the transfer of population that it became known as "the Great Migration"—and it would mold the culture of America in a mighty way. Who were these Puritan people? And why did they leave England in such a mass immigration?[2]

The name "Puritan" was originally a term of ridicule—applied to Christians who wanted to purify the Church of England of practices they deemed unbiblical. Their concerns were rooted in the Protestant Reformation. In 1517, Martin Luther, a Roman Catholic priest in Germany, had sparked the Reformation by calling for the Church to return to key biblical doctrines distorted or abandoned in the early Middle Ages. Luther and other Reformers preached salvation by God's grace through faith in Jesus Christ alone, rather than by a combination of faith and human works. They proclaimed the "priesthood of believers," teaching that any Christian should be able to read the Bible without the oversight of a minister or priest. They upheld the authority of the Bible over Church tradition and papal rulings, and they denounced the Church for "selling indulgences"—promising that a donation to the Church would lessen the punishment for sin in the afterlife.[3]

Church officials in Rome rejected Luther's call for reform and excommunicated him, but the Reformation surged across Europe, flooding much of it with spiritual revival—and dramatic political change. The Reformation's renewed preaching of the Gospel transformed hearts and minds, produced countless believers, and instilled them with the belief that everyone—even royalty—was subject to God's Higher Law as revealed by the Bible. Such teaching was unnerving to much of Europe's monarchy—perhaps even more troubling than the Reformation's challenge to Catholicism. In Portugal and Spain thousands of Protestants were executed. On a single day in 1572, as many as ten thousand were slaughtered in France. Among the major world powers—Spain, Portugal, France, and England—the Reformation took root and flourished only in England.[4]

It came to England during the reign of the mercurial King Henry VIII, who at first persecuted Protestants, then—when it suited his self-serving purposes—turned against the Catholics and established the Protestant Church of England in 1534. Much of England's population was ready for the Reformation, and embraced it. For the first time, the Bible was printed in English and became available to the common people. The Reformation suffered a deadly setback, however, under the five-year reign of Queen Mary I—who became known as "Bloody Mary" for her persecution of Protestants. English-language Bibles were ordered removed from the churches, and works by English Bible translators such as William Tyndale and Myles Coverdale were outlawed. Hundreds of Protestants were burned alive at London's notorious Smithfield execution site, and scores fled to the European continent—especially to Switzerland.[5]

There, the city of Geneva became a safe haven for exiled English Protestants and an incubator for Reformation ideals. In Geneva, leaders of the English Reformation were exposed to the brilliant Reformation theologian John Calvin. If Martin Luther was the Apostle Peter of the Reformation—launching a renewed spread of the Gospel—then John Calvin was the Reformation's Apostle Paul, spreading the biblical doctrines on which a Reformation faith was built. The exiled English Reformers in Switzerland studied and enthusiastically accepted Calvin's teachings, but not because Calvin pioneered any new ideas—Reformation believers placed nothing over the authority of Scripture. They became "Calvinists" because they believed Calvin's systematic theology reflected biblical truth.[6]

When Queen Mary sickened and died in 1558, she was succeeded by her half sister, Queen Elizabeth I. Less than a year into her rule, Elizabeth enacted a religious compromise of sorts with the Act of Supremacy and the Act of Uniformity. The Church of England was restored as the state church with fundamental Protestant doctrine and a degree of worship practices familiar to Catholics. The compromise aroused Protestant dissidents—the Puritans—who opposed remnants of Catholicism in the national church, and did not satisfy zealous Roman Catholics. Elizabeth's compromise ended the worst of England's sectarian violence, but neither Protestant nor Catholic dissidents would be spared sporadic persecution in the future. After attempts to overthrow the government by English Catholics, official policy toward Catholicism hardened and English Catholics would not regain full religious freedom for centuries.[7]

Meanwhile, the English Reformation thrived. Every church was now equipped with an English-language Bible, and crowds of Scripture-hungry people flocked there to read it. Affordable, small-sized personal editions of the English Bible were published in great numbers, and countless families acquired copies. England was transformed. "Sunday after Sunday, day after day," wrote British historian John Richard Green, "the crowds that gathered round the Bible in the nave of St. Paul's, or the family group that hung on to its words in the devotional exercises at home, were leavened with . . . a startling enthusiasm. The whole moral effect . . . was simply amazing. The whole nation became a church."[8]

Inspired by this extraordinary spiritual revival, the English people began to weigh everything according to the Bible—including government. Many came to believe that Christians were biblically obligated to submit to ruling authority—unless they were forced to choose between man's law and God's Higher Law. If that occurred, or if a ruler attempted to place himself above the Higher Law, resistance was not only biblically allowed, it was morally required. "In that obedience in which we have shown to be due to the authority of rulers," wrote John Calvin, "we are always to make this exception, indeed, to observe it as a primary, that such obedience is never to lead us away from [God], to whose will the desires of all kings ought to be subject, to whose decrees all their commands ought to yield, to whose majesty their scepters ought to be submitted." The fundamental doctrines restored by the Reformation, including a belief in the supremacy of Higher Law, were embraced by countless Christians in England—and by even greater numbers in Colonial America.[9]

In England, no group of believers was more committed to living according to the biblical worldview than the Puritans. They considered themselves Calvinists, as did the Presbyterians in Scotland and England, the Huguenots in France, and the Dutch Reformed in Holland. England's Anglicans also held to the fundamental doctrines of the Reformation but continued to observe the traditions and worship elements retained from Catholicism by Queen Elizabeth's compromise. The Church of England's Catholic-style practices posed no problem for many English Christians. Not so the Puritans. They believed the Roman Church had veered off course, equating papal rulings with God's Word and burdening believers with unbiblical, man-made dogmas.[10]

Most Puritans were plain English people—farmers, laborers, tradesmen, and merchants—although the movement originated with professors at Cambridge and Oxford universities. Puritan theology stressed salvation through personal faith in Jesus Christ as Lord and Savior, and personal discipleship based on the Bible. A Puritan worship service was devoid of ceremony, and emphasized reading of Scripture, prayer, and deep, meaty sermons. Puritan meetinghouses might feature columns and spires, but interiors were unadorned to keep the focus on hearing the Word of God. For Puritans, Christianity was more than a weekly observance; it was a lifestyle that reflected a personal relationship with Jesus Christ. "Let us walk honestly, as in the day," read a favorite Puritan Scripture passage, "not in rioting and drunkenness, not in chambering and wantonness, not in strife and envying. But put ye on the Lord Jesus Christ. . . ."[11]

Like the Pilgrim Separatists, mainstream English Puritans believed that every local congregation should be autonomous, independent of hierarchy and governed by its members—thus the Puritan movement also became known as the Congregational Church. Unlike the Separatists, mainstream Puritans felt compelled to remain within the Church of England—but they were committed to ridding it of any Catholic elements that could not be defended by Scripture. Their zeal to purify the official state church led Queen Elizabeth to view the Puritans at times with a degree of reserve. Her successor, King James I, viewed them with outright suspicion as "nonconformists." At issue was more than the Puritans' continuous criticism of the official government church. What rankled rulers most was the Puritans' belief in the biblical doctrine of equality—that every person, whether a prince or a pauper, was of equal value to God. If he was a Puritan, the poorest peasant in England considered himself a noble child of God.[12]

"The Puritan movement was essentially democratic," American scholar Ezra Parmalee Prentice observed. "Every individual stood without distinction of rank or fortune before his God. . . . Here, and not in Rousseau or the teachings of French philosophy, is the origin of the doctrine of the rights of man, and the establishment of government upon these principles was the beginning of a new social order. . . ." It was not a social order that appealed to the English monarchy. Some of England's rulers considered the Puritans a nuisance. Others viewed them as a serious threat. "Puritanism was not merely a religious doctrine," the famous political observer Alexis de Tocqueville would later note, "but corresponded in many points with the most absolute democratic and republican theories. It was this tendency which had aroused its most dangerous adversaries." As Scripture commanded, Puritans were generally loyal to the ruling authorities—

but their first allegiance was to an Authority that was higher and more sacred than human royalty.[13]

England's King James I viewed the Puritans as a troublesome menace. Like other English monarchs, he believed in the divine right of kings—that a monarch ruled by the will of God and therefore held final authority over both institutions and people. He realized the Puritan ranks were steadily increasing. What might they do if they someday deemed his rule to be unbiblical? In 1604, at a meeting called the Hampton Court Conference, he listened to Puritan complaints, and in a display of cooperation, he agreed to one request: he would support a new English translation of the Bible—a decision that would produce the King James Bible. He insisted, however, that the Puritans conform fully to the practices of the Church of England—which they believed they could not do. Weary of Puritan refusal to conform to the national church, the king at one point vowed: "I will make them conform themselves, or I will harry them out of the land, or else do worse."[14]

If England's Puritans felt uneasy with James I, his successor made them feel endangered. Charles I became king of England when his father died in 1625. He defended the divine right of kings even more forcefully than his father—and he despised the Puritans. Despite the opposition of Parliament, he married a French princess, Henrietta Maria, who was Catholic, and he directed the Anglican bishop of London, William Laud, to restore more Catholic-style worship practices into the Anglican Church. Laud was eager to comply: he privately hoped the Church of England would someday unite with the Roman Catholic Church, and he believed that restoring traditional Catholic practices might prepare the way for union. The Puritans were an outspoken obstacle boldly blocking fulfillment of Laud's dream.[15]

He preferred unmarried ministers, like the Catholic priesthood, and the Puritans objected. He advocated Catholic-style prayers for the dead, and the Puritans called it unbiblical. He ordered church members to kneel for communion; and the Puritans said it was worshipping the elements rather than the Lord. He required bowing at the church altar, and the Puritans said it was misplaced devotion. He implemented a relaxed observance of the Sabbath, and the Puritans considered it irreverent. He called for more ceremony in worship services, and the Puritans saw it as prideful. He required ministers to wear the Catholic-style surplice or tunic, and the Puritans insisted it was man-centered adornment. Better to have "begot seven bastards than to have preached without a surplice," one of Laud's agents warned. Tensions increased, and the Puritans felt increasingly threatened.[16]

When the king elevated William Laud to archbishop of Canterbury, the highest rank in the Anglican Church, the Puritans' concerns turned to alarm. Their fears soon proved justified. The archbishop ordered Puritans to fully comply with all Anglican worship practices. Most refused. In retaliation, he dismissed Puritan pastors from their congregations and stopped their salaries. Hundreds of Puritans were excommunicated. Puritan tracts and books were outlawed. Over time, the persecution worsened. Puritan leaders were hauled before the infamous Court of the Star Chamber, prosecuted without due process of the law, and sometimes tortured. Puritans who publicly criticized Church policy were whipped, placed in the pillory, then imprisoned. Some had their ears sliced off. Others had their noses slit. Many were branded on their faces with hot irons. One Puritan author had both ears severed, then was fined and imprisoned; when he wrote another critique from his cell, he was branded on both cheeks.[17]

Charles I meanwhile waged a bitter, prolonged conflict with the English Parliament, which had many Puritan and Presbyterian members. King and Parliament fought constantly over issues related to the divine right of kings verses the authority of Parliament as the people's voice. Finally, in January 1629, the king ordered Parliament dissolved and vowed to rule alone with absolute authority. He would do so for the next eleven years, in what became known as the "Eleven Years' Tyranny." Eventually, however, he would recall Parliament to obtain funding for a war in Scotland.[18]

When reassembled, Parliament and its Puritan leaders would promptly move to curb royal power. In 1642, the king would attempt to arrest opposition members—an act that would trigger the English civil wars. After a decade of warfare, the Parliamentary armies of Puritan Oliver Cromwell would prevail. Both Charles I and Archbishop Laud would be executed for treason, and the Parliamentarians would declare England a commonwealth republic. In the Restoration of 1660, however, the English people—who missed their monarchy—would demand that Charles II, the ruler's son, be crowned as king. England's Puritan era would end as it had begun, with a king on the throne, and a flood of secularism would sweep the nation.[19]

Tens of thousands of English Puritans would not be there to witness those events; instead, they chose to flee to America—with the seeds of liberty. As King Charles's displeasure with England's Puritans deepened, Puritan leaders looked westward toward the New World, and prayed for direction. They knew of the Pilgrims' New England venture, had heard of the hardships and the opportunities, and some concluded that a Puritan colony in America was their calling. The king was more than willing to rid England of Puritans. In March 1629, he granted the request of a Puritan group and issued an official charter for a grant of land in New England. It would be located adjacent to the Pilgrims' Plymouth settlement, although it would be much larger—and it would be called Massachusetts Bay Colony.[20]

The Great Migration began in 1630, as the first wave of English Puritan departed their homeland and surged toward the distant American shore. Like the settlers of Jamestown and Plymouth before them, the Puritan emigrants shared a consensus—the Judeo-Christian worldview—and the related appreciation for individual liberty and self-government so dear to the English people. Unlike the Jamestown and Plymouth colonists, however, they were prepared for the wilderness life they faced in North America. They were not so few in numbers that they risked the extermination the Pilgrims nearly suffered. Nor were their ranks initially restricted to men and boys, like Jamestown, or hampered like that colony by fortune-seekers, the desperate, and the destitute.[21]

The Puritans left England with their families, which added stability and commitment to their New World community. Their ranks were also hefty with the God-fearing English middle class—yeoman farmers, merchants, tradesmen, London lawyers, ministers, young professors from Oxford and Cambridge, and successful businessmen fortified by their fortunes. "They desired, in fact, only the best," wrote a knowledgeable observer, "men driven forth from their fatherland not by earthly want, or the greed of gold, or by the lust of adventure, but by the fear of God, and the zeal for a Godly worship." So many Puritan ships departed the English ports in the 1630s that England appeared to be emptying itself. "God hath sifted a nation," a Puritan preacher proclaimed, "that he might send choice grain into the wilderness."[22]

CHAPTER 5

"A City upon a Hill"

It would be "a City upon a hill"—a beacon of faith shining for the world to see. That was the vision described by John Winthrop, the first governor of Massachusetts Bay Colony, who shared it with the Puritan passengers of the ship *Arbella* in March 1630. Winthrop was a forty-two-year-old London attorney and justice of the peace. A proven leader, he was a book lover and an intellectual, with a modest, self-sacrificing attitude. He had suffered grief and hardship in his private life, but remained cheerfully optimistic, and those close to him spoke of his "tender and affectionate" nature. He was also a devout Puritan. His leadership would prove crucial to the Puritan colony, but it would extract a hard toll: he would lose his wife, two sons, and a daughter. It was like "passing through hell," he would later admit—but it was his calling, and in the end he would deem it God's work.[1]

He preached a layman's sermon to the *Arbella*'s passengers before their nine-week passage across the Atlantic. In it, he articulated the Puritan vision for New England. "For we must consider that we shall be as a City upon a hill," he said. "The eyes of all people are upon us." He was referring to Jesus' words in the

Sermon on the Mount: "Ye are the light of the world. A city that is set on a hill cannot be hid." Just as Christ called believers to become faithful models or "lights" to others, Winthrop and the other Puritans believed their New World community would be a "light" to the Old World they had left behind. If they were successful, others would follow. "Beloved," Winthrop told his shipmates, "there is now set before us life and good, Death and evil, in that we are commanded this day to love the Lord our God, and to love one another, to walk in his ways and keep his commandments . . . that the Lord our God may bless us in the land wither we go to possess it."[2]

Led by the *Arbella*, a fleet of Puritan ships reached what would become Massachusetts Bay Colony in June 1630. The sprawling colony lay to the north of the Pilgrims' Plymouth settlement and was much larger. Almost seven hundred Puritan passengers were aboard the *Arbella* and her three sister ships, and they would soon be followed by another thousand. Their large numbers and careful preparation helped ensure the colony's survival, but the Puritans also suffered death in the wilderness. More than two hundred died the first year, killed by scurvy contracted aboard ship, and "fevers" contracted when ashore. "It would assuredly have moved the most locked-up affections to tears," a Puritan survivor would recall, "had they passed from one hut to another and beheld the piteous case these people were in [and their] lamentation, mourning and woe. . . ." They endured the heartbreak and hardship as God's will, and persevered. "Thus it pleaseth the Lord still to humble us," Winthrop concluded. "I doubt not but he will do us the more good at the last."[3]

When healthy, they worked. They cleared sites in the wilderness and built towns—Charlestown, Watertown, Roxbury, Medford, and Dorchester. On a bayside site fed by a strong freshwater spring, they built a settlement named Boston, and in a single generation it expanded from village to town to city. In a single decade, they established more than fifty towns in the colony. Their zeal was encouraged by their self-image: they viewed themselves much like the Hebrews of the Old Testament entering the Promised Land. "We shall find," Winthrop had predicted, "that the God of Israel is among us." Jewish historian Gabriel Sivan would concur: "No Christian community in history identified more with the People of the Book than did the early settlers of the Massachusetts Bay Colony," he would write. "[They] believed their own lives to be a literal reenactment of the Biblical drama of the Hebrew nation . . . [and] instruments of Divine Providence."[4]

So motivated, the Puritans immediately went to work building their "City upon a hill." They were superbly equipped to do so. God had instilled man with a heart for work, they believed, and honest labor honored the Lord. "Whether therefore ye eat, or drink, or whatsoever ye do," Scripture advised, "do all to the glory of God." Puritans took that biblical admonition seriously, and worked zealously—not just for personal gain or obligation to human authority, but to glorify God. A believer, therefore, should do his best at every honorable task, they believed. "It is the singular favor of God unto a man that he can attend his occupation with contentment and satisfaction," counseled Puritan preacher Cotton Mather. So faithfully did the New England Puritans embrace the biblical work ethic that for generations to come it would be known as the "Puritan work ethic."[5]

Thus inspired and energized, the Puritans boldly seized the opportunities offered by the New World. Quickly, they built their Congregational meetinghouses—raising almost forty churches in the colony's first decade. Meanwhile, confident they were doing God's work, they established the free enterprise system with remarkable efficiency. They raised and sold crops and cattle, developed a flourishing fur trade, constructed a major shipbuilding trade, established a long-lasting fishing industry, opened trade with English colonies in the Caribbean, and exported tons of tobacco to England. Absorbing nearby Plymouth Colony, they expanded their towns, built up their ports, and grew their markets. In short order, the Puritans established a tradition of successful commerce that would eventually become a hallmark of the American people. The Puritans' faith-based zeal for work would inspire the American free enterprise system—which would one day become the envy of the world.[6]

Even so, the Puritans of New England would be depicted by postmodern American popular culture as "selfish rather than selfless, authoritarian rather than democratic, brutal rather than kindly, deceiving and pious hypocrites rather than vessels of faith." By the late twentieth century, the word *Puritan* would evoke in many an image of "a gaunt, lank-haired killjoy, wearing a black steeple hat." Such a negative image would stand in stark contrast to the view held by the American people and the nation's historians prior to the twentieth century. "In the popular mind," Northwestern University's Clarence Ver Steeg would note, "the Puritans [were once viewed as] the purest of men, the embodiment of all that was best in humankind . . . [renowned for] hard work, good judgment, faith, uprightness, unimpeachable motives, and the seat of representative government."[7]

Contrary to their grim, modern stereotype, most Puritans were optimistic, outgoing people who loved life. Not only did they read John Calvin's *Institutes*, they agreed with him when he wrote, "Shall the Lord have imbued flowers with such beauty, to present itself to our eyes, with such sweetness of smell, to impress our sense of smelling; and shall it be unlawful for our eyes to be affected with the beautiful sight, or our olfactory nerves with the agreeable odor?" God's world was meant to be explored, examined, and enjoyed, they believed, and Puritans typically displayed a zest for living. They were criticized by Quaker leader George Fox, for instance, not because they displayed joyless legalism—but because they so enjoyed "ribbons and lace and costly apparel."

Like most Englishmen of their day, they also loved field sports—hunting, fishing, archery, bowling, and even horse racing. "God would have our joys to be far more than our sorrows," proclaimed a Puritan proverb of the era.[8]

Life was not to be separated into the religious and the secular, they believed; instead, all of life should be Bible-based and God-centered—whether it was worship, family life, work, play, education, the arts, law, or government. Everything should be done in a manner that honored God—especially family life. God created the family even before he created the church, they believed, and it was designed as a blessing, the bedrock of society, and the training ground for youthful disciples of Christ. The focus of the family was meant to be spiritual, not just social, but marriage and children were seen as gifts from God. In radical contrast to their modern-day stereotype, Puritans believed husbands and wives were meant to enjoy physical intimacy. God obviously created sex for reproduction, they believed, but also to strengthen an unbroken bond of marriage. According to Puritan teaching, husbands and wives were to enjoy the marriage bed "with good will and delight, willingly, readily and cheerfully."[9]

Scripture ordained the husband as head of the family, they were taught, and he was biblically obliged to love his wife "even as Christ also loved the church." As leader of the family, he was also obligated to "train up a child in the way he should go" by providing biblical instruction and modeling morality. According to Puritan culture, fathers were responsible for providing spiritual instruction—as well as food, clothing, shelter, and education. The family flourished in Puritan New England, and the historic values that would define the American family for centuries were in large part the legacy of the Puritans' biblical faith. "The sense of spiritual fellowship gave a new tenderness and refinement to common family affections," according to English scholar John Richard Green. "Home, as we conceive it now, was the creation of the Puritan."[10]

The biblical principles at the center of Puritan life also caused them to place great value on education. Puritans were well educated for their day—some 130 of the first settlers were college graduates. They considered illiteracy almost sinful because it blocked access to the Bible. "So faith comes by hearing," advised the New Testament, "and hearing by the Word of Christ." Bible study was essential to the Christian life, the Puritans believed, and the responsible believer was obliged to read, write, and learn. "The Puritan scholar studied all history, heathen or Christian, as an exhibition of divine wisdom," historian Perry Miller would write, "and found in the temporal unfolding of the divine plan. . . ." As soon as they built their homes, the Puritans built schools. In 1647, the Massachusetts Bay Colony enacted legislation mandating that "every township within this jurisdiction, after the Lord hath increased them to the number of fifty householders, shall then forthwith appoint one within their towns to teach all such children as shall resort to him to write and read." When a township reached one hundred families, the law required its residents to establish a grammar school.[11]

The law was called the "Old Deluder Satan Act"—so named because the Puritans believed Satan used illiteracy as a weapon against biblical truth. "It being one chief project of that old deluder Satan to keep men from the knowledge of the Scriptures, as in former times by keeping them in an unknown tongue," the law stated, ". . . learning [shall] not be buried in the grave of our forefathers in church and commonwealth." For the same reasons—to know God's Word and to understand His creation—the Puritans established colleges in America. The first was Harvard University, in 1636. "Let every Student be plainly instructed and earnestly pressed to consider well," read the Harvard admissions requirements, "the main end of his life and studies is to know God and Jesus Christ which is eternal life (John. 17:3) and . . . the only foundation of all sound knowledge and learning."[12]

The Puritans also produced the first book published in America, the *Bay Psalm Book* of 1640, and the first textbook—the *New England Primer*. Written by an unknown Puritan in about 1690, the *New England Primer* used stories and passages from the Bible to teach reading skills and character training. More than three million copies would be put in the hands of schoolchildren over the course of a century, and its lessons would be recited by generations of Americans: "A—In Adam's fall We sinned all . . . B—Thy life to mend, God's Book attend . . . Z—Zacchaeus, he Did climb the tree, His Lord to see. . . ." The *Primer* also included the Lord's Prayer, the Apostles' Creed, and the Westminster Catechism, which was based on the Westminster Confession of Faith. The Confession was a comprehensive summary of biblical doctrine drafted under the direction of the English Parliament in 1646. Many of America's founding fathers would learn the concept of Higher Law by studying the Westminster Catechism in the *New England Primer*.[13]

Faith, values, commerce, education—all were established in Puritan New England with a biblical foundation. So were law and government—beginning even before the Puritans left the Old World. Back in England, John Winthrop and other Puritan leaders had signed what became known as the Cambridge Agreement. In it, they agreed to emigrate to New England—if they could bring their royal charter and governing authority with them. Thus, whether by Puritan prudence or royal neglect, the Puritans were allowed to establish a fully self-governing colony under the king's authority. Instead of working for a company back in England, the Puritans worked for themselves, and from the beginning their colony was both self-governing and faith-based.[14]

The Cambridge Agreement allowed them to establish a governing body called the Massachusetts General Court, which initially acted as both legislature and court system. Like the Plymouth Pilgrims, the Massachusetts Bay Puritans based their government on the biblical model of a covenant relationship. Just as God had established covenants with his people throughout the ages, according to Scripture, the "freemen" of Massachusetts Bay established a covenant between themselves and the government through the General Court. Local governments adopted the same model. Declared a typical Massachusetts Bay town covenant:

> *We Covenant with the Lord and with one another and do bind ourselves in the presence of God, to walk together in all his ways, accordingly as he is pleased to reveal himself to us in his Blessed word of truth. And do more explicitly, in the name and fear of God, profess and protest to walk as followeth through the power and goodness of the Lord Jesus Christ.*[15]

Such a covenant or constitution declared itself to be self-governing, a "Covenant with the Lord and with one another," and to be based on biblical principles—"his blessed word of truth." The proper form of civil government, Puritan leaders believed, was a representative democracy based on a biblical model. The New Testament book of Acts revealed how the early church selected its leaders, and thus provided a model for church and civil government. So did Old Testament passages such as Deuteronomy 1:13, in which God directed the Israelites to select leaders to represent them. Biblical grounds for resisting ungodly civil rule were found in the accounts of Old Testament prophets challenging godless kings, and when the Apostles defied a civil ban on preaching the Gospel by declaring, "We ought to obey God rather than men."[16]

Another major Puritan precedent for American law and government occurred in 1641, when the colony's General Court adopted a code of laws called the Massachusetts Body of Liberties. It was the first formal legal code in New England, and it would prove to be a cornerstone for American law and government. It contained a basic bill of rights, proclaiming the essential human rights of life, liberty, and ownership of private property. It also provided for equality under the law, free and regular elections, protection from self-incrimination, the right to jury trial, and a restriction against taxation without representation. Instead of citing legal restrictions as commonly done by the laws of the day, it proclaimed liberties. Through it, the people of Massachusetts Bay experienced an expanded level of political freedom not enjoyed back in England.[17]

According to the Body of Liberties, for instance, a husband could not strike his wife except in self-defense. "Everie married woman shall be free from bodilie correction or stripes by her husband," it proclaimed, "unless it be in his owne defence upon her assalt." By legally asserting such rights, the Puritans' Body of Liberties advanced English common law and established a crucial example for the development of future American law. "Puritans," Harvard historian George Bancroft would write, "planted in their hearts the undying principles of democratic liberty." In style and content, the Massachusetts Body of Liberties laid a foundation for the Declaration of Independence, the U.S. Constitution, and the Bill of Rights.[18]

Its author was a Puritan pastor. Ministers were expected to provide leadership in all areas of life in Puritan New England, including politics. The Reverend Nathaniel Ward drafted the Massachusetts Body of Liberties. He was an experienced English attorney and a brilliant writer as well as a clergyman. He based his work on the Magna Carta, English common law, and the Bible—which the Body of Liberties referred to as "the word of God." Included in this landmark bill of rights was an eleven-point "Declaration of the Liberties the Lord Jesus Hath Given to the Churches," which proclaimed the freedom of the church to teach biblical doctrine without government interference. "No Injunctions," it stated, "are to be put upon any Church, Church officers or member in point of doctrine, worship or discipline. . . ." The fundamental freedoms drafted by the Reverend Ward in the Body of Liberties would eventually echo across the ages—in the words of America's founding documents.[19]

Puritan-style self-government soon spread. In 1636, Pastor Thomas Hooker led a group of Puritans to Hartford and other frontier sites on the Connecticut River. A Puritan minister who had immigrated to New England three years earlier, Hooker led the creation of a three-town riverside community that eventually became the Colony of Connecticut. Hooker wanted the Connecticut settlements to model Massachusetts Bay, but with even greater political freedom. He cast aside the Bay Colony's requirement that voters be members of the Puritans' Congregationalist Church, arguing that it was unfair to unbelievers and weakened churches by attracting members who joined solely for political motivation. He also called for self-government in the Connecticut Colony, citing chapter one of Deuteronomy: "Take you wise men, and understanding, and known among your tribes, and I will make them rulers over you."[20]

In 1638, the Colony of Connecticut established a frame of government, the Fundamental Orders of Connecticut, which would become known as "America's first constitution." A sermon preached by Thomas Hooker helped inspire its creation. "The privilege of election, which belongs to the people," Hooker advised, ". . . must not be exercised according to their humors, but according to the blessed will and law of God." The Puritan framers of Fundamental Orders of Connecticut apparently followed Hooker's advice: The document would become a model for American Constitutional government, and featured this preamble:

> *For as much as it hath pleased Almighty God by the wise disposition of his divine providence . . . and well knowing where a people are gathered together the word of God requires that to maintain the peace and union of such a people there should be an orderly and decent Government established according to God,*

> *[we] enter into Combination and Confederation together, to maintain and preserve the liberty and purity of the Gospel of our Lord Jesus which we now profess, as also, the discipline of the Churches, which according to the truth of the said Gospel is now practiced amongst us; as also in our civil affairs to be guided and governed according to such Laws, Rules, Orders and Decrees as shall be made, ordered, and decreed. . . .*[21]

A year later, in the summer of 1639, a small group of Puritans from the nearby settlement of New Haven assembled in a settler's barn to—in the words of a participant—"consult about settling civil Government according to God." They too were led by a Puritan minister—the Reverend John Davenport. This handful of English exiles, gathered in a barn, established a self-governing democratic republic, which would become the Colony of New Haven. Eventually, it would merge with the Colony of Connecticut, but not before establishing another precedent for American democracy—the Fundamental Agreement of New Haven, which stated: "The Scriptures do hold forth a perfect rule for the direction and government of all men." Sixteen years later the colony's lawmakers enacted the New Haven Code of 1655, which drew approximately half of its seventy-nine statutes from the Old Testament, and required apprentices and children be taught "the main grounds and principles of Christian religion necessary to salvation."[22]

For a time, some Puritan colonies enacted statutes that duplicated the Old Testament's Levitical and Mosaic laws. So did the Colony of New Hampshire, which was not a Puritan colony. Established at about the same time as Massachusetts Bay, New Hampshire was founded by an Anglican, Captain John Mason, who was an English seafarer and cartographer. It developed under the shadow of larger Massachusetts Bay Colony, and alternated between being independent or under Massachusetts's jurisdiction until it became a royal colony in 1741. In 1680, New Hampshire enacted blasphemy and idolatry laws, which made it illegal if "any person within this province, professing the true God, shall wittingly and willingly blaspheme the holy name of God, Father, the Son, or Holy Ghost . . . [or] openly and manifestly worship any other god but the Lord God." The penalties were the same enforced by the Jews of antiquity.[23]

In 1643, representatives from the Puritan colonies of Massachusetts Bay, Plymouth, Connecticut, and New Haven banded together to organize a joint defense force and to resolve boundary disputes. They called their new association of colonies the New England Confederation or the United Colonies. It was Colonial America's first union of "states," and it established a political model for the future United States of America. Its governing charter was called the Articles of Confederation of the United Colonies of New England, and it began with these words:

> *Whereas, we all came into these parts of America with one and the same end and aim, namely to advance the Kingdom of our Lord Jesus Christ, and to enjoy the Liberties of the Gospel, in purity with peace . . . we conceive it our bound duty, without delay, to enter into a present Consociation among ourselves for mutual help and strength. . . .*

The United Colonies would provide a mutual defense, resolve border disputes, and, according to the Articles of Confederation, join in "preserving and propagating the truth and liberties of the Gospel."[24]

The New England Puritans had failings aplenty. They restricted political rights to church members, banished doctrinal dissidents, and at times appeared to have forgotten their former persecution as they persecuted others. Even so, their positive influence on the American nation of the future was extraordinary. America's long-held traditions of faith, values, family life, education, business, law, government, and the national work ethic were all shaped by the Puritans. So were many of America's cherished political freedoms—representative government, regular elections, ownership of private property, and self-government by the consent of the governed.[25]

Eventually, the Puritan culture dissolved into New England's mainstream Christianity, and some Congregational churches even succumbed to Unitarianism. Left behind, however, was a lasting legacy, as historian Samuel Eliot Morison would observe: "New Englanders, however they differed . . . had a common belief in the Bible as the guide to life." More than 150 years after the Great Migration, the treasured liberties championed by America's founding fathers would in great measure be the legacy of the New England Puritans. "These same principles," philosopher Alexis de Tocqueville would note, "unknown to the European nations or despised by them, were proclaimed in the wilderness of the New World and became the future symbol of a great people."[26]

CHAPTER 6

"God's Merciful Providence"

The young minister and his wife would soon stand for the first time on New England soil. It was a bitterly cold day in February 1630, and they had sailed from the English port of Bristol to Massachusetts Bay with twenty other passengers and a load of freight. The voyage had been so stormy that one crewman had been blown overboard in a gale. As the twenty-six-year-old Puritan clergyman filed off the ship with his wife, Mary, and the other weary passengers, he easily could have passed unnoticed in the crowd. If so, he was not overlooked for long: he would soon become the most controversial figure in New England. Some would embrace him with affection and loyalty; others would be stirred to anger and dismay. Throughout Puritan Massachusetts, he would provoke controversy—and he would forever affect the future American nation. His name was Roger Williams.[1]

He was personally welcomed by Massachusetts governor John Winthrop. The young preacher was a "godly minister," Winthrop had been told—said to be powerful in the pulpit. He would be a welcome addition to the colony's clergymen, Winthrop hoped. In short order, however, Roger Williams wore out his welcome. He quickly received a call as minister of a new Congregational church in Boston, but upon examination, he declined the offer. Like other mainstream Puritan churches, the Boston congregation was nonconformist but kept its official connection with the Church of England. Williams would have no part of it. The Church of England engaged in unbiblical practices, he declared, and membership in it was sinful. Almost immediately he became the most prominent dissenter in the Massachusetts Bay Colony.[2]

A native of London, Williams had been raised among England's Anglican gentry. His father was an affluent businessman and one of his wife's relatives was London's lord mayor. Williams was given a privileged education, and early in his childhood he displayed a gifted intellect. He also displayed a decidedly independent spirit. To his father's consternation, he declared himself a Puritan at age eleven. Gifted with a "natural inclination to study," he attracted the attention of the renowned English attorney and political thinker Sir Edward Coke, whose writings would later influence America's founding fathers. The great barrister agreed to mentor the precocious young Williams, who learned shorthand, took notes of Sunday sermons, and afterward preached them for Coke as an academic exercise.[3]

As Edward Coke's protégé, Williams was able to attend England's prestigious new Charterhouse School. Later, he graduated with honors from Cambridge University. He seriously considered practicing law as his famous mentor did; but instead, he chose to enter the ministry. He was ordained in the Anglican Church, although he fully embraced Puritan doctrine and opposed the concept of a state church. Befriended by some of England's principal Puritan leaders, he became the chaplain to a prosperous Puritan family.[4]

While a chaplain, he fell in love with a young woman of the English aristocracy who lived with her wealthy aunt. After proposing, Williams followed aristocratic etiquette and formally wrote the aunt for permission to wed. He was denied. Despondent at his rejection, he fell ill for a time. Then he displayed what would become a trademark temperament: he wrote the aunt again, this time assailing her with a sermon-style discourse that acknowledged her authority but questioned her salvation.[5]

Within a year, he married a former servant girl named Mary Barnard, who would bear him six children. The couple soon left England for America and the Puritan's "City upon a hill." There Williams exercised his convictions in his typical bold style, stirring controversy almost from the day he arrived. Centuries later, Roger Williams would be depicted by some as an early Enlightenment humanist at odds with narrow-minded Puritan bigots. He was "a rebel against all the stupidities that interposed a barrier betwixt men and the fellowship of their dreams," opined one twentieth-century historian. In reality, the opposite was true: Roger Williams believed the Puritans of Massachusetts were too worldly.[6]

The Enlightenment, the famed movement that celebrated human "reason" in contrast to the historic Judeo-Christian worldview, did sweep Western Europe near the end of Williams's life. Roger Williams, however, was hardly an Enlightenment humanist: he faulted the Puritan leadership not for being too strict, but for refusing to separate from the Church of England, which he thought was unbiblical. Not only should the Puritan congregations separate from the Anglican Church, he believed, but England should have no official state church. All denominations—all religious faiths—should be allowed free practice, he argued. By the time he emigrated to New England, Williams had acquired Anabaptist leanings, and in America those beliefs increased.[7]

Anabaptists, who would become known as Baptists in America, held to the fundamental doctrines of Christianity, and opposed infant baptism. The ordinance of baptism symbolized salvation through personal faith in Jesus Christ, they believed, and therefore was intended for believers alone, and not their children. Like Williams, Baptists supported freedom of religion and opposed the existence of a state church. Over the course of five years, Williams continuously and publicly criticized Massachusetts Bay's Puritan leadership. He continued to argue for separation from the Church of England, criticized Puritan restrictions on dissidents like himself, and opposed punishing colonists for disagreeing with Puritan doctrine and practices.[8]

Despite his constant public criticisms of Puritan practices, Williams's devout faith and endearing personality won the friendship of Puritan leaders such as William Bradford, Thomas Hooker, and John Winthrop. He accepted the pastorate of a church in Plymouth Colony, and for a time conducted a ministry with little controversy. After two years in the pulpit, however, even the easygoing Plymouth brethren began to object to some of his opinions, and he left. In 1633, he became an assistant, then the pastor at a church in Salem, but issues soon marked his ministry there, too. He preached that women should cover their heads when praying in church, argued that the local Indian tribes should be paid more for their lands, questioned certain worship practices as unbiblical, and even challenged the validity of Massachusetts's charter.[9]

Although a cloud of controversy often surrounded him, Williams wielded a keen intellect and an encyclopedic knowledge of Scripture that earned grudging respect from his adversaries—and enabled him to expose spiritual pride with near-surgical skill. "Oh remember it is a dangerous combat for the potsherds of the earth to fight against their dreadful Potter," he once admonished Massachusetts governor John Endecott for punishing dissenting Christians. "It . . . is a dreadful voice from the King of kings and Lord of lords [that says to you] 'why huntest thou me? Why imprisonest thou me? Why finest, why so bloodily whippest, why wouldest thou hang and burn me?' Is it possible [that you] hunt the life of my Savior and the blood of the Lamb of God? Sir, I must be humbly bold to say, that 'tis impossible for any man or men to maintain their Christ by the sword and worship a true Christ!"[10]

Williams continued to demonstrate against the Church of England and condemn Puritan leaders for not severing ties with it. By 1634, he was preaching that the king had no claim to the New World because it rightfully belonged to the Indians, and at one point he publicly referred to King Charles I as a liar. At the moment, the king was too distracted by his feud with Parliament to take notice of criticism from a faraway preacher. However, Williams's constant critiques and rash public comments unnerved Massachusetts's Puritan leaders. Allowing him to continuously disparage the king and the Church was intolerable, they concluded. So in 1635, the colony's General Court charged him with spreading "newe & dangerous opinions, against the authoritie of magistrates," and banished him from Massachusetts.[11]

He was slow to leave. After allowing more than ample time for his departure, Massachusetts authorities ordered officers to seize the controversial preacher and deport him to England. His friend John Winthrop, the governor, apparently sent him a warning, and Williams fled. He spent the winter with a nearby band of Narragansett Indians he had befriended. Williams had defended the Indians and had shared the Gospel with them—and they welcomed him when he was banished. The relationship proved beneficial to Williams in other ways: in 1636, he purchased a large tract of Indian land outside the jurisdiction of Massachusetts Bay. There, joined by other exiles from Boston and their followers, Roger Williams established a new colony.[12]

He called it Providence—so named because of "God's merciful providence to me in my distress," he said. "I designed it might be for a shelter for persons distressed for conscience," he would later write. Once again, the New England forest rang with the sounds of axes at work, as new settlers claimed land in Providence Plantation. They came because of a generous and democratic policy of land grants Williams offered—and because they wanted greater religious freedom. Massachusetts Bay and the other Puritan colonies were actually relatively tolerant for their day, but Providence Plantation did more than allow religious toleration. It grew into the Colony of Rhode Island—the first colony in America to grant full religious liberty.[13]

There, in the wilderness of Rhode Island, Williams moved from Congregationalist to Baptist. At his request, a layman baptized him by immersion. Then he baptized the layman—and set about baptizing others. His new congregation laid claim to being the first organized Baptist church in America. Alongside the Baptists, a diverse population of Christians arose in early Rhode Island, including a growing number of Quakers fleeing persecution, and a sizable body of Catholics. The colony also attracted some of America's first Jewish settlers, and an untold number of settlers who belonged to no church—all of whom were officially guaranteed full religious freedom by Rhode Island's government.[14]

It was the Reverend Roger Williams, with the help of influential friends, who engineered this unprecedented leap forward in religious freedom. In 1643, he made a lengthy lobbying trip to England, and exercised connections with the English aristocracy and Puritan community. The eventual result was an official charter for the Colony of Rhode Island by the authority of King Charles II, which declared that the colony's residents would enjoy religious freedom and even be excused from participation in the Church of England. The charter's provisions, like its language, were remarkably generous for the era:

> *Now, know ye, that we, being willing to encourage the hopeful undertaking of our said loyal and loving subjects, and to secure them in the free exercise and enjoyment of all their civil and religious rights, appertaining to them, as our loving subjects . . . and because some of the people and inhabitants of the same colony cannot in their private opinions, conform to the public exercise of religion, according to the liturgy, forms and*

ceremonies of the Church of England . . . our royal will and pleasure is, that no person within the said Colony, at any time hereafter, shall be any wise molested, punished, disquieted, or called in question, for any differences in opinion in matters of religion. . . .[15]

Such an offer was an extraordinary position for a government in the early seventeenth century, when religious persecution occurred throughout the world. Roger Williams's vision thus became reality in Rhode Island: he and others who shared his beliefs were free to worship outside the state church they so distrusted, and others were free to worship as they desired. Williams believed such an environment was not only a biblical expression of Christian charity, but would actually lead more people to faith in Christ. "It is the will and command of God that since the coming of his son the Lord Jesus," he wrote, "the most paganish, Jewish, Turkish, or anti-christian . . . men in all nations and countries . . . are only to be fought against with that sword which is only, in soul matters, able to conquer: to wit, the sword of God's Spirit, the word of God."[16]

To Williams, freedom of religion and the separation of church and state did not mean abandoning the biblical foundation of English law or suppressing every vestige of Bible-based morality in government; instead, it meant that there should be no government-sponsored denomination, such as the Church of England, and that everyone should be allowed to believe and worship according to his or her conscience. He did not originally intend to become a champion of religious liberty; he mainly wanted to purge Puritanism of its connection to the Church of England. "Williams backed into the principle of religious freedom," Colonial expert Clarence Ver Steeg would later observe, "not as one who would liberalize religion, but as one who would strive for a purer faith." Even so, he would enter history as one of the "earliest fathers of American democracy."[17]

He spent the rest of his life in Rhode Island, serving in the colonial legislature and as a three-term governor of the colony. He tried, vainly, to prevent New England's Indian wars, and held public debates with Rhode Island's Quaker leaders. Always, he was unconventional. Eventually, he announced that he was no longer a Baptist, but was merely a Christian "seeker." One area of faith in which he always remained consistent: he opposed government restrictions on the faith of anyone. As he had intended, the Colony of Rhode Island became a haven for all. Its colonists included a wide variety of Protestants, as well as Catholics, Quakers, a community of Jewish settlers from the Caribbean, the devout, the nominal, and the uninterested. Roger Williams died in 1683, almost eighty and active in Rhode Island's affairs until the end.[18]

His death occurred only six years before English Parliament passed the 1689 Act of Toleration, which granted freedom of worship to Protestant nonconformists. The Toleration Act did not apply to Quakers, Catholics, or Jews, who still faced restrictions, but it allowed dissidents such as the Puritans, Presbyterians, Dutch Reformed, and Baptists freedom to preach, teach, and worship outside the Anglican Church. Due to the Reverend Williams, such freedom already existed in large measure within the Colony of Rhode Island.[19]

Rash, provocative, brilliant, and devout, Roger Williams was convinced that Christians were called to demonstrate their faith in Christ by allowing the faith of others. He and his Rhode Island Colony thus set a standard for religious freedom that would someday be a hallmark of the future American nation. Freedom of faith would expand gradually but steadily in Colonial America. Even while mourners attended Roger Williams's funeral in 1683, three hundred miles to the south another crucial chapter in the saga of America's faith-based culture was unfolding in the new Quaker colony of Pennsylvania.[20]

CHAPTER 7

"The Holy Experiment"

William Penn found himself in a unique situation: The king of England owed him a lot of money. The debt had originally belonged to Penn's father, an admiral in the English navy, whose family connections with a mercantile empire had allowed him to amass a fortune. At the time, the future king—Charles II—was the duke of York, and Admiral Penn had loaned him a large sum at a critical time. Upon the admiral's death, ownership of the loan passed to his son. In 1681, two years before aging Roger Williams died in Rhode Island, William Penn decided to collect the debt he had inherited. Instead of money, Penn explained to the king, he wanted land in America—and the king granted his request. What emerged from the transaction was a colony named for Penn's father—Pennsylvania. Like Roger Williams in Rhode Island, William Penn sought full religious liberty, but not as a Baptist. William Penn was a Quaker, and his heart's desire was for a Quaker colony in Pennsylvania.[1]

Quakerism was a spin-off Puritan sect. It began in England in the early seventeenth century, and was founded by a shoemaker-turned-preacher named George Fox. The sect's theology was largely defined by Fox, and its unusual name also originated with him—indirectly. Sentenced to jail for his beliefs in 1650, Fox warned the presiding judge that he should tremble in fear of God for engaging in persecution. "You folk are the tremblers," the judge retorted, "you are the quakers." The name "Quaker" stuck. Although intended as an insult, it was accepted as the movement's nickname by Fox and the Society of Friends, as the Quakers called themselves.[2]

The Quakers carried dissent against the Church of England much further than did mainstream Puritans or the Separatists. They discarded Anglican and Puritan worship forms, abandoned structured church government, rejected baptism, communion, and some fundamental biblical doctrines—and promoted personal revelation, which they called the "inner light." They proclaimed pursuit of a simple life, and became known for their drab clothing and austere worship services. They also believed that government should be extremely limited in its influence over the individual, and staunchly opposed the existence of an official state church. At times, their public protests caused near riots.[3]

They were uncompromising in their faith and suffered prolonged persecution. In England, they were imprisoned by the thousands for declining to take oaths, ignoring the mandatory tithe to the Anglican Church, refusing to serve in the military, and often simply for assembling in worship. They took Christ's command to "love your enemies" as a call to pacifism but were determined in their nonviolent resistance. "The constables drove them from their meeting houses," historian Edward Channing would note, and "they went back through the windows; the constables pulled down the meeting houses, they met on the ruins; the constables bore the adults off to prison, the children met by themselves and worshipped in silence."[4]

They fled to America in droves. At first they were treated harshly there, too. Their unique beliefs unnerved Puritans and Anglicans alike, and at times the Quakers were intentionally provocative. One Quaker preacher ignited a near-riot in England by entering the city of Bristol astride a donkey in a Christ-like "triumphant entry," while supporters saluted him with hosannas. He was merely trying to symbolize Christ's entry into individual hearts, he claimed, but his tongue was bored with a hot iron and his forehead was branded with a *B* for blasphemy. In Massachusetts, a Quaker woman who was devoted to simplicity in the extreme interrupted a church service by stalking naked down the church aisle while loudly condemning the pastor.[5]

Such demonstrations were not typical, although many Quakers were willing to suffer for their beliefs. When banished from Boston by civil authorities in the 1650s, Quaker dissenters repeatedly returned, loudly denouncing Puritan policies in the streets, and disrupting Congregational worship services. They also refused to pay taxes and serve in the local militia. Early Colonial authorities viewed the Quakers as threats to the public order, and confrontational Quakers were punished by public whippings—which actually increased opposition to religious intolerance.[6]

In one celebrated case, a Quaker woman stoically endured ten lashes, then publicly forgave the executioner, causing public sentiment to shift in her favor. When exasperated Massachusetts officials hanged three Quaker protesters in 1659, they ignited an outpouring of public disapproval from the Puritan laity. Soldiers had to be deployed to control sympathetic crowds as the condemned Quakers walked hand in hand to the gallows "with great cheerfulness of Heart." The Quakers persevered, and gradually won religious liberty in England and America for themselves and others.[7]

As early as the 1620s, Quakers were grudgingly granted a degree of religious toleration in New Netherland, the Dutch colony that occupied modern New York Bay with its capital, New

Amsterdam, on the site of modern-day New York City. The Dutch Reformed Church was the official state church of Holland and its colonies, but Dutch authorities allowed the emigration of Puritans, Baptists, Lutherans, Catholics, Quakers, and a small community of Jewish refugees from Portuguese Brazil. Peter Stuyvesant, New Netherland's brash governor, originally tried to devise "a friendly way" to force the Jews to leave, but under pressure from the colony's sponsor, the West India Company, he relented and allowed the Jews to worship in their homes. He was less lenient with Lutheran emigrants, barring their worship services and deporting their pastor, and he considered the Quakers to be "an abominable heresy." However, support for the Quakers—and religious freedom—received a precedent-setting boost from a community of Dutch Christians.[8]

In the 1650s, when a group of poor Quakers arrived in New Netherland, Christians in the Flushing settlement on Long Island attempted to house the needy newcomers. Governor Stuyvesant threatened to punish anyone aiding Quakers, but the Flushing believers drafted a formal protest called the "Remonstrance against the Law against Quakers." It argued that Christians had a biblical obligation to assist those in need, regardless of their beliefs, based on Christ's command that "whatsoever ye would that men should do to you, do ye even so to them." They respectfully explained to the governor that they were compelled to obey God's Law rather than his:

> *Master, we are bound by the Law to do good to all men, especially to those of the Household of faith . . . so love, peace and liberty extending to all in Christ Jesus condemns hatred, war and bondage. [Our] desire is not to offend one of his little ones in whatsoever form, name or title he appears in, whether Presbyterian, Independent, Baptist or Quaker . . . desiring to do unto all men as we desire all men should do unto us . . . for our Savior saith this is the Law and the Prophets.*

The Dutch Christians in Flushing did not convince the governor, but they did establish an important precedent for Colonial America—tolerance for those of other beliefs as an expression of Christianity.[9]

It was a legacy soon transferred to English America. In 1664, an English naval flotilla arrived off New Amsterdam and forced the Dutch colony's surrender without firing a shot. New Netherland became the English Colony of New York—named for the Duke of York, who later became King James II. After the transfer of power, New York's first English governor, Richard Nicolls, established English-style government with what was called the "Duke's Laws," which reflected the Judeo-Christian foundation of English law. Nicolls introduced the Church of England as the official state church in New York, but continued and expanded New Netherland's tradition of religious tolerance. The amount of religious freedom granted Catholics varied according to who was in power, but the Colony of New York was comparatively tolerant toward Catholics, Jews, and Protestant dissenters—including Quakers.[10]

Such was the environment in England and America when William Penn began his quest for a Quaker colony. Born in London in 1644, and raised in an upper-class home near the Thames River, he was considered "religiously inclined" even as a child. His parents were prominent Anglicans, but Penn declared himself a Puritan as a teenager. At Oxford University, where his father sent him for an aristocrat's education, he was exposed to Quaker teaching. Handsome, articulate, and bright, he became a leading critic of the state church among Oxford's students, and was expelled from school for his nonconformist protests. Exasperated, his father sent him to Paris in the hope that he would become enamored with secular culture rather than Quakerism. Instead, young Penn wound up studying at a French Huguenot academy, where his nonconformist tendencies were reinforced.[11]

His father summoned him back to London, arranged for him to receive military training, then enrolled him in the study of law—at which he excelled. Then, at age twenty-one, Penn was sent to Ireland to oversee one of the family estates—far away from England's Quakers. He found a body of Friends there, however, and was influenced by the powerful preaching of a Quaker leader named Thomas Loe. Soon he too was preaching Quakerism, and was jailed by Irish authorities for participating in a raucous public protest. His father managed to secure his release, brought him back to London, and banished him from home. Penn obeyed, explaining that he could not forsake his beliefs. Eventually, his father came to respect Penn's Quakerism as a matter of conscience, and the two were reconciled.[12]

Back in England, he continued preaching and protesting—until English authorities imprisoned him in the Tower of London. Undeterred, he turned to book writing, producing books on Quaker doctrine, a popular work on Christian discipleship entitled *No Cross, No Crown*, and an important work on religious liberty. At one point, the Anglican bishop of London reportedly offered to arrange his freedom if Penn would recant his Quaker beliefs. "My prison shall be my grave, before I will budge a jot," Penn is said to have replied. "For I owe obedience of the Conscience to no mortal man." Despite his bold resistance, Penn was soon freed from the Tower by the intervention of influential family friends.[13]

In 1670, his father died and left him a large inheritance, which he used to help defend the Friends from persecution. He also employed his superb legal skills, becoming a leading advocate of individual rights. The Quaker community and others close to him respected his integrity, and he maintained the respect of many in England's ruling class. Others, however, dismissed him as a Quaker fanatic—one prominent critic called him "a poor, shallow, half-crazed creature." His contribution to Colonial American culture and the growth of religious liberty, however, was substantial.[14]

Through an unusual series of events, in 1673 he was asked to serve as a trustee to a proposed Quaker colony in America. It was called West Jersey, and was located in the western region of modern New Jersey. King Charles II had granted the territory between New England and Maryland to his brother, the Duke of York, who in turn had given two noblemen the region comprising modern New Jersey, which they named for the island of Jersey in the English Channel. To entice settlers into their colony—and profit from quitrent payments—the colony's two proprietors offered religious liberty to all colonists, freedom still unavailable in England. Profits were slow in coming, however, so one proprietor sold his share to the Quaker group. It became West Jersey, with the remaining territory known as East Jersey.[15]

In 1677, approximately two hundred settlers arrived in West Jersey equipped with an official charter of government called the Concessions and Agreements of the Proprietors, Freeholders, and Inhabitants of West Jersey. It guaranteed legislative self-government and a bill of rights for the West Jersey colonists—including religious freedom. No person, it stated, "shall be in any ways molested, punished, disquieted or called into question for any difference in opinion or practice in matter of religious concernments." It provided much greater religious liberty than was available in England at the time—and its author was said to have been William Penn. It was a mighty precedent for faith and freedom—and Penn knew it. "There we lay a foundation for after ages to understand their liberty as Christians and as men," he wrote, ". . . for we put the power in the people."[16]

East Jersey, as the eastern colony was temporarily known, offered a similar guarantee of religious freedom, although—like some other colonies—it placed political restrictions on Jews and Catholics. East and West Jersey would be merged by royal decree in 1702 and would collectively become the royal Colony of New Jersey. By then, the appeal of self-government and religious liberty had attracted not just Quakers, but a wide range of

Protestants—Congregationalists, Anglicans, Baptists, Lutherans, German Reformed, Dutch Reformed, and a large and influential population of English Presbyterians. There too, in small but significant numbers, were Jews and Catholics.[17]

William Penn influenced Colonial American culture in a serious way with the West Jersey colony, but he made an even greater impact with the founding of Pennsylvania. The king officially granted the colony to Penn on March 4, 1681. It would prove to be more than ample payment for the sixteen thousand English pounds the king had borrowed from Penn's father. It was a huge territory—more than three times the size of New Jersey—and a year later, the land that would someday become the state of Delaware was temporarily added to the grant. If King Charles II was generous, he was also shrewd: far fewer Quakers would be left to annoy him in England. Penn drafted a Charter of Liberties for Pennsylvania, which provided fundamental freedoms, including a guarantee that all who believed in God would "in no ways be molested or prejudiced for their religious Persuasion or Practice in Matters of Faith and Worship, nor shall they be compelled at any Time to frequent or maintain any religious Worship, Place or Ministry whatever."[18]

The Colony of Pennsylvania would be, in Penn's words, a "Holy Experiment"—a faith-based colony that offered expanded religious liberty to everyone. To William Penn, it was all done in the name of Christ. "True godliness does not turn men out of the world," he wrote, "but enables them to live better in it; and excites their endeavors to mend it; not to hide their candle under a bushel, but to set it upon a table in a candlestick. . . . Christians should keep the helm, and guide the vessel to port; not . . . leave those that are in it without a pilot." He offered generous terms to emigrants: a penny an acre bought a two-hundred-acre farm, and two hundred English pounds bought a five-thousand-acre estate with a town lot in Philadelphia—the capital city that Penn had neatly laid out around checkerboard squares. Most of the colony's first settlers were Quakers, but others soon came in large numbers—Presbyterians, Lutherans, German Reformed, Mennonites, French Huguenots, Anglicans, Baptists, Amish, Catholics, and a large Jewish community that developed in Philadelphia. It was a colony infused with people of biblical faith.[19]

Unlike the Puritans, who believed that laws and law enforcement were necessary to restrain humanity's sinful nature, Quakers considered mankind to be essentially good, so Penn and others launched the Colony of Pennsylvania with scant laws. A crime wave of sorts soon made them reconsider the need for law and order. To deal with the sins that beset the colony's growing population, Quaker authorities implemented an expanded criminal code that resembled Puritan laws in the Massachusetts Bay Colony. Despite its growing pains, the colony flourished. It exceeded the neighboring Colony of New York in population by 1700, and Philadelphia became the largest city in Colonial America. Again, based on their literal acceptance of the New Testament admonition to "love your enemies," the colony's Quaker leadership also established respectful and peaceful relations with Pennsylvania's Native Americans, an example that was followed by few other colonies.[20]

William Penn and the colony's administrators had less success keeping the peace between colonists in Pennsylvania and Delaware. Although the Delaware territory was administered as part of the Colony of Pennsylvania, its settlers were diverse and independent-minded. A half century earlier, Delaware was the site of a short-lived Swedish colony named New Sweden. It had been ruled by the Dutch, then the English (it was administered by the governor of New York), then added to William Penn's Pennsylvania grant. Many Delaware settlers were Anglicans or dissenters and issues abounded between them and the Pennsylvania Quakers.[21]

In 1701, Penn agreed to a separate legislature for Delaware, which eventually became a separate colony. As with West Jersey and Pennsylvania, Penn attempted to make Delaware a model of religious liberty, which he made a principal feature of Delaware's charter. "Because no people can be truly happy, though under the greatest Enjoyment of Civil Liberties, if abridged of the Freedom of their Consciences, as to their Religious Profession and Worship," it stated, ". . . no Person or Persons inhabiting this Province or Territories, who shall confess and acknowledge One almighty God, the Creator, Upholder and Ruler of the World . . . shall be in any Case molested."[22]

Pennsylvania's Quaker population was eventually outnumbered by non-Quakers, which resulted in a shift in political leadership as well. Pennsylvania would long be considered the "Quaker Colony," but Quakers became the religious minority. Even so, the Quakers' "Holy Experiment" in Pennsylvania reinforced Colonial America's Judeo-Christian values and became a model for religious liberty. William Penn, the Puritan-turned-Quaker whose biblical faith inspired the founding of three colonies, lived until age seventy-five. In his final years, he proposed another grand concept for America. England's leaders ignored it, but it too proved to be visionary. His proposal? A union of all the American colonies, governed by a colonial congress.[23]

CHAPTER 8

"For Our Saviour and Our Sovereign"

Lord Baltimore had already failed once. Now he wanted to try again? His real name was Sir George Calvert—his title was Lord Baltimore—and he too had a vision for land and liberty in America. Sir George was Catholic, and he yearned for a Catholic colony in America where English Catholics could flee the restrictions of Anglican England. While Puritans worried that the Church of England was too Catholic, Calvert and other devout Catholics were convinced it was not Catholic enough. A Catholic colony in America, he believed, offered greater freedom for English Catholics. Sir George had been a high-ranking member of the court during the reign of King James I, and he was viewed with favor by James's son and successor, King Charles I. In 1629, just as the Puritans' Great Migration was beginning, he appealed to King Charles for a land grant to establish his colony.[1]

He had already tried—and failed—to establish the colony of Avalon or Ferryland in Newfoundland, but his efforts were stymied by harsh weather and French raiders. In a warmer climate and at a safer location, he believed, his Catholic colony could prosper. Charles I was sympathetic to Sir George's proposed colony. Although he officially headed the Church of England, he had married a French princess, Henrietta Maria, who was a devout Roman Catholic. Charles called himself a "Catholic," but an Anglican one, not a Roman Catholic, and allowed the queen to practice her faith in a court chapel, although those outside her entourage could not. In 1632, as Puritans were pouring into New England, Charles I granted Calvert's petition for a colony in America. He ordered it named for his Catholic queen, leading English Protestants to speculate that it was really named for the Virgin Mary.[2]

The Colony of Maryland would be established on the north shore of the Potomac River and would share a southern border with Virginia. It was not officially a Catholic colony—the Church of England was the national church in all of England, including the colonies—but Catholicism would be tolerated there and its leadership would be predominantly Catholic. Sir George Calvert had just cause for celebration, but he never saw his dream fulfilled. As the colony's charter was being prepared, he died. His oldest son, Cecilius Calvert, became the second Lord Baltimore and the lord proprietor of the new colony. The younger Calvert would never set foot in Maryland; he would rule from afar—but he would do so capably. Maryland would not go the way of Newfoundland's Avalon Colony: it would make a fortune for the Calvert family, and for many it would become the Catholic haven Sir George Calvert had envisioned.[3]

As lord proprietor of Maryland, Cecilius Calvert financed a recruitment campaign for the colony, promising "prosperous success" for all who would emigrate to America. In November 1633, approximately three hundred settlers boarded the *Ark* and the *Dove*—ships outfitted by Calvert—and departed England for Maryland. Led by Cecilius's brother, Leonard Calvert, who was the colony's first governor, they consisted mainly of English laborers and indentured servants. About twenty were aristocrats of the ruling class—"gentlemen adventurers," they were called.

They were accompanied by wives and children, who would give the colony stability and growth. Also on board were two Catholic priests and two lay missionaries—all Jesuits. To avoid controversy and arousing Anglican officials, Cecilius left recruitment of ministers to the colonists—although he did ask Church officials in Rome to make priests available if the Catholic colonists wanted them. They did, and thus the first colonists were accompanied by the four Jesuits, who were officially listed among the "gentlemen adventurers."[4]

Ironically, most of the passengers bound for the Catholic colony were Protestants: in contrast to England's Puritans, few Catholics wanted to settle in wilderness America, so Protestants were needed to make the colony financially successful. "By far, the greater part were heretics," reported one of the Jesuit priests. The majority of the expedition's ruling class were Catholic, while most of the laborers and indentured servants were Anglican. Therefore, from the beginning, the Catholic colony of Maryland contained a majority of Protestants. Even so, after decades of restrictions in Anglican England, Roman Catholics who were willing to emigrate now had the opportunity to fashion a Catholic-led colony in America much as the Puritans were doing in New England.[5]

Before the expedition left England, Cecilius Calvert met with his brother and other colony officials. They must "suffer no scandal nor offence to be given to any of the Protestants," they were told. "Roman Catholics," the lord proprietor cautioned, were "to be silent upon all occasions of discourse concerning matters of Religion. . . . And this to be observed on land as well as at Sea." It was easier said than done. At sea, the two-ship flotilla was battered by a hurricane-strength storm, which ripped away the *Ark*'s mainsail, broke her rudder, and left the ship rolling uncontrollably atop towering swells. The frightened passengers prayed aloud, according to one of the Jesuits, with the Catholics beseeching "the Blessed Virgin . . . St. Ignatius . . . St. Michael and all the guardian angels," while the Protestants were busy "calling directly upon

God." When doom seemed imminent, the storm suddenly abated, and Catholic and Protestant alike had reason to give thanks.[6]

In March 1634, the *Ark* and the *Dove* made landfall in Maryland on the western shore of Chesapeake Bay. Governor Calvert claimed the colony "for our Saviour and for our Sovereign Lord the King of England." The Jesuit priests celebrated Mass on the site—"a thing which had never been done before in that part of the world," observed a participant—and the Protestants also held a worship service. "After we had completed the Sacrifice, we took upon our shoulders a great cross, which we had hewn out of a tree," reported one of the priests, "and . . . with the assistance of the governor and his associates, and the other Catholics, we erected a trophy to Christ the Saviour, humbly reciting on bended knees the litanies of the Sacred Cross with great emotion."[7]

It was a scene reenacted repeatedly when early English colonists first set foot on American soil. Whether Anglicans in Virginia, Separatists at Plymouth, Puritans at Massachusetts Bay, Catholics in Maryland, or others who followed—upon reaching America's wilderness shores, pioneer English colonists typically enacted the same ceremony: they thanked God for safe passage across the Atlantic, then dedicated their colony to God and king. Catholic Maryland was no different. "It was thus in a religious spirit, and in accordance with the spirit of all who had preceded them," observed a nineteenth-century historian, "that the Maryland adventurers said their prayers, and took possession of the country for their Savior and for the English King."[8]

At a site up the Potomac River, Governor Calvert and his colonists established a settlement—the colony's capital—which they named St. Mary's City. The Jesuit priests exercised their religious freedom immediately by taking the Gospel to the region's Native Americans. Eventually, Maryland's Indian nations, like those throughout America, would be overwhelmed by the advancing European civilization—peacefully or otherwise. Initially, however, some tribes in Maryland apparently welcomed the Catholic missionaries and the Gospel they bore. One Jesuit reported to his superiors that Chitomacon, the "king" of Maryland's Piscataway tribe, had been converted to Christianity and baptized with his family. "For my part," the priest wrote, "I would rather, laboring in the conversion of these Indians, expire on the bare ground, deprived of all human succor, and perishing with hunger, than once think of abandoning this holy work of God. . . ."[9]

As they built their colony at St. Mary's City and elsewhere in Maryland, Catholic and Protestants worked together to forge a common culture despite the conflicts and suspicions of the day. The cooperative atmosphere was due in large part to the informal policy of religious toleration established by Cecilius Calvert, who followed the model his father had tried to implement at his short-lived Newfoundland colony. Maryland's charter cited "a laudable and pious Zeal for extending the Christian religion" as a motive for colonization, and Calvert established an oath of office for the colony's governors requiring them to support broad religious freedom for the day. Under the oath, the governor vowed that he would not "directly or indirectly, trouble, molest or discountenance any person whatsoever, professing to believe in Jesus Christ . . . [nor] make any difference of persons in conferring offices, rewards or favors for or in respect to their said religion."[10]

The Calverts also offered Maryland's colonists more self-government than was afforded to their countrymen back in England. The colony's charter granted ruling authority to the colony's lord proprietor—with the "Advice, Assent and Approbation" of a legislative assembly. The colony's charter thus set a precedent for American government by stating that Maryland's colonists would have a legislative voice. They exercised it promptly. When, as lord proprietor, Cecilius Calvert attempted to enact a series of laws, including capital punishment for idolatry and blasphemy, the

Maryland Christians rejected them and asserted their rights to make law through the legislature. After some wrangling, the lord proprietor agreed and granted the Marylanders an unusually broad degree of self-government through their legislative assembly.[11]

As the Maryland Colony grew, its Protestant population came to outnumber Catholics by three to one. No Catholic world power—not France, Spain, or Portugal—granted freedom of religion to Protestants, or allowed them to hold office. Maryland's Catholic administration did so, however: numerous Protestants were seated in the colony's legislature. Like his brother, Maryland's lord proprietor, Governor Leonard Calvert was Catholic, and thus the colony was administered by Catholics, but Protestants held real power in the legislative assembly. Together, Catholics and Protestants thus governed early Maryland, and the colony's opening era was marked by peace. Eventually, however, old sectarian fears and suspicions were aroused in the colony, mainly by outsiders and new colonists. Tensions increased during the English civil wars, as many Catholics sided with King Charles I and the Royalists, while many Protestants, especially dissenters, backed the Parliamentary forces.[12]

In 1645, Richard Ingle, a sea captain accused of piracy, raided St. Mary's City with two warships, claiming to act in the name of Parliament. Denouncing Maryland's lord protector as a Royalist, he and his crews plundered the town, burned several houses, seized stores of tobacco, and imprisoned Catholic leaders and priests. Governor Leonard Calvert fled to Virginia, and back in England, Cecilius Calvert gave up his colony as lost. Leonard Calvert had not given up, however, and two years later the governor returned to Maryland with a small army, drove out the insurgents, and restored order. In 1649, in order to restore stability to the colony, reassure Protestants, and protect Catholics, Cecilius Calvert presented the colony's legislature with an exceptional legislative proposal for the day. If passed, it would turn Maryland's informal toleration of religious freedom into law.[13]

It was officially called the Act Concerning Religion—better known as the Toleration Act of 1649—and the legislators did pass it. In a unique exercise for Colonial America, Maryland's Catholic and Protestant leaders jointly enacted a statute providing expanded religious freedom. "Forasmuch as in a well governed and Christian Commonwealth matters concerning Religion and the honor of God ought in the first place to be taken into serious consideration and endeavored to be settled," it proclaimed, "no person professing to believe in Jesus Christ shall from henceforth be any ways troubled, molested or discountenanced for or in respect of his or her religion . . . nor in any way compelled to the belief or exercise of any other Religion against his or her consent."[14]

Although it protected religious liberty for Protestants and Catholics alike, it did not extend freedom of religion to everyone—Jews and Quakers were not officially included, for instance. Nor were the rights afforded Catholics to be long-standing: within a few decades, politics, sectarian strife, a burgeoning Protestant population, and government promotion of England's state church penalized all who were not Anglican and erased Maryland's distinction as a Catholic haven. America's Catholics would eventually be afforded full freedom of religion, and the Roman Catholic Church in turn would also accept the coexistence of other faiths. For its day, Maryland's Toleration Act was an exceptional achievement, and laid a keystone precedent for religious liberty in America. As with Roger Williams and William Penn, Cecilius Calvert was not motivated merely by pragmatic politics: he too was following the biblical principle: "whatsoever ye would that men should do to you, do ye even so to them."[15]

That principle would eventually make freedom of faith a hallmark of American democracy. In 1669, it received an important boost from the Bible-based constitution of a newly created colony far south of Maryland. In April of that year, English colonists on the surviving vessel of an original three-ship flotilla reached the coast of present-day South Carolina after a disastrous voyage from England. Led by an eighty-year-old Puritan governor they had recruited in Barbados, they established the first permanent colony in South Carolina, on the site of modern Charleston. Eventually, their colony would become two colonies—North and South Carolina—both bearing a form of the Latin word *Carolus* to honor England's King Charles II.[16]

The king had granted the Colony of Carolina to eight English noblemen—the lords proprietors—for supporting him and the restoration of the English monarchy following the English civil wars. The settlers who reached the Carolina Colony in 1670 brought more than just supplies and fortitude: they were backed by a charter pledging official "zeal for the propagation of the Christian faith," the Fundamental Constitutions of 1669, which would be a faith-based model for the future American nation. Anthony Ashley Cooper, an English earl and one of the lords proprietors, was the constitution's official author, but its real author was a brilliant English philosopher and pioneer political scientist named John Locke.[17]

Locke would eventually become known as "the philosopher of the American Revolution" because of his tremendous influence on America's founding fathers. His classics, such as *Two Treatises of Government* and *The Reasonableness of Christianity as Delivered in the Scriptures*, emphasized God's Higher Law and Natural Law as the basis for English law and government. The generation of leaders who would craft America's founding documents would be schooled in Locke's writings. Even earlier, however, Locke helped define American law and government through the Carolina Colony's Fundamental Constitutions, which he came to draft through his close association with Lord Ashley Cooper. Locke, who was also trained in medicine, was Lord Ashley's personal physician, and once performed a rare surgical procedure that saved his life.[18]

When the lord proprietor needed a constitution for the Carolina Colony, he turned to Locke. The Fundamental Constitutions not only paved a path of self-government for other founding documents to follow, it dramatically advanced the cause for religious liberty. While he drew from a range of sources in his writings, John Locke was guided first and foremost by biblical doctrine. "The holy Scripture is to me, and always will be, the constant guide of my assent," he wrote, "and I shall always hearken to it, as containing infallible truth. . . ." The son of devout Puritans, he recorded his personal profession of faith in *Vindication of the Reasonableness of Christianity*. "There is a faith that makes men Christians," he wrote, "[and] this faith is the believing of Jesus of Nazareth to be the Messiah . . . receiving Him for our Lord and King promised and sent from God."[19]

"As a philosopher, Locke was intensely interested in Christian doctrine," twenty-first-century Locke scholar Jeremy Waldron would conclude, "and . . . he insisted that most men could not hope to understand the detailed requirements of the law of nature without the assistance and teachings of Jesus." The "law of nature" consisted of the laws by which God created and sustained the universe. It included both physical laws and mankind's sense of right and wrong, and was properly understood only by the revelation of Scripture—the Higher Law. Locke followed the historic Christian tradition that some called the "creator-redeemer distinction," which was reemphasized by Martin Luther in the Reformation. It held that government should respect and acknowledge the Creator God of the Bible but should never attempt to coerce its citizens to accept God's plan of redemption.[20]

John Locke's constitution reflected that biblical worldview and launched the Carolina Colony with "liberty of conscience" guaranteed for all—Protestants, Catholics, Jews, and "Heathens." The truth of Christianity was strong enough to prevail if other expressions of faith were freely allowed, Locke believed, and the constitution so stated. Furthermore, Christians had a biblical obligation to share the Gospel of Jesus Christ with unbelievers; to deny them that opportunity by excluding them would be a "great offense to Almighty God and [a] great scandal to the true religion we profess," the constitution stated. Therefore, broad religious freedom was extended to all, including the colony's Native Americans, as a faithful expression of love for Christ. Hence, the constitution promised:

> *Jews, Heathens and other dissenters from the purity of the Christian religion, may not be scared and kept at a distance from it, but by having an opportunity of acquainting themselves with the truth and reasonableness of its doctrines, and the peaceableness and inoffensiveness of its professors, may be good usage and persuasion, and all those convincing methods of gentleness and meekness, suitable to the rules and designs of the gospel, be won over to embrace, and unfeignedly receive the truth. . .*[21]

Subsequent constitutions would govern South and North Carolina as the two colonies developed, but the Fundamental Constitutions of 1669 sent forth a powerful message: settlement was open to Christians of various persuasions—and to others. And they came. Anglicans of the national church were initially the most numerous, but the Carolina Colony's religious liberty attracted growing numbers of Baptists, Presbyterians, French Huguenots, and Quakers. Carolina's open door also enabled a significant Jewish community to develop there. Fears of collusion with Spanish enemies in Florida caused Catholic immigration to be discouraged for a time; but even so, the impact of the Carolina Constitution extended beyond its legal lifetime. A century later, when America's founding fathers looked to John Locke's writings as a model for a nation, they would also look to Carolina's Fundamental Constitutions of 1669.[22]

Under its influence, the Colony of North Carolina, officially established in 1712, became home to a host of Christian dissenters—Presbyterians, Lutherans, Moravians, Baptists, Huguenots, Quakers, and others—who eventually outnumbered members of the Church of England in the colony. The colony of Georgia—last of the thirteen to be settled—also attracted a tide of dissenters. Founded by English humanitarian James Oglethorpe in 1732, it began as a haven for former prisoners freed from debtors' prisons in England. As a buffer colony to Spanish Florida, Colonial Georgia also needed a rapid influx of settlers—and a policy of religious freedom similar to the Carolina Colony helped attract them.[23]

The Church of England would remain the official state church in Colonial America until the Revolution, but its membership was eventually surpassed in numbers by dissident denominations—Presbyterians, Congregationalists, Baptists, Lutherans, Dutch Reformed, and others. Virginia remained an Anglican stronghold, and the state church remained strong in other southern colonies. Everywhere, however, the Church of England was disliked by many because the government penalized other denominations and implemented taxes to support it. As discontent with British rule increased on the eve of the Revolution, many Americans viewed the Anglican Church with disdain as an arm of the government.[24]

Even faithful Anglicans frequently resisted the national church. One Anglican congregation in Maryland refused to accept a Church-appointed pastor, and locked the church door when the preacher arrived, forcing him to climb through a window to claim the pulpit. When an unwanted minister preached his first sermon in an Anglican church in New York, a Presbyterian parson began preaching in a field outside the church—and half the Anglican audience defected to the outdoor pulpit. Like the New York congregation, Colonial Americans voted with their feet—and many walked away from allegiance to an official government denomination. When Anglican leaders pushed for an American bishop on the eve of the Revolution, it provoked a continental controversy, and opposition was widespread even among Anglicans. There would be no "Church of America" like the Church of England.[25]

Amid the profusion of Christian denominations in Colonial America, a pattern gradually emerged: First came religious tolerance, eventually followed by full religious liberty. "Religious tolerance had been brought about by a medley of religious faiths such as the world had never seen before," historian John Richard Green would note. Over time, the old animosities of Europe began to subside. The fear born of past persecutions gradually faded. There would be no Spanish Inquisition in America—no execution sites bloodied by hundreds of victims like London's Smithfield. Americans would not stand for it. Religious liberty would become one of the touchstones of liberty in America.[26]

Through a diversity of Bible-based beliefs, Colonial America firmly founded its culture, laws, and government on the Judeo-Christian worldview. That common faith was clearly expressed in the founding documents of all thirteen American colonies:

- ✦ The Massachusetts Bay Colony's charter recorded an intent to spread the "knowledge and obedience of the only true God and Savior of mankind, and the Christian faith," much as the Mayflower Compact cited a commitment to "the Glory of God, and Advancement of the Christian faith."
- ✦ Connecticut's Fundamental Orders officially called for "an orderly and decent Government established according to God" that would "maintain and preserve the liberty and purity of the Gospel of our Lord Jesus."
- ✦ In New Hampshire, the Agreement of the Settlers at Exeter vowed to establish a government "in the name of

Christ" that "shall be to our best discerning agreeable to the Will of God."

- Rhode Island's colonial charter invoked the "blessing of God" for "a sure foundation of happiness to all America."
- The Articles of Confederation of the United Colonies of New England stated, "Whereas we all came into these parts of America with one and the same end and aim, namely, to advance the Kingdom of our Lord Jesus Christ and to enjoy the liberties of the Gospel . . ."
- New York's Duke's Laws prohibited denial of "the true God and his Attributes."
- New Jersey's founding charter vowed, "Forasmuch as it has pleased God, to bring us into this Province . . . we may be a people to the praise and honor of his name."
- Delaware's original charter officially acknowledged "One almighty God, the Creator, Upholder and Ruler of the World."
- Pennsylvania's charter officially cited a "Love of Civil Society and Christian Religion" as motivation for the colony's founding.
- Maryland's charter declared an official goal of "extending the Christian Religion."
- Virginia's first charter commissioned colonization as "so noble a work, which may, by the Providence of Almighty God, hereafter tend to the . . . propagating of Christian Religion."
- The charter for the Colony of Carolina proclaimed "a laudable and pious zeal for the propagation of the Christian faith."
- Georgia's charter officially cited a commitment to the "propagating of Christian religion."[27]

Colonial America was constructed, one colony at a time, on two pillars—faith and freedom. It was an extraordinary combination, rare in history, and it bequeathed unprecedented opportunities to the American people. "Possessed of security and quiet, abundance of land, a free market for their staples, and, practically, all the rights of an independent state," historian George Bancroft would write, ". . . the colonists enjoyed all the prosperity which a virgin soil, equal laws, and general uniformity of condition and industry, could bestow. Their numbers increased; their cottages were filled with children, as the ports were with ships and emigrants." America was forged in faith, and it was a land like no other.[28]

CHAPTER 9

"The Great Awakening"

Jonathan Edwards stood behind the pulpit and looked down at the people in the pews. They sat shoulder to shoulder in the cramped Congregational meetinghouse, and they did not appear very worshipful. It was a summer evening—July 8, 1741—in the small town of Enfield, which was located on the Connecticut-Massachusetts border. The crowd in the meetinghouse appeared restless, even irreverent to some, and one observer thought they acted "thoughtless and vain"—as if they had come to church for entertainment. Doubtlessly, some did; and others probably came out of curiosity. All of them were there to hear the Reverend Edwards preach.[1]

Edwards had come to town with a reputation: He was the grandson of the Reverend Solomon Stoddard, a famous Puritan preacher, and he had acquired an increasing amount of fame himself. He now held his late grandfather's pastorate at Northampton, Massachusetts, and he was said to be brilliant—an "intellectual giant," some called him. As a child, he had been homeschooled by an intellectual mother and a minister father who had graduated from Harvard. Satisfying his scholarly childhood inquiries apparently required the entire family: he was the sole son among ten sisters, and the older siblings also helped tutor him. As a boy, he carefully conducted and documented scientific experiments, and wrote a scholarly essay on the habits of the "flying spider." When he was ten years old, he composed a "semi-humorous tract on the immateriality of the soul." At age twelve, he was accepted as a student at Yale University.[2]

There, he flourished. He mastered John Locke's *Essay Concerning Human Understanding* at age fourteen, finding it delightful—worth more to him, he said, than "handfuls of silver and gold." He enthusiastically embraced Newtonian science, captivated by the concept that distant stars were really blazing suns encircled by planets. The study of science, he concluded, was a disciplined and delightful examination of God's creation. At seventeen, he graduated from Yale as valedictorian and head of his class. He then plunged into the study of theology, spending two years at divinity school. While there, he surrendered his life to Jesus Christ as Lord and Savior. From that point forward, instead of succumbing to intellectual pride as might be expected for an acclaimed genius, he humbly vowed "to lie low before God, as in the dust; that I might be nothing, and that God might be all."[3]

After finishing divinity school, he briefly ministered to a Presbyterian congregation in New York, returned to Yale briefly as a tutor, then joined his grandfather at Northampton Congregational Church as an associate pastor. He married a devout, sweet-spirited woman named Sarah Pierpont, and assumed the pastorate at Northampton upon his grandfather's death in 1729. As minister of one of the largest churches in Massachusetts, he received ample opportunity to preach and write, and his published sermons drew international attention. He habitually rose daily at 4 A.M. for a thirteen-hour workday of prayer and Bible study, reading the Hebrew lexicon and other works, and for sermon preparation. Often, he wandered through the nearby forest, praying and jotting down notes about topics that came to mind. He earned wide respect as a scholar and theologian, and eventually would be named president of what would become Princeton University. Despite all his accomplishments, his heart's desire was to witness a spiritual revival in Colonial America.[4]

Many believed it was desperately needed. When Jonathan Edwards came to preach in Enfield that summer night, more than 130 years had passed since the founding of Jamestown. A full century had passed since the Great Migration had spilled ranks of God-fearing Puritans into the New England wilderness. The Judeo-Christian worldview was still the consensus philosophy of Colonial America, but many Christian leaders feared that America's foundational faith was faltering. Prosperity, security, and the distractions of a progressive culture had dulled Christianity in the Colonies, they believed, and the American people had grown lukewarm in their faith.[5]

The frontier lacked churches and clergy, and was notorious for its rowdy lifestyle. America's cities were little better, some believed. Among the urban elite, deism—with its view of a disinterested, impersonal God—was growing fashionable, and the squalor and hardship of slum neighborhoods bred secular indifference. Throughout the Thirteen Colonies, eighteenth-century Americans seemed to be drifting from the faith of their fathers. "In short, the old established religious habits and customs were crumbling under the impact of changing social conditions," historian Carl Bridenbaugh would later write, "and secularism was slowly, almost imperceptibly, filtering into the minds and actions everywhere. . . ." A Pennsylvania pastor fretted that "the people were very generally through the land careless at heart, and stupidly indifferent about the great concerns of eternity." A minister from Vermont concurred: "The difference between the church and the world was vanishing away," he lamented. "Church discipline was neglected, and the growing laxness of morals was invading the churches."[6]

The spiritual decline even affected Puritan New England. There, some blamed the slippage on Jonathan Edwards's grandfather, who had led a movement within the Congregational Church to adopt what was known as the Halfway Covenant. Church membership was required for many civil rights in Colonial America, which leavened the church rolls with members motivated less by faith and more by a desire to obtain political rights. The Halfway Covenant met lukewarm aspiring members halfway, according to supporters, by granting church membership to people of moral reputation, children of members, and those who had been baptized as infants—without requiring a personal testimony of faith in Christ. Stoddard believed the Halfway Covenant was an act of grace that could lead the lukewarm to salvation.[7]

Edwards, however, saw the Halfway Covenant as an unbiblical compromise of faith, and he rejected it. The church doors should be open to all, he believed, but church membership was meant solely for professing Christians. Salvation, he taught, did not come by good works, moral living, or intellectual knowledge. Jonathan Edwards, the consummate intellectual, taught that salvation came from a changed heart, and not merely by intellectual assent—not from "a head stored with notions and speculations," as he put it. "If the great things of religion are understood," he preached, ". . . they will affect the heart." In the Gospel of John, Jesus told Nicodemus, "Ye must be born again," and Edwards taught likewise. Salvation, he preached, came by God's grace through personal faith in Jesus Christ as Lord and Savior—a salvation experience. Church membership, he believed, should depend on a credible testimony of personal faith in Christ.[8]

Not all agreed—even in Edwards's home church. Many viewed church membership as a right, and resented Edwards's position. Eventually, the congregation would remove him as pastor at Northampton. When dismissed, he would go about God's work elsewhere, initially taking his wife and eight children into the New England backcountry to pastor a modest church for the Mohican Indians. His reputation as a minister, theologian, and scholar would not be diminished—his greatest published works would come later, as would his call to the presidency of Princeton. All of that lay far in the future when he came to preach in Enfield in 1741. His appearance drew a crowd because of his prominence—and because of reports about extraordinary events occurring under his ministry at Northampton.[9]

Six and a half years earlier, in 1734, the first stirrings of a culture-changing event occurred in Edwards's church. Some of the congregation's young people had responded to his salvation message by holding prayer meetings, where they prayed for revival in their church and elsewhere. In December 1734, six people in Northampton had suddenly prayed to receive Christ. More conversions had followed. Within a few months, the number was averaging about thirty a week. News of a revival in Northampton spread to surrounding communities, attracting visitors to the Northampton church, and more people came to Christ. Within six months, approximately three hundred people were said to have professed faith in Christ, including almost every adult in town. Northampton and the surrounding region were transformed.[10]

"In the spring and summer that followed, the town seemed to be full of the presence of God," Edwards would report. "Our assemblies were then beautiful. Our public praises were greatly enlivened. Our young people, when they met, were wont to spend their time talking about the love of Jesus Christ. . . . They had now abandoned their frolicking, their night-walking, their impure language and lewd songs. And among all, whether young or old, there was seen to be a change in their habits of drinking, tavern-haunting, profane speaking and extravagance of apparel. Notoriously vicious persons have been reformed. The wealthy, the fashionable, the great beaus and fine ladies, have relinquished their vanities."[11]

From Northampton, the revival spread to other towns in the Colony of Massachusetts—to South Hadley, Suffield, Sutherland, Deerfield, Hatfield, Northfield, Springfield, and Longmeadow. Everywhere it occurred, the revival changed communities. People took a new interest in reading the Bible. Worship services increased in attendance on the Lord's Day. Feuding colonists settled their differences. Argumentative neighbors apologized to each other. Neglected debts were repaid. Families and friends were reconciled. "It was a time of joy in families on account of salvation being brought unto them," Edwards would recall, "parents rejoicing over their children as new born, and husbands over their wives, and wives over their husbands."[12]

Edwards recorded the Northampton revival in a booklet titled *A Faithful Narrative of the Surprising Work of God in the Conversion of Many Hundred Souls in Northampton.* It became an international bestseller and helped spur faraway revivals in England, Wales, and Scotland. Englishman John Wesley, founder of Methodism, read it while walking from London to Oxford. "Surely, this is the Lord's doing," he penned in his diary, and credited the Northampton revival for helping establish the Methodist Church. "Edwards' preaching at Northampton," historian Samuel Morison would write, "was the womb of all modern revivalism in the Protestant churches of the English-speaking world." In the summer of 1741, when some expected the Northampton revival to abate, it came anew to Connecticut, beginning in Enfield.[13]

When the impatient audience in the meetinghouse that night peered up at the famous Jonathan Edwards, they saw an ordinary-looking preacher—tall, slender, dignified. Some thought he looked "scholarly," and others described his eyes as "piercing," but there was nothing hypnotic or mesmerizing about his appearance. Nor was he a dramatic speaker. His pulpit delivery had more of a teacher's cadence than a preacher's, but his quiet, measured tones captured attention—and he spoke with authority. "Besides his logic, there was his strong and realizing faith," a fellow New England preacher recalled. "God, heaven, hell, the sinfulness of sin, the beauty of holiness, the glory of Christ and the claims of his gospel were as substantial realities to his mind and heart as the valley of the Connecticut or the mountains of Berkshire. He spoke of them accordingly, and made them seem real to his hearers."[14]

His message seemed real at Enfield that night. It was titled "Sinners in the Hands of an Angry God," and it was about the wrath of God. It was not a typical Jonathan Edwards sermon—he usually preached on more cheerful topics, such as the perfection of Christ. His text came from Deuteronomy 32:35—"their foot shall slide in due time"—and the ultimate point of his sermon was God's redeeming love and the escape He offered from the penalty of sin. Edwards did not pound the pulpit or engage in thundering, bombastic oratory. The sermon was delivered soberly and with his characteristic gentle and precise eloquence—but it fell upon its hearers like the gust of a mighty wind.[15]

"Your wickedness makes you, as it were, heavy as lead," Edwards told them.

> *[The] sun does not willingly shine upon you to give you light to serve sin and Satan; the earth does not willingly yield her increase to satisfy your lusts; nor is it willingly a stage for your wickedness to be acted upon; the air does not willingly serve you for breath to maintain the flame of life in your vitals, while you spend your life in the service of God's enemies. . . . There are the black clouds of God's wrath now hanging directly over your heads, full of the dreadful storm, and big with thunder; and were it not for the restraining hand of God, it would immediately burst forth upon you.*[16]

Only the love of God prevented them from immediately receiving the penalty for sin, Edwards explained. "The sovereign pleasure of God, for the present, stays his rough wind," he told them, "otherwise it would come with fury, and your destruction would come like a whirlwind, and you would be like the chaff of the summer threshing floor." It was a sermon directed not only to professing nonbelievers, but also to those who claimed salvation through church membership, good works, or moral living. "However you may have reformed your life in many things," he cautioned, "and may have had religious affections, and may keep up a form of religion in your families and closets, and in the house of God, it is nothing but his mere pleasure that keeps you from being this moment swallowed up in everlasting destruction."[17]

Freedom from the wages of sin, he preached, came only by being "born again" through personal surrender to Jesus Christ. "Thus, all you that never passed under a great change of heart, by the mighty power of the Spirit of God upon your souls; all you that were never born again, and made new creatures, and raised from being dead in sin, to a state of new, and before altogether unexperienced light and life, are in the hands of an angry God. . . . Therefore, let everyone that is out of Christ now awake and fly from the wrath to come."[18]

"What shall I do to be saved?" some in the audience began to cry. "Oh, I am going to Hell," others moaned. "Oh, what shall I do for Christ?" others asked aloud. A wave of weeping swept through the ranks of the meetinghouse crowd. At one point, the collective crying became so loud that Edwards had to stop preaching and request silence. "Men and women could not support themselves," an eyewitness would pen in his diary, "but grasped the pillars of the church or were kept from falling by those about them. . . ." Several pastors who were attending the service arose and began ministering to the people, receiving professions of faith in Christ as they moved through the congregation. "The Power of God was seen," one would later marvel,

". . . and, Oh, the cheerfulness and pleasantness of their countenances. . . ." Finally, the transformed crowd sang a hymn, prayed, and filed out of the meetinghouse—but that would not be the end of it.[19]

Beginning at Enfield that summer evening in 1741, a mighty wind of change swept through New England, then to other colonies, and, eventually, to all thirteen. It was the greatest spiritual revival in American history, and became known as the "Great Awakening." It would reinvigorate a biblical faith for decades to come in Colonial America, affecting the common and the affluent alike, and permeating city, town, village, and frontier. "The Great Awakening," asserted Pulitzer Prize–winning historian Vernon Parrington, "was the single movement that stirred the colonial heart deeply during three generations." The revival was unleashed full-force that night at the Enfield meetinghouse, but it arose almost simultaneously in various locations. A similar swell of Christian conversions had occurred in the Middle Colonies through the preaching of evangelists Theodore Frelinghuysen and Gilbert Tennent, and other outbreaks of revived faith occurred elsewhere. Meanwhile, the Great Awakening's most famous evangelist was also at work—and through him, the revival would sweep across Colonial America like a mighty gale.[20]

CHAPTER 10

"It Seem'd as if All the World Were Growing Religious"

Benjamin Franklin watched the famed evangelist preach with a mixture of admiration and reservation. The acclaimed preacher was his friend, and as America's leading publisher, Franklin was interested in publishing his sermons. However, he was not personally excited by the minister's message. Although he approved of religion in general and Christianity in particular, Benjamin Franklin readily admitted that he was not a Christian. Even so, he marveled at the young preacher's eloquence and the power of his voice, which easily reached the crowd of thousands attending the outdoor assembly. He admired his minister friend for his personal integrity and his extraordinary speaking ability, but Franklin did have one reservation: despite his generous nature, he did not want to give away any money this day.[1]

"I perceived he intended to finish with a collection," Franklin would later recount, "and I silently resolved that he should get nothing from me. I had in my pocket a handful of copper money, three or four silver dollars, and five pistols in gold. As he proceeded, I began to soften, and concluded to give the coppers. Another stroke of his oratory made me asham'd of that and I determin'd to give the silver; and he finish'd so admirably, that I empty'd my pocket wholly into the collector's dish, gold and all." The persuasive young minister's name was George Whitefield. He would soon become the most famous preacher in Colonial America, and the power of his preaching—as witnessed by Benjamin Franklin—would help fuel the nation-changing phenomenon called the Great Awakening.[2]

Unlike Jonathan Edwards, George Whitefield was neither an intellectual nor a scholar, and his childhood stood in contrast to Edwards's studious and disciplined upbringing. Whitefield was an English tavern keeper's son, raised in an unchaste and hardscrabble lifestyle. Education had little appeal to him, and he quit school to work at the family inn. Later, however, after a stint of mopping floors and emptying chamber pots, he realized the value of education and returned to school. With the help of friends, he managed to enter Oxford University—although by his own admission his early interests were loose women and heavy drinking. At Oxford, he met John Wesley and his brother Charles, and felt drawn to join their Holy Club—the forerunner of Methodism.[3]

Like other Methodists, who were so named for their methodology of disciplined Bible study and discipleship, Whitefield was ridiculed by other students and threatened with expulsion by school officials. He withstood it all, remained in the Holy Club, and in the spring of 1735, surrendered his life to Jesus Christ. He experienced an overwhelming sense of God's forgiveness, which he called his "new birth." From that moment onward he believed, like Jonathan Edwards, that salvation in Christ was evidenced by a born-again experience. His attitude toward life changed, and so did his lifestyle. He visited prisoners in jail. He ministered to the ill. He tried to help the poor. And he began to preach.[4]

His first sermon was at an Anglican church in his hometown of Gloucester. He was a twenty-one-year-old ministerial student, but those who heard him in the pulpit were struck by the power of his preaching. Upon graduation, he began preaching in Anglican churches, and within a year—at age twenty-two—he was a household name throughout England. Offered a prominent assistant pastor's post in London, he instead sailed for the American colony of Georgia as a missionary in 1738. There—in what would be the first of seven stays in America over a thirty-year period—he preached, established schools, and launched an orphanage that would be a lifelong ministry. In 1739, back in England as an ordained Anglican minister, he earned national celebrity for his preaching. His fellow ministers welcomed him initially but came to resent his fervent, emotional style and his insistence that a "new birth" in Christ was required for salvation. They also complained that the "motley throngs" attracted to his preaching crowded out regular worshippers and siphoned donations that could have gone to the local church.[5]

At times, he was a study in contrasts: His contact with unbelievers—"the lost"—was marked by warmth and affection, but he could be brash and quarrelsome with fellow clergy. He found time for anyone who sought personal counsel, but his hapless administrative ability caused problems for his beloved Georgia orphanage. His ministry was supported at times by affluent sympathizers in England and America, but he loved the working class and always preached in the plain language of the common people. He helped fund his orphanage with income from a plantation that utilized slavery, but publicly admonished slave owners for allowing slaves to live in substandard living conditions, and insisted that he be allowed to preach to the slave community. He became a beloved figure to slaves and black freedmen, and he in turn declared his joy "to see black and white . . . praising the name of the Lord."[6]

In the face of all the criticism, he remained supremely confident of his calling as an evangelist. When pastors complained that his preaching made their members overly impassioned in the name of Christ, he cited it as evidence that many ministers needed to be born again. "The reason why congregations have been so dead," he frankly pronounced, "is because dead men preach to them." Although some Anglican ministers supported his efforts—and some even announced that they had indeed experienced the "new birth" through his preaching—most remained critical of his techniques. "I am sorry to see you here," said an Anglican minister who encountered Whitefield on a city street. "So is the devil," Whitefield retorted.[7]

Such rejection by the clergy of the national church proved to be a blessing. Whitefield turned to the dissidents—the Presbyterians, Congregationalists, Baptists, Lutherans, Dutch Reformed, and others who had come to compose the majority of the common people in eighteenth-century America. And he took his preaching outdoors—attracting outdoor audiences of gigantic size for the day. Crowds of 8,000 were common. Larger assemblies of 10,000 to 15,000 were recorded. One appearance in Boston drew an estimated 20,000 people. To accommodate the massive crowds, he preached from atop scaffolding, which enabled his booming voice to be heard by all. He was a commanding figure, tall, slender, and able-bodied, although a childhood bout of measles had left him with a habitual squint. His most memorable physical attribute, however, was his voice: its power was astonishing. Benjamin Franklin once tried to scientifically measure it and concluded that Whitefield could project his voice with enough range to reach 30,000 people in an open-air setting.[8]

He was a master of the scriptures and could present biblical truths with simple and piercing applications for his audiences. In the pulpit, he was agile in his gestures, graceful in his mannerisms—and unforgettably dramatic. A famous English actor of the day said he would willingly pay a fortune if he could only say "Oh!" as effectively as George Whitefield. "When he spoke," a fellow Englishman wrote, "and they heard his strong but sweet voice, exquisitely modulated to express the deepest, strongest passion, or the soberest instruction, or the most indignant remonstrance, they stood charmed and subdued. Then his message was so solemn and so gracious . . . and he believed it, and loved it, and wanted them to accept it. . . . Quietness and attention reigned through all the host while, for perhaps an hour and a half, he spoke."[9]

Seemingly equipped with inexhaustible energy, he rose daily at precisely four in the morning and retired at exactly ten o'clock each evening. Often traveling by horseback, he preached from Georgia to Massachusetts, drawing gigantic crowds everywhere. For decades, he averaged preaching forty hours a week. On one tour of New England, he traveled eight hundred miles and preached more than 175 sermons. In advance of his appearances, horse, wagon, and foot traffic crammed the roads, and his preaching sites were packed hours before his arrival. By the time he departed, communities small and large had been transformed by the Gospel message.[10]

In Philadelphia, Whitefield joined evangelists William and Gilbert Tennent for a public preaching crusade that attracted tens of thousands. In its wake, Philadelphia was saturated with new believers, and daily life in America's largest city was dramatically altered. "It is wonderful to see the change soon made in the manners of our inhabitants," observed Benjamin Franklin. "From being thoughtless or indifferent about religion, it seem'd as if all the world were growing religious, so that one could not walk thro' the town in an evening without hearing psalms sung in different families of every street." Whitefield saw the unprecedented response as the work of God's Holy Spirit. So did countless common Americans—especially those who experienced the "new birth" under Whitefield's preaching.[11]

One who did, a Connecticut farmer named Nathan Cole, preserved an account of the experience:

I was in my field at work. I dropped my tool that I had in my hand and ran home and run through my house and bade my wife get ready quick to go and hear Mr. Whitefield preach at Middletown, and ran to my pasture for my horse with all my might fearing that I should be too late to hear him. I brought my horse home and soon mounted and took my wife up and went forward as fast as I thought the horse could bear, and when my horse began to be out of breath, I would get down and put my wife on the saddle and bid her ride as fast as she could and not stop or slack for me except I bade her, and so I would run until I was much out of breath, and then mount my horse again, and so I did several times to favor my horse. We improved every moment to get along as if we were fleeing for our lives, all the while fearing we should be too late to hear the sermon, for we had twelve miles to ride double in little more than an hour. . . .

I saw before me a cloud or fog rising. I first thought it came from the great river, but as I came nearer the road, I heard a noise something like a low rumbling thunder and presently found it was the noise of horses feet coming down the road and this cloud was a cloud of dust made by the horses feet. It arose some rods into the air over the tops of the hills and trees and when I came within about 20 rods of the road, I could see men and horses slipping along in the cloud like shadows, and as I drew nearer it seemed like a steady stream of horses and their riders, scarcely a horse more than his length behind another, all of a lather and foam with sweat, their breath rolling out of their nostrils in the cloud of dust every jump.

Every horse seemed to go with all his might to carry his rider to hear news from heaven for the saving of souls. It made me tremble to see the sight, how the world was in a struggle. I found a vacancy between two horses to slip in my horse; and my wife said how our clothes will be all spoiled see how they look, for they were so covered with dust, that they looked almost all of a color coats, hats, and shirts and horses.

I heard no man speak a word all the way three miles but everyone pressing forward in great haste and when we got to the old meeting house there was a great multitude; it was said to be 3 or 4000 of people assembled together, we got off from our horses and shook off the dust, and the ministers were then coming to the meeting house. I turned and looked towards the great river and saw the ferry boats running swift forward and forward bringing over loads of people; the oars rowed nimble and quick, everything—men horses and boats—seemed to be struggling for life; the land and banks over the river looked black with people and horses. . . .

When I saw Mr. Whitefield come upon the scaffold he looked almost angelical, a young, slim slender youth before some thousands of people with a bold undaunted countenance, and my hearing how God was with him everywhere as he came along it solemnized my mind, and put me into a trembling fear before he began to preach; for he looked as if he was clothed with authority from the Great God, and a sweet solemn solemnity sat upon his brow. And my hearing him preach gave me a heart wound; by God's blessing my old foundation was broken up, and I saw that my righteousness would not save me. . . .[12]

As the Great Awakening swept through the Thirteen Colonies, countless thousands of Colonial Americans shared a "new birth" experience similar to Nathan Cole's. The new converts to Christ included adults and children, men and women, the aged and infirm, churchgoers and the unchurched, the religious and the irreverent, whites, blacks, and Native Americans. Some conversions occurred quietly, thoughtfully. Others were emotional and dramatic: "I saw (or thought I saw) light inexpressible dart down from heaven upon me, and shone around me for the space of a minute," a New York slave named James Gronniosaw recounted. "I continued on my knees, and joy unspeakable took possession of my soul."[13]

George Whitefield and Jonathan Edwards were the most famous preachers of the Great Awakening, but the revival was also fired by the preaching of others, such as the Tennents, Samuel Davies, William Robinson, Daniel Marshall, Shubal Stearns, Devereux Jarratt, and numerous local and itinerant ministers. "I preached at Mr. James Fay's on Luke 19:9, to a great multitude and it pleased God to give it some success," a New England preacher named Ebenezer Parkman wrote in his diary in 1742. "As soon as the exercise was over, Deacon Fay broke forth in a loud voice, with tears of joy, and blessed God that he saw this day. . . . The rest of the people seemed so inclined to religious matters, that they did not go away. Many tarried to discourse on the affairs of their souls, and hear of the experiences of one another."[14]

The Great Awakening left Colonial America awash in a flood of faith. "The general carriage and behavior of people were soon very visibly altered," reported an eighteenth-century pastor. "Those awakened were much given to reading in the Holy Scriptures and other good books. . . . The subjects of discourse almost always, when any of them were together, were the matters of religion and great concerns of their souls." The American frontier remained more rowdy than righteous, and America's largest cities still had notorious neighborhoods, but daily life throughout the Thirteen Colonies clearly reflected a renewed biblical perspective. The Great Awakening transformed the hearts and minds of the American people.[15]

The revival's long-term practical impact was dynamic. "When the joy and relief of sudden conversion subsided," observed twentieth-century historian Cedric Cowling, "most converts felt a strong sense of obligation, at first to God and then to the community at large. They were receptive and educable; young male converts were eager to become ministers and begin proselytizing. . . ." In New England alone, the revival spurred the founding of more than 150 new churches. A new wave of missionary activities was unleashed. New ministries to the poor were created. A faith-based movement to end slavery arose. Orphanages were established, and ministries to educate Native Americans and freed blacks developed.[16]

The revival inspired the establishment of a parade of new colleges: Princeton, Columbia, Brown, Rutgers, Dartmouth, and others—all dedicated to instilling knowledge from a biblical perspective. In rural Pennsylvania, revivalist William Tennent opened his modest Log College, which attracted some of Colonial America's brightest minds and helped democratize American higher education. Everywhere, Colonial Americans eagerly sought greater knowledge of God and his creation. The wealthy amassed libraries of theological works; the common people passed around published sermons. More devotionals, catechisms, pamphlets, and sermons were published in the wake of the revival than all works of history, law, and science combined. Rich and poor alike enthusiastically read the Bible and Christian classics such as *Pilgrim's Progress* and Foxe's *Book of Martyrs*. On the streets and in the fields, average Americans knowledgeably discussed various theological topics.[17]

In America's cities, church steeples defined the skylines and lifted the cross above the hubbub of daily life. Church bells pealed with regularity. In town and country alike, the most popular form of "entertainment" was a worship service. A visiting preacher with even a regional reputation might attract a crowd of hundreds or thousands. In Southern colonies, where the population was dispersed, affluent planters sometimes rode for hours by horseback to attend church, not just for the social and business benefits, but from a genuine desire to assemble for worship. On the Colonial frontier and in the backcountry, people routinely hiked as much as twenty miles—sometimes barefoot—to hear an itinerant preacher. "The poor people are hungry after the Word, and ready to devour me," an itinerant preacher wrote from the South Carolina backcountry in 1768. "Here I found a vast Body of People assembled—Such a Medley! Such a mixed multitude of all Classes and Complexions I never saw."[18]

A renewed appreciation for the Sabbath followed in the wake of the revival. On Sundays, business simply ceased. Outside the frontier, few places tolerated Sunday revelry, drinking, or gambling—or even unnecessary travel. Boston's streets were so empty on Sundays that the rare loiterer could expect to be questioned by law enforcement officers. Even in cosmopolitan New York City, the law restricted Sunday traffic to worship-related travel. A day of worship, rest, and family life, claimed an observant New Englander, "not only gives seriousness and poise to character . . . but it [also] teaches self-control, self-knowledge [and] self-respect." A popular American adage of the day noted of the Sabbath: "Keep this, keep all; lose this, lose all." In eighteenth-century America, Sundays were quiet and restful, and a faithful Sabbath observance became a distinctive characteristic of the American people.[19]

Despite the obvious benefits of the Great Awakening, opposition to it continued—and not just from the clergymen of England's national church. More than a few Congregationalist and Presbyterian ministers rejected its emotionalism, mass assemblies, and emphasis on a personal "born-again" experience in Christ. So did some pastors from other denominations. An Anglican clergyman spoke for many critics when he denounced the revival's converts: "There are so many absurdities committed by them, as wou'd shock one of our Cherokee savages," he opined. "One on his knees in a Posture of Prayer—Others singing—Some howling—These Ranting—Those crying—Others dancing, Skipping, Laughing and rejoicing. . . . Is there anything like this in the Church of England?"[20]

Revival supporters became known as "New Lights." Opponents were called "Old Lights." Churches divided into New Light and Old Light congregations. The revival also created broader distinctions within America's Protestant denominations. Those who held to a belief in the authority of Scripture, the Trinity, the deity of Christ, and the need for a "new birth" salvation experience would become known as Evangelicals. Some Old Lights were devoted to those fundamental doctrines but rejected revival emotionalism and its nondenominational appeal. Other Old Lights, who believed that intellectual reason and experience were superior to the revelation of Scripture, also dismissed the revival. In response to the Great Awakening, many Old Lights began to refer to themselves as theological "Liberals" and developed a distinctive identity within American Christianity.[21]

The Great Awakening also defined political distinctions in Colonial America. Many Old Lights worried that the revival threatened the existing social order and political establishment. Most troubling to them, a modern Colonial scholar would note, was "the evangelical stress on a common humanity in which each soul, however humble, communed directly with God on the same equal plane as everyone else." Some Old Lights were convinced that the revival's Bible-based teaching that everyone was equally valuable to God encouraged "republican and mobbish principles and practices." In some places, Old Light pastors encouraged sympathetic civil authorities to enact restrictions on revival activities and supporters. Fearful of challenges to the established order, many Colonial officials were more than willing to comply.[22]

Old Light sentiment persuaded the Connecticut legislature to pass a series of laws designed to repress the revival. Itinerant ministers who preached without an invitation from established clergy could be fined and expelled from the colony. Another law intended to discourage preaching by revival converts required ministers to have college degrees. New Light pastors were jailed for officiating at weddings and were forbidden to conduct baptisms. A born-again Connecticut lawyer named Elisha Paine was jailed for public preaching but continued to draw large crowds by preaching from an open jailhouse window. To protest such actions, some New Lights stopped paying the mandatory tax supporting the Church of England, and were arrested and jailed. In one Connecticut county, the local jailhouse had to be enlarged to accommodate the number of protesters who were arrested.[23]

Most Americans resented such repression. In Connecticut, the swelling ranks of New Lights voted the antirevivalists out of office. They put a majority of New Light supporters in the Colonial assembly and replaced the Old Light governor. Born-again and newly motivated by the Great Awakening, countless Americans joined or became more active in new or existing churches—mainly the ones that supported the revival. Already by the mid-eighteenth century, Protestant dissenters outnumbered members of the national church, and the Great Awakening dramatically swelled their ranks. Scores of new converts, including many from the Anglican Church and Old Light Congregational churches, joined New Light congregations—especially the New Light Presbyterians and the Baptists.[24]

Presbyterians surged in numbers throughout Colonial America, even in former Anglican strongholds such as South Carolina and Virginia. Their ranks were boosted by a wave of immigration from Scotland and by a large influx of Scots-Irish immigrants. Descendants of Scots who had settled in northern Ireland, the Scots-Irish emigrated to Colonial America in vast numbers, settling in America's seaboard cities, in the sparsely settled southern Piedmont, and on the Appalachian frontier. Likewise, America's Baptist population dramatically expanded, especially on the frontier. In Virginia, where the Church of England remained strongest, authorities sometimes broke up Baptist worship services and whipped Baptist preachers, but such tactics failed to slow Baptist growth there or elsewhere. Other dissenter denominations grew also, until the great majority of Colonial American church members were in Protestant congregations outside the Church of England.[25]

While it encouraged denominational diversity, the Great Awakening also established an extraordinary unity of faith in Colonial

America. Despite denomination differences, essential Christianity reigned throughout the land. "In kindling the religion of the heart in the great mass of plain people," historian Merle Curti would conclude, "the revivals gave a broader base to the Christian heritage. Thus the intellectual life of the colonists—their views of the universe, of human nature, and of esthetics, their social and political ideas—was shaped in large measure by Christian patterns of thought." Americans came to expect biblical values to be reflected in the institutions of the day—the church, education, the arts, business, law, and government. "The key principle," American scholar Daniel Dorchester would note, "was that the government, civil and ecclesiastical, is constituted and administered upon the Bible as the source of knowledge and authority. . . ." Philosophically, in the mid-nineteenth century, Protestant, Catholic, and Jewish Americans alike had a common consensus—the Judeo-Christian worldview. It was the cultural glue that united Colonial America's melting-pot culture.[26]

In renewing the influence of the biblical worldview, the Great Awakening also increased Americans' awareness of the biblical principle of equality before God—and the God-given inalienable rights that Higher Law bestowed on every individual. Many Americans—especially the New Light multitude in the dissenter denominations—began to apply biblical principles to Colonial American politics. For the free exercise of their Great Awakening faith, they were willing to resist London-based Colonial authority throughout the Thirteen Colonies. Likewise, when authorities with the government's national church sought to install an American bishop, Americans blocked it with outspoken intercolonial opposition. "For the first time," historian Harris Starr would write, "the American people . . . sought to limit ecclesiastical and political authority and advocated freedom of conscience and individual liberty."[27]

Due largely to the Great Awakening, the political base in Colonial America on the eve of the American Revolution was not some secular organization—it was the local church. Likewise, Colonial America's most influential leader was not a politician, merchant, banker, journalist, or performer—it was the preacher of the local church. The church was the center of family life in eighteenth-century America, and the direction of the local pastor was generally heeded with respect. Unlike the French Revolution, with its humanistic hostility to Christianity and clergy, its lawless violence, and its inevitable reign of terror, the American Revolution would be a genuine quest for liberty that was fueled, disciplined, and restrained by the rule of law—the Higher Law of the Bible. "God hath given to every Man," said New England minister Solomon Paine, "an unalienable right . . . and hath blessed them that appeared to stand uprightly for the Liberties of Conscience. . . ."[28]

Jonathan Edwards died in 1758, soon after taking the presidency at Princeton University. Weary and weak from work, he contracted a deadly fever from a smallpox inoculation. At the end of his days, in addition to the president's duties, he was preaching on Sundays and teaching a class in theology. In 1770, George Whitefield also died on his mission field, struck down in Newburyport, Massachusetts, by exhaustion and an asthma attack following a two-hour sermon. He died on the Lord's Day, and was buried under the pulpit of the town's First Presbyterian Church. By one estimate, he had preached more than eighteen thousand sermons. The extraordinary revival that Edwards and Whitefield had helped launch left Colonial Americans with an unprecedented unity, a common appreciation for their God-given, inalienable rights, a motivation to resist abusive authority, and an established national consciousness—all based on the Judeo-Christian worldview. A nation-making Revolution was approaching. Equipped by a heritage of liberty and prepared by the Great Awakening—America would be ready.[29]

CHAPTER 11

"Where the Spirit of the Lord is, There is Liberty"

It was Patrick Henry's twenty-ninth birthday, but celebration was the last thing on his mind. He was a newly elected freshman member of the Virginia House of Burgesses, meeting in Williamsburg, and already he was about to engage in a historic confrontation. It was May 29, 1765, and in moments he would confront not only the most powerful members of the House of Burgesses—but also the full might of the British Empire. The issue was the Stamp Act, a controversial new law enacted by the British government that imposed taxes on paper-related products—licenses, newspapers, pamphlets, college diplomas, almanacs—even playing cards. Official Stamp Act agents would be appointed to ensure compliance with the new law, the British government announced, and violators would be prosecuted without the right to a jury trial.[1]

From Massachusetts to Georgia, Americans in 1765 were outraged—not by the tax itself, but because the Stamp Act was widely viewed as a government attack on American liberty. Colonial America was not allowed representation in the British Parliament—there were no elected officials there to speak on behalf of the American people. They were officially English citizens, but they had no political voice in Britain's national legislature. King and Parliament had always respected that political reality, and had refrained from imposing direct taxation on a people who had no recourse against it. In recent years, however, under the reign of King George III—who had taken the throne in 1760—the Mother Country had increased its involvement in the lives of Colonial Americans.[2]

The Stamp Act of 1765 was the latest and most controversial action by king and Parliament—a direct tax on all thirteen colonies even though America had no representation in Parliament. Now the cry of "No taxation without representation!" rang throughout Colonial America. It was voiced in the colonial assemblies, bantered in coffeehouses, inked in newspapers and printed pamphlets, and proclaimed from church pulpits. Americans questioned the intent of the unprecedented Stamp Act. Was it merely the first of many direct taxes? Would it lead to erosion of Colonial America's treasured heritage of liberty? Countless colonists were certain it was a threat to the political freedom long enjoyed by Americans. By late May 1765, when Patrick Henry braced himself for a confrontation in the Virginia legislature, the Stamp Act controversy had become a full-scale political crisis on both sides of the Atlantic.[3]

The crisis had its roots in events that occurred two years earlier on the far rim of the American frontier. There, on May 16, 1763, an outpost of British troops at Fort Sandusky in the Ohio Country was slaughtered by a war party of Wyandot Indians. Within a week, a larger garrison in wilderness Michigan was attacked with brutal losses by Ojibway warriors. The massacres were the opening battles of Pontiac's Rebellion, an Indian uprising in the Ohio Country that was led by the Ottawa war chief whose name it bore. Every British army post on the far northwestern frontier was destroyed, and Pontiac even attacked major British garrisons at Detroit and Fort Pitt. By year's end, British troops had suppressed the uprising, but Pontiac's Rebellion greatly disturbed British leaders in London.[4]

What most troubled the king and Parliament was not the casualties of war—they were accustomed to troop losses. Their gravest concern was the likelihood that additional military forces might be needed in America. More troops meant more expenditures, and the timing was poor. Just that year, the Peace of Paris had ended Britain's Seven Years War with France, which was known in America as the French and Indian War. The British victory had forced the surrender of Canada and most lands east of the Mississippi River, ending France's era as a major North American power. Britain now ruled the seas, the subcontinent of India, and most of North America. It was a spectacular triumph, but it came at a great price: Britain was almost bankrupt. The years of war had nearly doubled the national debt, and now it appeared more spending might be required to secure the American frontier. King George and Parliamentary leaders agreed: the American Colonies needed to be taxed.[5]

As a preliminary, the king issued the Proclamation of 1763, which reduced the number of British troops in America by drastic action: it closed the western frontier. Since 1607, Americans had been expanding the frontier westward—and now they were forbidden to settle west of the Appalachians. Those already living in the Ohio Country were ordered "forthwith to remove themselves." America's expansive western frontier would be left to the Indian tribes, who presumably would battle each other for possession instead of fighting British troops. Americans who hoped to acquire land on the frontier were advised to move instead to newly acquired Canada. There, London proclaimed, they "would be useful to their Mother Country, instead of planting themselves in the Heart of America . . . to the infinite prejudice of Britain."[6]

To most Americans, the Proclamation of 1763 was unwarranted punishment. It not only shut down the opportunity for a new start on the western frontier, it also struck many Americans as evidence of "mercantilism"—a government policy designed to discourage Colonial development and reduce America to a resource farm for the Mother Country. It was soon followed by an unpopular indirect tax on trade—the American Revenue Act of 1764—which was called the "Sugar Act" in the Colonies. It placed duties on sugar and molasses, required increased accountability from the American shipping industry, and threatened strict enforcement. As Colonial resentment increased, London added an even more intrusive law: the Quartering Act of 1765. It required cities and towns to garrison and supply British troops, and empowered army officers to commandeer taverns, inns, or unoccupied buildings for temporary troop quarters.[7]

Americans were incensed. For more than 150 years, the British government had left the Americans to fend for themselves—and largely govern themselves. It was a disinterested, laissez-faire style of government—"happy neglect" some called it—and now it was suddenly changing. American colonists had been taxed by their colony's legislature in the past, but they had representation in the Colonial legislatures. Occasionally the monarchy had requested revenues from a colony's governor, who in turn sometimes forwarded the request to the colony's legislature. Now, however, the national government wanted to impose direct taxes on American colonists without granting them representation in Parliament.[8]

While Americans viewed their colonies as almost autonomous, most members of Parliament believed Parliamentary authority outranked a colony's legislature and the terms of its original charter. George III, meanwhile, believed both king *and* Parliament outranked every colony, and that by the divine right of kings, God granted him authority over the institutions and people of his realm—with some exceptions for Parliament. Americans generally respected the distant monarchy; many were surprised at the king's support for the unpopular series of laws, and believed Parliament had misled him. Even so, they were angered by the new restrictions and taxes—especially direct taxation of the Stamp Act. Benjamin Franklin, who eventually came to view the new taxes as "cruel and unjust," spoke for many Americans when he declared that Parliament "had really no right at all to tax them." By imposing a direct tax on Colonial Americans without representation in Parliament, he charged, the British government had chosen "compulsion over persuasion."[9]

In March 1765, despite widespread American opposition, Parliament had enacted the Stamp Act—with enforcement scheduled to begin the following November. On May 29, 1765, the Virginia House of Burgesses had the opportunity to become the first legislative assembly in America to take official action against the Stamp Act. It appeared to Patrick Henry, however, that most of Virginia's legislators were ready to give up and let the moment pass, even though they believed the Stamp Act violated a century and a half of American freedom. Now that it had officially become British law, they were reluctant to speak against it and risk charges of disloyalty toward king and Parliament. Patrick Henry might have been expected to sit still and be quiet like a typical freshman legislator. But that was not his way. He had grown up in the Virginia backcountry, and like many frontiersmen, he preferred to face threats head-on.[10]

At age eighteen, he married a poor backcountry bride named Sarah Shelton, and sweated uselessly on a hardscrabble farm for several years. A failure as a farmer, he became a storekeeper, but failed at that. He returned to the plow, and failed again. Desperate, he took up the study of law. "He could not dig," an early biographer would observe, "neither could he traffic, but perhaps he could talk. Why not get a living by his tongue? Why not be a lawyer?" It was a natural fit: young Patrick Henry proved to be master of the courtroom. In three years, he had handled more than a thousand cases, and had won most of them, including cases defending the freedom of Baptists and other dissenters. His quick mind, sharp instincts, and courtroom savvy were exceeded only by the mastery of his oratory. He was an unexcelled public speaker. His words were eloquent, his timing was superb, his voice was powerful, and his presence was dramatic—all of which were rendered even more memorable by his backcountry accent.[11]

In 1763, he earned fame throughout Virginia for a skillful courtroom defense of Colonial rights in a case called the Parson's Cause, which propelled him to the House of Burgesses. There, amid legislative debate on the Stamp Act crisis, he opened an old law book to a blank page, jotted down several points opposing the Stamp Act—and asked to address the assembly. As he waited his turn to speak, he looked anything but commanding: tall, lanky, and dressed in outmoded attire, he had the look of the frontier about him. The polished, veteran legislators from Virginia's affluent Tidewater region took one look and dismissed him as a "rustic and clownish youth . . . without training or experience in statesmanship."[12]

Others had also underestimated him. Patrick Henry's roughhewn, youthful appearance was deceptive: he was confident in what he believed, and when he spoke in public, an astonishing transformation occurred. Those in the country courtrooms had seen it, and now so did Virginia's assembled lawmakers. From this "rustic and clownish youth" poured forth a "torrent of eloquence"—a unique mastery of logic and language. Those who witnessed it described it as "bold, grand and overwhelming." Patrick Henry—frontier youth, failed farmer, unsuccessful merchant, and country lawyer—stood alone that day in the Virginia legislature and defended the God-given liberty of all Americans with matchless skill and oratory.[13]

The colonists, he proclaimed, deserved "all the privileges, franchises and immunities" that belonged to citizens of the

Mother Country—rights that were guaranteed by the faith-based Colonial charters. Only a Colonial legislature that was elected by the people had the "exclusive right and power to lay taxes and impositions" upon Americans—not the king or Parliament. Taxation without representation, he charged, was an attempt to "destroy British as well as American freedom." Aside from laws enacted by their elected representatives, "the inhabitants of this colony, are not bound to yield obedience to any law or ordinance whatever designed to impose any taxation whatsoever upon them." Those who claimed otherwise, he asserted "shall be deemed an enemy." No Colonial legislators had taken such a stand against king and Parliament, but now Patrick Henry called on his fellow Virginians to become the first. His words provoked a firestorm of debate—and would alter history. How, some wondered, did a novice Colonial lawmaker—"without training or experience"—possess the wisdom and fortitude to stand against the mighty British Empire?[14]

The answer lay in Patrick Henry's past: he *was* trained—tutored in the principles of Higher Law and trained in the tradition of righteous resistance. His father, John Henry, was a well-educated Scotsman, a militia officer, and a frontier judge. He enforced a rigorous homeschool regime for young Henry, who was known as a "book-hating boy" eager to abandon study for lure of the woods. Under the tutelage of his father and an Anglican minister uncle, Henry was drilled in enough Latin to last a lifetime, along with other academic disciplines. The formative instruction that apparently molded him most, however, was instilled by a New Light Presbyterian preacher named Samuel Davies. Young Patrick was formally raised as an Anglican—baptized in his uncle's church—but his mother, Sarah Syme Henry, was a devout Presbyterian who made sure he worshipped regularly with her at Davies's nearby church.[15]

Henry was deeply influenced by the dynamic Presbyterian pastor, who shaped the thinking of an entire generation of Americans on the eve of the Revolution. "There was nothing weak, frail, sick, effeminate or enervated about the average parson of colonial days," nineteenth-century historian Frank Child would note. "They could study twelve consecutive hours when the opportunity came, for the reason that a good many other hours had been spent in the open air walking, fishing, planting, riding, harvesting or attending to similar activities." Ministers were often the best-educated people in their communities, and many Americans were exposed to the issues of their day from Sunday sermons and the shared knowledge of their pastor. "It was the parson who lived among books and directed the current of thought," according to Child. "He was a spiritual man, living in close fellowship with his Master. Strong in body and mind, compelled to be practical and disciplined in spirituality, the parson . . . became on many occasions the great political force . . . always pressing with disinterested purpose toward such issues as he deemed wisest and best."[16]

It was an apt description of Patrick Henry's mentor. In 1747, Samuel Davies had come to Virginia from his native Delaware. A twenty-three-year-old Presbyterian missionary and church-planter, he was charged with discipling born-again believers in the glow of the Great Awakening. In Anglican Virginia, Presbyterians, Baptists, Quakers, and other dissenters still faced harassment and restrictions. Ministers had to be licensed by the government, itinerant preaching was outlawed, and violators were often jailed. Davies disarmed authorities with his diplomacy, legal knowledge, and intellect, however, and successfully pressed Virginia officials for expanded religious freedom under England's 1689 Toleration Act. When Virginia's House of Burgesses resisted, he organized backcountry Presbyterians to lobby the legislature. Virginia's Baptists soon followed the same tactics, and the coalition finally forced the colony's Anglican lawmakers to extend religious freedom to dissenter denominations.[17]

Davies's political success was matched by his church-building efforts, which expanded the Presbyterian population of Virginia and neighboring North Carolina. In the pulpit he was acclaimed as an American George Whitefield, although he had an intellectual bent more like Jonathan Edwards and would also eventually become president of Princeton. His sermons were widely published and generated a huge following throughout Colonial America. In them, he emphasized the biblical obligation of believers to selflessly serve the public good and resist tyranny. "Religion without Public Spirit and Benevolence," Davies proclaimed, "is but a sullen, selfish, sour and malignant Humour for Devotion, unworthy of that sacred Name."[18]

Christians were to be the "salt" and "light" that preserved society and lit its way with loving leadership, he taught. Without biblical direction and discipline, he counseled, political freedom would eventually dissolve into sinful self-indulgence. Patriotism would then become "monstrous . . . atheistical . . . irreligious," and would contain "no more real Goodness in it, than the instinctive fondness of a Brute for its Young." In a sermon titled "The Curse of Cowardice," Davies denounced the "sly hypocritical coward" who would seek public service for self-enrichment or self-promotion. Genuine, unselfish patriotism could only be inspired, he preached, by a heart that was yielded to Jesus Christ and motivated by "the Agency of the Holy Spirit." Christians were therefore morally obligated to provide the leadership necessary for effective "publick Spirit and Piety."[19]

The lessons in leadership instilled in Colonial Americans by Samuel Davies and other public-minded ministers were still fresh when the Stamp Act crisis erupted. Well schooled in the Judeo-Christian worldview, many colonists recognized the threat to American liberty and attempted to resist it. Likewise, just as Colonial America's foundation of faith inspired resistance, it also restrained it. Amid the outrage over the Stamp Act, disorders *did* occur: offices and homes of governmental officials were looted in some places, a mob broke out the windows of an Anglican church in Connecticut, Stamp Act agents were tarred and feathered, and New York's lieutenant governor felt it necessary to seek safety on a British warship. Those were the excesses of the Stamp Act crisis, however, and while some Americans took to the streets, most went to their churches.[20]

As the center of Colonial life, the local church was where Americans turned in time of crisis. There they prayed. They worshipped. And they looked to their pastor for direction. Catholic congregations were still almost too few to count, and most Anglican ministers were reluctant to confront the government they served—but countless Protestant pastors unleashed the power of the pulpit against the Stamp Act. It was a remarkably unified protest: New Lights, Old Lights, Evangelicals, and Liberals all generally agreed that the Stamp Act was an assault on inalienable rights, a break with English common law, and a brash attempt to supplant Higher Law with man's law. "Brave followers of the Lamb," preached New Light pastor Joseph Bellamy, "lay aside every weight, and, with your hearts wholly intent on this grand affair, gird up your loins, and with all the spiritual weapons of faith, prayer, meditation, and watchfulness . . . sacrifice every earthly comfort in the glorious cause. . . ."[21]

The most influential pulpit protest of the Stamp Act crisis came from the Reverend Jonathan Mayhew, the liberal pastor of Boston's West Congregational Church. His sermon bore a ponderous title—"A Discourse Concerning Unlimited Submission and Non-Resistance to the Higher Powers"—and it had been preached and printed before. No matter. Reprinted in Colonial newspapers at the height of the crisis, it dramatically influenced American opinion. "We may very safely assert these two things in general, without undermining government," Mayhew pronounced. "One is, that no civil rulers are to be obeyed when they enjoin things that are inconsistent with the commands of God. . . . [D]isobedience to them is a duty, not a crime. . . . Another thing that may be asserted with equal truth and safety is, that no government is to be submitted to at the expense of that which is the sole end of all government—the common good and safety of society." To obey an ungodly law, Mayhew concluded, " 'tis treason against mankind, 'tis treason against common sense, 'tis treason against God."[22]

Mayhew's call to resistance would become known as "the morning gun of the Revolution," and it would echo from countless other American pulpits. Taxation without representation, Colonial pastors preached, violated the inalienable rights of Americans and was "nothing less than . . . vile, ignominious slavery." They reminded their congregations of the biblical obligation to God's Higher Law—"We ought to obey God rather than men." Some cited Reformation theology. When ungodly rulers "attack God's Word" or persecute the people in their care, wrote Reformation leader Huldrych Zwingli, Christians were morally obligated to "resist them, and, if needful, depose them. . . ." Acting in the role of Old Testament prophets, many preachers cried that America's Colonial charters were modeled on the covenants of the Old Testament and thus had legitimately established liberty in the land.[23]

Patrick Henry presented a similar argument to the Virginia House of Burgesses: the colony's liberty had been ensured by a covenant-like charter, and Parliament had no valid grounds to usurp it. As a disciple of Samuel Davies, he was well prepared to defend the Higher Law. His faith in Christ, Henry once wrote, was what "I prize far above all this world has, or can boast." He was never "ostentatious" about his faith, but was "always ready to avow it and defend it," according to biographer Moses Tyler. "To the very end of his life, his most sacred convictions and tenderest affections seem to have been on the side of the institutions and ministers of Christianity. . . ."[24]

At home, Henry routinely read to his family from the works of Thomas Sherlock, a leading eighteenth-century Christian apologist, whose works, Henry vouched, "removed all my doubts about the truth of Christianity." Alarmed to see French-style humanism becoming fashionable among some of Virginia's young legislators, he once reprinted and distributed Christian apologist Soame Jenyns's *View of the Internal Evidence of the Christian Religion.* As for the faddish deism in which a few of his contemporaries dabbled, Henry dismissed it as "but another name for vice and depravity" that faded before the truth of Scripture. "I am," he said, "much consoled by reflecting that the religion of Christ has, from its first appearance in the world, been attacked in vain by all the wits, philosophers, and wise ones, aided by every power of man—and its triumph is complete." Of the Bible he once said, "Here is a book worth more than all the other books that were ever printed."[25]

On that day in May 1765, as Colonial Americans struggled to mount a defense against the Stamp Act, young Patrick Henry rose before the Virginia House of Burgesses and challenged his fellow legislators to lead the resistance. His seven-point resolution proclaimed the Colonial case against taxation without representation, and boldly raised a standard for American resistance to London authority. "Like the Reverend Samuel Davies enacting the solemn division of Judgment Day before his enthralled congregation, so did Henry create the spectacle of virtuous liberty triumphant over oppression," a biographer would observe. After a fierce debate, most of Henry's resolutions passed, barely. On both sides of the Atlantic, they became known as "Virginia Resolves." The colony's legislature alone had "sole and exclusive right and power to lay taxes . . . upon the inhabitants of this Colony," they proclaimed, stating that the people of Virginia were "not bound to yield obedience to any law" by which Parliament tried to tax them. The Virginia House of Burgesses became the first Colonial legislature in America to take action against the Stamp Act.[26]

Colonial American newspapers reported the story, and Virginia became a heroic model of resistance to Americans everywhere. So did Patrick Henry—not just for the resolutions he authored, but mainly for the dramatic words he spoke in the heat of debate. "Many threats were uttered," he would later recall, "and much abuse cast on me. . . ." He finally retorted with a reminder of the fate that had befallen two earlier rulers charged with tyranny: "Caesar had his Brutus," he proclaimed. "Charles the First, his Cromwell and George the Third—may profit from their example!" Bedlam erupted in the legislative chamber, accompanied by shouts of "Treason! Treason!" Unfazed, Henry boldly responded, "If this be treason, make the most of it." Later, he apologized for his words—his passion for the cause of "Dying Liberty" led him to speak rashly, he said. Then, his duty done, he mounted his horse and headed west toward the Virginia backcountry. Ahead awaited the welcome of home and family; in the future awaited the fame of a founding father.[27]

Other Colonial legislatures followed Virginia's lead, and officially denounced the Stamp Act. Committees of Correspondence were created to maintain communications between the Colonial legislatures and help formulate unified action. In Massachusetts, the legislature passed a measure inviting the other colonies to send official representatives to a Stamp Act Congress in New York City. Nine colonies agreed and dispatched delegations. The Stamp Act Congress convened in October 1765 and crafted a unified Colonial response called the "Declaration of Rights and Grievances." It stated that "taxation cannot be constitutionally imposed upon [the American colonies] but by their respective legislatures," and urged Parliament repeal the Stamp Act. More importantly, it served as a model of what an intercolonial congress might accomplish.[28]

Another model was provided by America's Presbyterian and Congregational ministers, who formed a clergyman's congress in the wake of the Stamp Act. Within a year of the Stamp Act, it convened in Elizabeth Town, New Jersey, and drew thirty-one delegates from Connecticut, Pennsylvania, New York, and New Jersey. They united to develop an intercolonial strategy for protecting America's religious and political liberties. The concept originated with Ezra Stiles, a Congregationalist minister in Connecticut, who would later serve as president of Yale University. Eventually, Congregationalist and Presbyterian clergy from a majority of colonies would attend the congress, or serve on its committees of correspondence. Although its actions were nonbinding, critics in both Britain and America saw the clergymen's congress as a Calvinist scheme to promote American independence. According to some American royalists, the "principles of religion and polity" practiced by America's Presbyterian and Congregationalist ministers "were equally adverse to those of the established Church and Government."[29]

Meanwhile, a Colonial boycott of British goods was implemented to place economic pressure on Parliament, and the American cause was boosted by the unexpected efforts of an influential English lobbyist—the Reverend George Whitefield. Just four years from his death, the famous revivalist was still widely admired in Great Britain and thus potentially wielded powerful political influence. Whitefield's old friend Benjamin Franklin and Massachusetts leader John Adams enlisted him in the campaign to repeal the Stamp Act. By some accounts, he may have lobbied both Parliament and the king—echoing the calls of America's pulpits, legislators, and people with a uniquely powerful voice. "I thought that this people would submit to the Stamp Act," one of America's royal governors advised London. "But the publishing of the Virginia resolves proved to be an alarm bell to the disaffect." Confronted by this economic pressure, political protests, and public outrage—all fanned from American pulpits—the king and Parliament finally conceded: in 1766, the infamous Stamp Act was repealed.[30]

Throughout Colonial America, church bells pealed, crowds

assembled, bonfires blazed, and artillery salutes were fired. Again, Americans went to their churches. There, they observed thanksgiving services, filled their sanctuaries with hymns of praise, and looked again to the pulpit for direction. "Welcome to these shores again," the Reverend Jonathan Mayhew proclaimed in an address to "Liberty" delivered at his Boston church. "Long mayest thou reside among us, the delight of the wise, good and brave. . . ." He knew from Scripture, he told his congregation, "that the Son of God came down from heaven to make us free indeed, and that 'where the Spirit of the Lord is, there is liberty.'" It was a time for thanksgiving, Mayhew noted. "How great are our obligations . . . to the Supreme Governor of the world. He hath turned our groans into songs, our mourning into dancing. He hath put off our sackcloth, and girded us with gladness." For a time, repeal of the Stamp Act produced a season of relief and celebration in America—but more groans, mourning, and sackcloth lay ahead.[31]

CHAPTER 12

"An Appeal to God and the World"

They marched two by two in silence. Tramping down Boston's Pearl Street on a moonlit winter night, they made an odd-looking army. Most were costumed as if they were theater Indians: some were wrapped in blankets, some were outfitted with feathers, many had faces camouflaged with sooty "war paint." Their long double line was composed of men and boys, about seventy in number, and most of them carried an ax or a hatchet. Trailed by a crowd of hundreds, they marched like men on a mission, heading resolutely for Griffin's Wharf on Boston Harbor. There, with their ranks bolstered by volunteers from the crowd, they were issued brief commands by their leaders. Obediently, they separated into three groups and each boarded a different ship—the *Dartmouth*, the *Eleanor* and the *Beaver*.[1]

For three hours, with the efficiency of men accustomed to hard labor, they worked the ships' block and tackle, lifting 342 hefty wooden chests from the ships' holds. Speaking little as they worked, they used their axes and hatchets to crack open the chests, then emptied their contents into the harbor waters below. It was English tea—ninety thousand pounds of it. Nothing else was taken, and a lock they broke was replaced on the spot. When a pilferer from the crowd packed his pockets with loose tea, he was cuffed, booted, and sent running. Except for one man knocked unconscious by a ship's hoist, no one was hurt. Finally, when all the tea was floating in the harbor, the ships' decks were swept clean and the "Indians" dispersed. Organized as a nonviolent protest, the raid was intended to defy what was seen by many as British tyranny. It would become famous as the Boston Tea Party.[2]

It occurred on the evening of December 16, 1773—seven years after the British government had repealed the Stamp Act. The euphoria unleashed by repeal of the Stamp Act in 1766 had faded quickly. Americans soon learned that the same day Parliament repealed the Stamp Act, it enacted the Declaratory Act, which declared that Parliament had the authority to impose any laws it deemed proper on the American colonies—"in all cases whatsoever." Colonists who felt threatened by the Stamp Act would witness the power of king and Parliament again—and soon. A year later in 1767, Parliament enacted the Townshend Acts, which levied taxes on a wide range of imported items—glass, lead, paper, paints, and tea. It was "the same medicine in another bottle," concerned Americans complained.[3]

Colonial leaders reacted promptly. A new boycott of English goods was organized, and Colonial legislatures again took action. The Massachusetts legislature denounced the Townshend Acts as taxation without representation and dispatched a formal "circular letter" to the other colonies, calling for united resistance against the government. In response, the colony's royal governor dissolved the Colonial legislature. More ominously, in October 1768, British warships landed two regiments of troops in Boston. In 1769, the Virginia House of Burgesses condemned the Townshend Acts with a series of resolutions, and it too was officially dissolved by the colony's governor. British authorities could not stop America's boycott of British goods, however, and by 1770, British merchants were beseeching Parliament for relief.[4]

The king and Parliament finally conceded. Like the Stamp Act, the Townshend Acts were repealed—except for one commodity. Britain had a new prime minister, Lord Frederick North, and he agreed with the king that a total repeal would be a sign of weakness. The tax on tea would remain in place, they decided. It would stand as a reminder to the Americans of royal authority. "America must fear you before she can love you," proclaimed Lord North. "I will never think of repealing it," he vowed, "until I see America prostrate at my feet."[5]

Relations between Colonial America and the Mother Country continued to sour. In 1770, a street brawl erupted between citizens and British soldiers in New York City. In March of the same year, a British guard at Boston's customs house hit a mouthy young laborer with a gun butt. A growing crowd of men and boys began pelting the sentry with snowballs, prompting him to summon reinforcements. An ugly confrontation occurred, and the soldiers opened fire, killing five civilians and wounding six. The troops were later exonerated by a Massachusetts jury, but the "Boston Massacre," as it became known, provoked widespread unease among Americans.[6]

Two years later, in 1772, another sensational confrontation occurred. A group of disgruntled Rhode Island sailors and merchants seized a British customs schooner, the *Gaspee*, put its crew ashore, and set fire to the vessel. In response, British officials vowed to prosecute all perpetrators in England, not in America. Even colonists who condemned the *Gaspee* burning viewed the British response as an erosion of Colonial rights. Soon afterward, Massachusetts colonists learned that the colony's judges would hereafter be salaried by the British government, and not by the colony, making them accountable to London alone.[7]

Meanwhile, in the spring of 1773, Americans learned of another controversial British policy—the Tea Act. It was enacted by Parliament to bail out the troubled British East India Company, a commercial giant dealing in cotton, silk, indigo, opium, and tea. One of its problems was a surplus of tea—seventeen million pounds of it—which sat unsold in English warehouses. The company's financial fortunes affected the British national economy, and the firm had important friends in Parliament. To help the ailing giant, Parliament passed the Tea Act, which allowed the East India Company to sell its surplus tea in Colonial America at reduced prices. The deal meant cheaper tea for the colonists but it also undercut American merchants and threatened to hurt local business. As a further boost to the ailing company, Parliament removed the tea tax on British exporters but kept it in place for American importers.[8]

Already, many Americans had given up tea drinking to protest the tea tax. Now they asked why the tea tax should be tax-exempt for British exporters, but not American importers. They also resented the unfair monopoly given the East India Company at the expense of American merchants. To many, British tea had become a symbol of British oppression. In Charleston, tea cargoes were left to rot on the docks; in New York and Philadelphia, tea ships were sent back to Britain. In Massachusetts, now a tinderbox of Patriot resentment, eight thousand people assembled outside Old South Church on the night of December 16, waiting to learn if the colony's royal governor would send back three shiploads of tea that had arrived in Boston. The governor refused. When the news was announced, the crowd and the camouflaged "Indians" were ready, and someone shouted, "Boston harbor a teapot tonight!" Three hours later, ninety thousand pounds of British tea was floating in Boston harbor.[9]

The mastermind behind the Boston Tea Party was the principal leader of the Patriot movement in Massachusetts—Samuel Adams. In the seven years following repeal of the Stamp Act, as Americans felt increasingly threatened by the Mother Country, Samuel Adams was always at the center of the storm, defending Colonial rights. By 1773, he was the best-known champion of liberty in Colonial America. Eventually, generations of Americans would know him as the "Father of the Revolution." Amid the tensions racking Colonial America in 1773, however, he was not viewed with universal admiration—especially by British leaders and their Loyalist supporters.[10]

"Damn Samuel Adams!" wrote a Massachusetts Loyalist. "Every dip of his pen stings like an horned snake." Said another: "I doubt whether there is a greater incendiary in the King's dominion." As early as 1764, when the Sugar Act was enacted, Adams was among the first to cry "No taxation without representation." He assumed a key role in protesting the Stamp Act in Massachusetts, and led the opposition to the Townshend Acts in the colony's legislature. After the Boston Massacre in 1770, he successfully petitioned the colony's royal to reduce the presence of British troops in Boston to avoid future confrontations.[11]

In 1772, he and Joseph Warren, another Patriot leader, formed a Committee of Correspondence to alert Massachusetts's population to potential threats and organize any necessary resistance. The mission of the committees, Adams wrote, was the preservation of "the rights of the colonists, and of this province in particular, as men, as Christians, and as subjects." Within months, Adams and Warren had skillfully established committees in more than a hundred villages and towns—and the model spread to other colonies. By dispatch riders, on foot, by ship, and through newspapers, the Committees of Correspondence became an efficient rapid-response system, which enabled America's Colonial legislatures to meet challenges from London with unified action. To Patriots, Samuel Adams was a friend and protector; to British officials, he was Colonial America's chief troublemaker.[12]

In some ways, Samuel Adams seemed an unlikely leader. A cousin of John Adams, he was descended from Puritan emigrants—"virtuous, independent, New England farmers." One of twelve children, he was born and raised in Boston within a family known for its faith. From his father, Samuel Sr., a political activist and a member of the Massachusetts legislature, Adams learned government principles and political savvy. His mother, Mary, a "pious and devoted woman," deeply influenced his personal faith. Young "Sam" Adams, as he became known, was often inattentive to the practical side of life, but his intelligence and engaging personality served him well.[13]

At age fourteen he entered Harvard. He immersed himself in classical literature, reportedly learned Latin and Greek, and became devoted to John Locke's works. Even as a student, according to a nineteenth-century biographer, he was impassioned about liberty: "The few fragments that remain written in a boy's hand [and] his favorite topic for debate in college . . . speak in one tone—liberty! liberty! liberty!" He graduated with honors, then successfully pursued a master's degree. Always, he respected the authority of Higher Law: his master's thesis was titled "Whether it be lawful to resist the Supreme Magistrate, if the commonwealth cannot otherwise be preserved?"[14]

After Harvard, he considered the ministry but concluded he did not have a call. He tried several professions, succeeded at none of them, and wound up working in the family malt house—which he lost through mismanagement after his parents' deaths. While respected for his "strict integrity and blameless morality," he had no interest in moneymaking and was willing to live in "honorable poverty." He married a minister's daughter, who tragically died early and left him with two children to raise. In his forties, he married a loyal, sympathetic woman named Elizabeth Wells, who cheerfully tolerated old clothes and a leaky roof so her husband could champion Colonial liberty. It was in the realm of politics that Samuel Adams discovered his genius. "Politics came as natural to Samuel Adams as the air he breathed," noted an observer: "not the petty politics that plots and plans for place and patronage, but the great politics that is the practical side of statesmanship."[15]

At the time of the Boston Tea Party, he was fifty-one years old, prematurely gray, but robust despite a slight tremor of the hands and face attributed to palsy. He could be a "delightful and entertaining companion," but he was not a flatterer or backslapper. Serious-minded and determined, he possessed the rare ability to command a situation at precisely the most opportune moment. Often, however, he remained in the background, while skillfully resolving issues and planning strategy. In defense of his beliefs, he could be courageous. The British commander in Boston reportedly once confronted him with a veiled threat, then followed with the offer of "great gifts and advancement" if he sided with the king. "Sir, I trust I have long since made my peace with the King of Kings," Adams responded. "No personal consideration shall induce me to abandon the righteous cause of my country."[16]

"What gives him his influence?" George III once fretted aloud to his court officials, who sometimes referred to the political opposition in Colonial America as "Sam Adams' conspiracy." Adams's inspiration, if not his influence, came from his faith—he was the embodiment of a Puritan warrior from the days of Cromwell and Charles I. Fearless and relentless on the political stage, he was devout and mild-mannered at home. His children reportedly idolized him, and his loyal wife described him as a "tender husband." His political opponents would have been incredulous to witness his nightly ritual when home: there, according to an early biographer, he would habitually gather his family in a "little circle each night [to] listen to the Divine Word." He was devoted to the faith of his fathers, and to the apostolic cry of the early church: "We must obey God rather than men!" Sam Adams, it was said, was "the Last Puritan."[17]

Ironically, his first public position was tax collector. Typically, he bungled the job and created a budget deficit. His financial fumbling was largely forgotten, however, when he publicly took the lead in opposition to the Sugar Act. Elected to the Massachusetts legislature during the Stamp Act crisis, he quickly rose to clerk of the House, and emerged as the colony's leading proponent of Colonial rights. A prolific writer, he authored a barrage of influential newspaper editorials that shaped the thinking of the day. While Loyalist leaders dismissed the colony's common people as "scum" and "rabble," Adams courted their support with celebrations, bonfires, and fireworks displays.[18]

He was a master at organizing public protests, political rallies, and parades, and was backed by Boston's Sons of Liberty, a rowdy, pro-independence political club composed largely of laborers, which had chapters in every colony. Admirers saw him as a courageous freedom fighter, defending Colonial rights in the legislature, in the newspapers, and in the streets. Critics accused him of inciting mobs, manipulating politics, and stirring emotions—all in the name of American liberty. Regardless of his methods, over the course of a decade Sam Adams emerged as the premier champion of freedom in Colonial America. John Adams, who knew his cousin's strengths and weaknesses, praised him. "He is the most elegant writer, the sagacious politician, and celebrated patriot of any who have figured in the past ten years," Adams said.[19]

"[All] men are equally bound by the laws of nature, or to speak more properly, the laws of the Creator," Sam Adams wrote in a typical editorial. "They are imprinted by the finger of God on the heart of man . . . and confirmed by written revelation. In the state of nature, every man hath an equal right by honest means to acquire property, and to enjoy it; in general, to pursue his own happiness. . . . [The] people *alone* have an incontestable, unalienable and indefeasible right to institute government; & to reform, alter, or totally change the same when their protection, safety, prosperity and happiness require it."[20]

It was those "unalienable and indefeasible" rights they believed they were defending when Sam Adams's Patriot protesters dumped the detested British tea into Boston Harbor. King George III and the British Parliament disagreed. They were outraged, and the king vowed that Massachusetts would be made to display "the obedience which a colony owes its Mother Country." In early 1774, Parliament responded with a series of punitive measures that became known in America as the "Intolerable Acts." One of the acts, the Boston Port Bill, forcibly closed the port of Boston to commercial shipping except for food, fuel, and military supplies. Not until the king was satisfied that the government and the East India Tea Company had been amply compensated by the people of Massachusetts would the colony's economic lifeline be reopened. Other laws gave the king more control over the colony's government and outlawed unauthorized town meetings.[21]

Americans elsewhere looked to Massachusetts and wondered if the same fate awaited them. Their fears were soon stoked by more action by Parliament. A revised Quartering Act gave British troops the right to seize any unoccupied structures for barracks in *any* colony, and a new law called the Quebec Act granted lands to Canada that had been claimed by Massachusetts, Connecticut, and Virginia. It also placed Canada under a highly centralized government in which almost every action was subject to a veto by the king. Parliament reserved the right to enact a wide range of taxes on Canadians, who were also denied the right of jury trials in civil cases. Many Americans began to question if the same restrictions placed on Canada would eventually be imposed on the American colonies.[22]

To enforce the Boston Port Bill and the Intolerable Acts, London replaced Massachusetts's civilian governor with a military officer, General Thomas Gage, who commanded the British army in North America. To back up General Gage, more red-coated

British troops were soon marching through Boston's streets. Gage had been posted to America for a long time, and had married into a prominent New York family, but viewed the common people of Massachusetts as a "despicable rabble" bent on rebellion. He believed Americans needed the heavy hand of authority, and his orders were clear: he was to enforce "full and absolute submission" on the people of Massachusetts.[23]

"The die is now cast," vowed King George: "the colonies must either submit or triumph." Submission, however, was not what most Americans had in mind, especially in Massachusetts. In mid-May 1774, shortly before the port of Boston was due to be closed, Samuel Adams presided over a town meeting of the Committees of Correspondence from eight Massachusetts towns and the city of Boston. They voted to dispatch a "circular letter" written by Adams, publicly pleading for the support of every American colony and calling for a united Colonial protest against the Intolerable Acts. "This attack," Adams wrote, "though made immediately upon us, is doubtless designed for every other Colony who shall not surrender their sacred rights and liberties . . ." The delegates to the town meeting passed a measure denouncing the Intolerable Acts for their "injustice, inhumanity and cruelty," and proclaimed that "we, therefore, leave it to the just censure of others and appeal to God and the world."[24]

Over the summer of 1774, as Adams's plea for help spread through the colonies, Americans responded with an outpouring of sympathy and support. The "cause of Boston is the cause of us all," became the common cry, and the people of Colonial America became unified as never before. For the first time, many began to blame George III as much as Parliament for attacking American liberty. The king, many now came to believe, was brazenly attempting to put his law above the Higher Law of God. In Philadelphia, volunteer fund-raisers sent aid to Boston for families left unemployed by the port closing. Dockworkers in Marblehead, Massachusetts, offered to work free unloading any ships bringing goods for Boston into their port. Planters in South Carolina sent a cargo of rice. A town in Connecticut donated a flock of sheep. New Yorkers raised money. So did farmers in Virginia. Quakers in Pennsylvania raised more than 2,500 English pounds—a small fortune.[25]

In Virginia, the news from Boston arrived as the colony's House of Burgesses was convening. Patriot leader Richard Henry Lee hastily assembled an impromptu caucus of like-minded legislators that included Patrick Henry and a young lawyer named Thomas Jefferson. Huddled in the capitol's empty legislative chamber, the determined band plotted a strategy to assist Massachusetts and defend American liberty. Their solution: a day of "Fasting, Humiliation and Prayer" in Virginia on June 1, the day Boston's port would be closed. Henry and Jefferson researched Puritan fast day proclamations from a century earlier and used them as a model for the resolution.[26]

"We were under conviction of the necessity of arousing our people from the lethargy into which they had fallen," Jefferson would later recall. Given the devotion of the day, a call for prayer was much more likely to pass the legislature than a political proclamation. It would unite Virginians in an act of faith, while protesting the government's punishment of Massachusetts. As he helped draft the prayer resolution, did Patrick Henry think about the lessons he had learned from his old mentor, Samuel Davies? "The rising generation did not remember, as Henry did, how Samuel Davies had raised patriotic fervor," historian Henry Mayer would note. In its final, Puritan-inspired language, the resolution called on Virginians everywhere "devoutly to implore the Divine Interposition for averting the heavy Calamity, which threatens Destruction to our civil Rights, and . . . to give us one Heart and one Mind firmly to oppose, by all just and proper Means, every Injury to American Rights."[27]

On May 24, 1774, the House of Burgesses passed the fast day resolution without changing a word and with no dissenting votes. The legislators would officially observe the day, it was agreed, by marching together to the local Anglican church for prayer. The resolution was quickly printed as a flyer—a "broadside" in the vernacular of the day—distributed on the streets of Williamsburg, and carried by dispatch riders to villages and towns throughout Virginia. It energized Patriot support in Virginia like a "shock of electricity," according to Thomas Jefferson. It also shocked Virginia's royal governor, the Earl of Dunmore, who showed up in the legislative council chambers with the broadside in hand. The proposed day of prayer and fasting was an insult to the king and Parliament, he pronounced. As punishment, he ordered the House of Burgesses dissolved.[28]

Undeterred, the Virginia legislators trudged over to the nearby Raleigh Tavern, where they reassembled in the Apollo Ballroom. There, eighty-nine censured Virginia lawmakers—Patrick Henry, George Washington, Peyton Randolph, Richard Henry Lee, and Thomas Jefferson among them—drafted a new resolution. In it, they declared that "an attack, made on one of our sister colonies . . . is an attack made on all" and politely criticized London for "the unconstitutional principle of taxing the colonies without their consent." Patrick Henry fretted that the response was "much too feeble," but it concluded with an understated but epic recommendation for "deputies from the several colonies of British America, to meet in general congress." The document's polite language belied its importance. The dismissed lawmakers, meeting in the makeshift chamber of a Williamsburg eatery, had done the unprecedented: they became the first legislative body in America to call for creation of an American congress.[29]

Other legislatures followed their example, and by various means selected delegates for the proposed assembly. Only Georgia refrained. Its leaders feared Britain would retaliate by withholding troops needed to subdue an Indian uprising. In Massachusetts, the legislature recommended a time and a place for the congress to convene—September in Philadelphia. General Gage, now military governor of Massachusetts, tried to disband the colony's legislature before it could pick delegates to the Congress. Samuel Adams had the doors to the legislative chamber locked, however, and personally pocketed the key, preventing the governor's order from arriving until delegates were selected. Adams's circular letter to the other colonies—his "appeal to God and the world"—had triggered the events leading to creation of the First Continental Congress. Sam Adams had long yearned for such an assembly, and now he viewed its creation with deep satisfaction. "May God inspire that intended body with Wisdom and Fortitude," he wrote a friend, "and unite and Prosper their Councils."[30]

CHAPTER 13

"The Love of Liberty is Interwoven in the Soul of Man"

On a Monday afternoon in late August 1774, Samuel and John Adams stepped down from their carriage and set foot in Philadelphia for the first time. Neither man had ever traveled outside New England. For more than two weeks, they had been on the road from Boston to Philadelphia, and they now arrived in America's largest city "dirty, dusty, and fatigued." They were also unquestionably exhilarated. Both were members of the Massachusetts delegation to the First Continental Congress, which would soon convene in Philadelphia's Carpenters' Hall. They had left home in grand style, riding in a coach pulled by a team of four horses, accompanied by coachmen, two assistants on horseback, and two mounted guards.[1]

In city and town along their long route, they had been celebrated as honored dignitaries, welcomed by tolling church bells, greeted by local officials, treated to lavish feasts, and, on at least one occasion, honored by a cheering crowd and an artillery salute. The Continental Congress now preparing to convene in Philadelphia was the talk of Colonial America, and its newly named delegates were the celebrities of the day. Sam Adams was the more renowned of the two cousins, but John Adams was also prominent and accomplished. A respected Boston attorney and Massachusetts legislator, he too was a leading advocate of American liberties in his colony, although he did not have his cousin's national fame. In contrast to Sam Adams, who arrived in Philadelphia wearing clothes donated by his friends, John Adams was a model of New England propriety and frugality.[2]

A man of average height, somewhat stout, he was known for a receding hairline, a face that flushed easily, a scholar's appetite for knowledge, a temperamental nature, and boundless energy. A major similarity: Like his cousin, John Adams was devout. While Samuel Adams was a Calvinist evangelical, John Adams was a theological Liberal in the manner of his mentor, the Reverend Jonathan Mayhew, whose *Unlimited Submission* sermon had so inspired Americans during the Stamp Act crisis. Some historians would later describe John Adams as a Unitarian, or a deist, perhaps because his family had his body reinterred at a Unitarian church several years after his death. Adams, however, professed to be a Christian all of his life. In the words of his twenty-first-century biographer, historian David McCullough, John Adams was "a devout Christian and an independent thinker." Although positioned on the opposite end of Protestant Christianity's theological spectrum from his cousin, John Adams firmly fashioned his life and his politics on the Judeo-Christian worldview.[3]

He too had considered the ministry as a young man, but instead chose a career in law. A Harvard graduate, he built a legal practice, married a bright soul mate named Abagail Smith—who would bear him five children—and earned respect as a Massachusetts legislator. Always, he read, and often in Latin. He dismissed classical works of philosophy as a "disappointment," and recorded "disgust" at some of Plato's thinking. His favorite work was *Paradise Lost* by Puritan intellectual John Milton, and at one point he studied the Bible by copying its chapters into a daily journal.[4]

He was always eager to hear a well-prepared sermon, and

while in Philadelphia for the Continental Congress, he tried to attend several worship services every Sunday. "The Christian religion is," he once wrote, "above all the religions that ever prevailed or existed in ancient or modern times, the religion of wisdom, virtue, equity, and humanity . . . it is resignation to God, it is goodness itself to man." He fancied the English theologian William Paley, an eighteenth-century apologist whose works included *Evidences of Christianity*, and he also followed latitudinarian theology, which held that truth was best determined by human reason and the revelation of Scripture.[5]

Always, he treated the Bible with respect. "Suppose a nation in some distant region should take the Bible for their only law-book," he once speculated.

> *Every member would be obliged, in conscience, to temperance and frugality and industry; to justice and kindness and charity towards his fellow men; and to piety, love, and reverence, towards Almighty God. In this commonwealth, no man would impair his health by gluttony, drunkenness, or lust; no man would sacrifice his most precious time to cards or any other trifling and mean amusement; no man would steal, or lie, or in any way defraud his neighbor, but would live in peace and good will with all men; no man would blaspheme his Maker or profane his worship; but a rational and manly, a sincere and unaffected piety and devotion would reign in all hearts. What a Utopia; what a Paradise would this region be!*[6]

Like his cousin and most Americans, John Adams viewed the Higher Law of God as the ultimate authority and the foundation for human liberty. "The right of the colonies," he once wrote, "was traced not merely to the charters, to Magna Carta, and the English constitution, but to the law of God and nature; to the common and primitive rights of mankind." He was no deistic, rationalistic radical, seeking to fuel a revolution that would topple the traditions of Western thought and culture. He was instead a man of law and order, and like most other members of the Continental Congress, he sought independence and nationhood that would be based on the principles of Scripture. "From a sense of the government of God," he wrote, "and a regard for the laws established by his providence, should all our actions for ourselves or for other men primarily originate. . . ."[7]

Were there not deists, humanists, and rationalists within the Continental Congress? Indeed so, according to John Adams, but they were few in number. Deism accepted the existence of Supreme Being, but only as a disinterested and inactive observer of his creation. Humanists believed that man, not God, was the authority over all things and the central focus of life. Rationalism was an expression of the humanist worldview and claimed that the chief source of truth was human reason, rather than revelation and faith. Deism and humanism had become fashionable among Europe's elite during the recent Age of Enlightenment, but their influence was insignificant in Colonial America. "Actually, European deism was an exotic plant in America, which never struck roots into the soil," Harvard historian Perry Miller would observe. " 'Rationalism' was never so widespread as liberal historians . . . have imagined."[8]

The drift toward Enlightenment philosophies in America was smothered by the impact of the Great Awakening, which reinforced Judeo-Christian thought as the overwhelming consensus among eighteenth-century Americans. "When secularism and religious indifference had begun to make headway among the humble ranks of society," historian Merle Curti would conclude, "the Great Awakening checked these tendencies." Decades after the Revolutionary War, an aging American veteran was questioned about the philosophical origins of the Revolution. His answer reflected the heart of Colonial America. Was the Revolution inspired, he was asked, by the famous philosophers of the Enlightenment—Montesquieu, Rousseau, Spinoza, Voltaire? He reckoned he had never heard of any of them, he replied, and explained that his reading had been restricted to "the Bible, the Catechism, Watts's Psalms and Hymns, and the Almanac."[9]

Such too was the consensus of the Continental Congress. As members of America's educated elite, the delegates included a few whose personal beliefs lay far outside the mainstream, according to John Adams. Among them was an occasional "Universalist" or "Priestleyan"—even one or two "Deists and Atheists"—but they were the tiny minority, said Adams. The great majority of delegates reflected the theological makeup of Colonial America: some Catholics, some Quakers, but mostly Protestants: Presbyterians, Congregationalists, Baptists, Lutherans, German Reformed, and a large number of Anglicans. Despite denominational differences and a smattering of skeptics, the common philosophical foundation of the Continental Congress was a Bible-based faith.[10]

That shared perspective was the common denominator among the delegates meeting in Carpenters' Hall. "What composed that army of fine young fellows that was then before my eyes?" John Adams would later recall. Despite their differences and diversity, the delegates to the Continental Congress had generally been "educated in the general principles of Christianity, and the general principles of English and American liberty," according to Adams. That shared faith was also the consensus on which the founding fathers would build a new nation. "The general principles on which the fathers achieved independence," Adams would note, "were the only principles in which that beautiful assembly of young men could unite, and . . . what were these general principles? I answer, the general principles of *Christianity*."[11]

The heritage of faith that united the Continental Congress was grounded in "the law and the prophets" of the Old Covenant, revealed in the apostolic message of the New Testament, forged in the persecution of the early Church, reformed by extraordinary events in Wittenberg, Geneva, and London, and planted afresh in a new world by chaplains at Jamestown, Separatists and Puritans in New England, believers in the havens of Maryland, Rhode Island, and Pennsylvania, faithful Anglicans patiently ministering in the southern colonies, and Great Awakening revivalists such as Jonathan Edwards, Samuel Davies, and the "forgotten founding father," George Whitefield. It was a remarkable legacy of Bible-based faith that equipped, disciplined, and united the delegates of the Continental Congress for "such a time as this."[12]

The second-day vote to open the Continental Congress with prayer and scripture established a pattern as well as a precedent: throughout the challenges, perils, and turmoil of the unfolding crisis and the War for Independence that would follow, Congress would continue to act on those "general principles" of faith as defined by John Adams. The words of Psalm 35 that rang through Carpenters' Hall, inspiring Adams and others, would also prove prophetic: "Plead my cause, O LORD, with them that strive with me; fight against them that fight against me. . . . Let them be confounded and put to shame who seek after my soul; let them be confused and put to shame who devise my hurt. . . ." Who among the delegates to Congress on that extraordinary day in 1774 could have imagined the pride and power of the mighty British army "brought to confusion" on fields of fire with names like Trenton, Saratoga, and Cowpens? Who could have imagined the king's colors placed in surrender and the disciplined ranks of British redcoats "confounded and put to shame" in an obscure pasture at a faraway place called Yorktown?[13]

As the Continental Congress began its deliberations in Philadelphia, Americans in growing numbers saw the actions of king and Parliament as threats to their inalienable rights of life and liberty.

"The Love of Liberty is interwoven in the Soul of Man, and can never be totally extinguished," Samuel Adams wrote at one point, "and there are certain periods when human patience can no longer endure indignity, and oppression. The spark of liberty then kindles into a flame. . . ." As Congress sought a solution to the crisis with the Mother Country, that "flame" of liberty again blazed from America's pulpits. Just as Americans had looked to their ministers for leadership and direction in the Stamp Act crisis of 1765, they did so again in the 1770s. In Philadelphia, John Adams wrote home, "the clergy here of every denomination . . . thunder and lighten every Sabbath." Again, America's preachers unleashed the power of the pulpit in defense of Higher Law and American liberty.[14]

As they did so, they did not excuse their own people for the political wildfire ablaze in the land. Through the crisis between king and colonies, some preached God was chastening Americans for the besetting sins of city slums and godless behavior in the remote regions of the western frontier. "It should be an invariable rule with Christians," declared the Reverend William Tennent III, "to regard the Hand of God in every Thing which happens, but especially in public Calamities." New York pastor John Henry Livingston concurred: "There are certain national virtues which bring national blessings, and national sins which produce national evils." Some clergymen still believed King George was being misled by a "malignant faction" in his court, and many still counseled "earnest Supplications . . . for our King and all in authority."[15]

Amid the outrage over the Intolerable Acts, however, respect for George III wilted, and growing numbers of clergymen held the king responsible for suppressing inalienable rights. Leading the charge were America's Calvinist pastors, especially the Presbyterians. George III resembled the pharaoh of Egypt, said Reverend Montgomery, and "seems not to know us as his children." Connecticut pastor Stephen Johnson warned that a "proud, arbitrary, selfish and venal spirit of corruption" within the king's court would force Americans to choose between "slavery or independency." Harvard's president, the Reverend Samuel Langdon, said the actions of King and Parliament revealed a "prevalence of vice" and had "changed the whole face of things in the British government."[16]

Pastors from other dissenter denominations—Congregationalists, Baptists, Lutherans, Dutch and German Reformed—joined ranks with the Presbyterians in holding the king accountable. The most popular sermon of the era was titled "An Oration on the Beauties of Liberty," and was the work of a Baptist lay preacher named John Allen. Originally preached at Boston's Second Baptist Church in 1772, it was published and widely circulated in 1774, and became enormously popular and influential throughout the American Colonies. Based on an Old Testament text from the prophet Micah, it issued a stirring call for Americans to protect and preserve their God-given liberty:

> *Liberty! Who would not prize it? Who would not adore it? It is the finished work of Heaven! The glory of omnipotence! The majesty of God! The display of his power, wisdom and perfection. All nature bespeaks it! . . . O this is Liberty divine . . . Is it not the image of Jehovah? The resemblance of the God whom we adore? Therefore, if there be any vein, any nerve, any soul, any life or spirit of liberty in the sons of America, shew your love for it, guard your freedom, prevent your chains; stand up as one man for your liberty; for none but those who set a just value on this blessing are worthy [of] the enjoyment of it.*[17]

From Georgia to New Hampshire, the colonists were reminded from pulpit and pamphlet that liberty was an inalienable right according to the Natural Law of creation, and the Higher Law of Scripture. Every human being, kings included, was subordinate to God's law, Colonial pastors preached, and it was obvious from its providential past that America had a God-ordained future. Like the Jews of the Old Testament, many pastors taught, the Americans were a chosen people. The Puritan vision of America as a "City upon a hill" no longer belonged to New England alone—it had become embraced by all of America. Presbyterian pastor John Carmichael spoke for many in America when he preached that "out of these present tumults, disturbances and commotions, a great and mighty empire may rise up in the western world, for King Jesus."[18]

On both sides of the Atlantic, American ministers in the 1770s became known as the "black regiment," so described for the common black clergyman's attire and the army-sized influence they wielded. Increasingly, America's black regiment—especially the Calvinists—reminded Americans that their first priority was the Higher Law of God. In 1774, as the British Parliament discussed conditions in the colonies, a knowledgeable member tried to explain the American mind-set to his fellow lawmakers. "If you ask an American who is his master," he advised, "he will tell you he has none, nor any governor, but Jesus Christ. I do believe it and it is my firm opinion that the opposition to the measures of the legislature of this country is a determined prepossession of the idea of independence." On the eve of the Revolution, the collective call from America's pulpits was an age-old cry of Bible-based resistance: "No king but Jesus."[19]

The First Continental Congress remained in session for almost two months, from September 5, 1774, until adjournment on October 26. Every colony except Georgia sent delegates. Some wanted reconciliation with Britain, others sought compromise, and some supported independence. By the time they adjourned, however, the delegates had overcome their differences enough to make an important show of unity. They rejected a compromise by Pennsylvania delegate Joseph Galloway—the Galloway Plan—

which proposed a type of Colonial parliament with veto power given to the king. They passed a measure called the Declaration and Resolves, which condemned the Intolerable Acts and the Quebec Act, asserted American rights to "life, liberty and property," and declared taxation to be the sole right of the Colonial legislatures. They also established what was called the Continental Association, through which each colony agreed to suspend trade with Great Britain.[20]

Their most important action was endorsement of the Suffolk Resolves, a series of resolutions enacted in Massachusetts by a convention of delegates from Boston and other towns in Suffolk County. Although pledging loyalty to the king, the Suffolk Resolves declared the Intolerable Acts to be illegal under British law, urged Massachusetts's colonists to withhold taxes from the royal government as a protest, advised the people of the colony to field an armed militia for self-defense, and recommended suspending all trade with the Mother Country. The resolves also stated that "it is an indispensable duty which we owe to God, our country, ourselves and posterity, by all lawful ways and means in our power to maintain, defend and preserve those civil and religious rights and liberties, for which many of our fathers fought, bled and died, and to hand them down entire to future generations."[21]

Before adjourning, the Continental Congress issued a lengthy public address to "the People of Great Britain," explaining Colonial America's position and pledging continued loyalty to king and Parliament—as long as America's inalienable rights were respected. "The cause of America," Congress declared, "is now the object of universal attention: it has at length become very serious. This unhappy country has not only been oppressed, but abused and misrepresented. . . . Know then, that we consider ourselves, and do insist, that we are and ought to be, as free as our fellow-subjects in Britain, and that no power on earth has a right to take our property from us without our consent."[22]

In a similar public "Memorial" issued to the American colonists, Congress summarized America's grievances, and asserted biblical justification for the defense of inalienable rights—which Congress described as "the rights of men, and the blessings of liberty" that were due all people. "In every case of opposition by a people to their rulers, or of one state to another," Congress proclaimed, "duty to Almighty God, the creator of all, requires that a true and impartial judgement be formed of the measures leading to such opposition; and of the causes by which it has been provoked, or can in any degree be justified: That neither affection on the one hand, nor resentment on the other, being permitted to give a wrong bias to reason, it may be enabled to take a dispassionate view of all circumstances, and settle the public conduct on the solid foundations of wisdom and justice." Congress thus invoked support for Higher Law as justification for resisting British abuse of power. If London refused to address Colonial concerns, Congress vowed, it would reassemble in Philadelphia next May.[23]

In February 1775, the British Parliament took up the grievances presented by Congress. Sir William Pitt, a highly respected former British prime minister, advocated reconciliation with the American colonies. British troops should be withdrawn from Boston, he advised, the Continental Congress should be officially recognized by the British government, and Parliament should not attempt to impose any taxation without the consent of America's colonial legislatures. His proposal was decisively rejected; instead, Parliament declared the colony of Massachusetts to be in a state of rebellion. Soon afterward, in the Virginia House of Burgesses, Patrick Henry recommended immediately placing his colony "into a posture of defense." When some legislators objected to war preparation, Henry sadly predicted: "There is no longer any room for hope. . . . An appeal to arms and the God of hosts is all that is left us!" He concluded his speech with a dramatic vow that American schoolchildren would memorize for generations to come: "I know not what course others may take, but as for me, give me liberty or give me death!"[24]

In Massachusetts, meanwhile, the British commander, General Gage, began fortifying defensive positions in the Boston area. In response, the Massachusetts legislature established a Provincial Congress, named Patriot leader John Hancock as its president, and gave him authority to call out militia forces if needed. Gage then sent a solemn dispatch to London: military action might be necessary, but it would likely provoke a war. Perhaps, he suggested diplomatically, it might be wise to seek reconciliation with the Americans. George III was aghast—he wanted resolution, not reconciliation. In April 1775, Gage received orders to do what was necessary for "re-establishing government" in Massachusetts. On the night of April 18, more than seven hundred British troops marched out of Boston, headed westward. They had orders to arrest John Hancock and Samuel Adams, who were overnight guests at a minister's home in Lexington, and to raid a depot in Concord where the militia stored military supplies.[25]

At dawn the next morning, April 19, 1775, British troops reached Lexington. There they encountered a force of militia volunteers on the village green. Outnumbered, the Americans began backing away—when someone fired a shot. The British opened fire, killing eight Americans and wounding ten. The surviving Americans retreated, and the British moved on to Concord, where they destroyed arms and equipment as planned. Somehow the courthouse and a blacksmith shop caught fire. The smoke attracted increasing numbers of Massachusetts militiamen, and some took a stand on a bridge on the edge of town.[26]

The British fired on them, too, leaving two Americans dead. This time the militia delivered an effective return fire, however, killing three British soldiers and wounding nine. The Americans withdrew, and the British filed out of Concord, heading back to Boston. On the line of march, however, they were repeatedly attacked by American troops firing from cover, frontier-style. The British were reinforced at Lexington, and began looting and burning civilian homes as they retreated. Enraged, the militia increased their numbers and their fire, and the British march became an ongoing battle, with a trail of British dead and wounded left behind. By the time the British troops reached the safety of Boston, they had suffered 273 dead and wounded, compared to American losses of ninety-five. The American War of Independence had begun.[27]

Warned of the approaching British troops, Samuel Adams and John Hancock escaped capture. As they were leaving town, they heard the gunfire and saw the smoke of battle rising in the distance. "Oh! What a glorious morning is this!" Adams reportedly exclaimed. He realized the political battles were now over: as King George had said, "The die is now cast. The colonies must either submit or triumph." News of Lexington and Concord came to John Adams while he was at his home near Boston. Somberly, he took up his pen and recorded his thoughts. "It is Arrogance and Presumption in human Sagacity to pretend to penetrate far into the Designs of Heaven," he wrote. "But, I can't help depending upon this, that the present Calamity . . . is intended to bind the Colonies together. . . ." Far to the south, in Patrick Henry's Virginia, the news interrupted a provincial council in Fredericksburg. The Virginians adjourned their meeting but put aside their customary closing, "God save the King!" Instead, they cheered, "God save the liberties of America!"[28]

CHAPTER 14

"Thou Hast Brought a Vine Out of Egypt"

The delegates to the Second Continental Congress filed past the handsome columns and whitewashed walls that graced the sanctuary of Philadelphia's Christ Church. Quietly, they seated themselves in the sanctuary's boxed pews. The Anglican church was a Philadelphia landmark, and its lofty brick bell tower lifted the church steeple a towering 196 feet above the city skyline. It was July 20, 1775, and the delegates were present at Christ Church for a momentous national event. The Congress had officially declared this summer day to be a day of "public humiliation, fasting and prayer." Concerned about the "impending danger and public calamity" that warfare had brought to the American colonies, the Continental Congress had recommended that "Christians, of all denominations" set aside this day to pray for America—and, following their own advice, the delegates had voted to observe the day of prayer by worshipping together.[1]

The Second Continental Congress had convened in Philadelphia on May 10, 1775, in the wake of Lexington and Concord. Cheering crowds and tolling bells welcomed the delegates, but now militia companies were drilling on Philadelphia's broad streets. Congress met this time in the Pennsylvania State House, which lay just down the street from Carpenters' Hall and offered more room. Housed in a tower above the stately brick structure was a huge bell—famously named the "Liberty Bell" later—and on it was scripture from the book of Leviticus: "Proclaim liberty throughout all the land unto all the inhabitants thereof." Now, even more than when Congress had adjourned back in October, the scripture seemed relevant to the business conducted in the legislative chamber below.[2]

When Congress was gaveled into order, some old members were missing, and new ones were present as replacements. Among the new faces were John Hancock of Massachusetts, Benjamin Franklin representing Pennsylvania, and Thomas Jefferson of Virginia. Again, twelve colonies sent delegations, but eventually Georgia too would be represented. Hancock was selected as president of the Second Continental Congress, and the delegates set about deliberating strategy for defending what some now called "the United Colonies." Should they let each colony defend itself with militia forces? Or should they try to form some kind of American army? Soon after Congress convened, news came that militia troops under Ethan Allen had captured a principal British stronghold, Fort Ticonderoga, on New England's Lake Champlain, and information gathered at the fort indicated the British intended to make an attack from Canada. In Boston, meanwhile, thousands of New England militia now confronted General Gage's British army, and more bloodshed could erupt at any time.[3]

In early June, John Adams proposed that Congress officially accept the militia forces at Boston as an American army. Several days later, the Congress agreed, establishing the Continental Army. On June 15, the Congress unanimously named Virginia delegate George Washington to head it as commander in chief. A Virginia planter and legislator, Washington was a veteran militia officer from the French and Indian War, and also had spent years overseeing Virginia's frontier defenses. An Anglican, Washington was a quiet but serious believer. Upon his appointment to commander in chief, he wrote his wife, Martha, that "it has been a kind of destiny that has thrown me upon this service. . . . I shall rely, therefore, confidently on that Providence which has heretofore preserved and been bountiful to me. . . ."[4]

Washington departed for Boston immediately to take command of American forces there, but fighting began before he could arrive. On June 17, the British army had attacked Patriot positions at the Battle of Bunker Hill. It was a British victory, but to the surprise of British commanders, it took three assaults and more than a thousand casualties to drive the Americans off the hill. Two weeks later, Washington reached Boston and took formal command of American forces there—now the Continental Army. The fighting in Massachusetts aroused a mighty outpouring of support for the defense of American liberty, but Congress intended to try once more to achieve reconciliation with London.[5]

In early July, the Continental Congress passed what would become known as "the Olive Branch Petition," which was authored by Pennsylvania delegate John Dickinson, a prominent Patriot leader and an impassioned advocate for reconciliation. In respectful tones, the Olive Branch Petition made a direct appeal to King George III, asking him to suspend hostile actions in America until the current crisis could be resolved. The same week, the Continental Congress also adopted the Declaration of the Causes and Necessities of Taking Up Arms, which was coauthored by Dickinson and Thomas Jefferson and stated the case for American resistance.[6]

It stopped short of calling for American independence—many delegates still hoped for reconciliation—but it did declare the colonists' willingness to fight rather than surrender their liberty: "We fight not for glory or conquest. We exhibit to mankind the remarkable spectacle of a people attacked by unprovoked enemies, without any imputation or even suspicion of offenses. . . ." The declaration also clearly stated the colonists' prevailing belief that America had "grown up" according to the will of God and with his "Divine favour."

> *We gratefully acknowledge, as signal instances of the Divine favour toward us, that his Providence would not permit us to be called into this severe controversy, until we were grown up to our present strength, had been previously exercised in war-like operation, and possessed of the means of defending our-selves.*

As preached so often from so many American pulpits in the preceding years, the declaration affirmed a belief in the righteousness of the American cause and a conviction that God would enable the people of America to resist tyranny.

> *With hearts fortified with these animating reflections, we most solemnly, before God and the world, declare that, exerting the utmost energy of those powers which our beneficent Creator hath graciously bestowed upon us, the arms we have been compelled by our enemies to assume, we will, in defiance of every hazard, with unabating firmness and perseverance, employ for the preservation of our liberties. . . .*

The declaration concluded with a congressional statement of faith on behalf of the American people. They would not be alone, it confidently predicted, as they faced the full might of the British Empire.

> *With an humble confidence in the mercies of the supreme and impartial Judge and Ruler of the Universe, we most devoutly implore his divine goodness to conduct us happily through this great conflict, to dispose our adversaries to reconciliation on rea-*

sonable terms, and thereby to relieve the empire from the calamities of civil war.[7]

The "calamities of civil war" were fresh in the minds of the delegates when they observed the congressional day of prayer and fasting: it followed Bunker Hill's bloody harvest by just a month. It was the first of many "fast days" called by the Continental Congress. The date had been picked by the delegates on June 7, and the resolution recommending "public humiliation fasting and prayer" had been authored by John Adams, with assistance from delegates William Hooper and Robert Treat Paine. Congress unanimously approved it:

> *This Congress, therefore, considering the present critical, alarming and calamitous state of these colonies, do earnestly recommend that Thursday, the 20th day of July next, be observed, by the inhabitants of all the English colonies on this continent, as a day of public humiliation, fasting and prayer; that we may, with united hearts and voices, unfeignedly confess and deplore our many sins; and offer up our joint supplications to the all-wise, omnipotent, and merciful Disposer of all events . . . that virtue and true religion may revive and flourish throughout our land; and that all America may soon behold a gracious interposition of heaven. . . .*

The resolution concluded by suggesting how Americans might observe the special day: "And it is recommended to Christians, of all denominations, to assemble for public worship, and to abstain from servile labour and recreations on said day." Congress had the fast day resolution published in newspapers and distributed as a handbill. Throughout the American colonies, countless pastors read it from the pulpit and encouraged their congregations to properly observe the day of prayer. John Adams was exultant at the prospect. "We have appointed a continental fast," he wrote home. "Millions will be upon their Knees at once before their great Creator, imploring his Forgiveness and Blessing . . ."[8]

Americans observed the day of prayer seriously and respectfully. In Philadelphia, the usual weekday bustle was oddly absent. The city's streets were empty and quiet. Elsewhere in Colonial America the day was similarly observed. Americans quietly observed the day at home, or assembled in their churches for appropriate services of worship. America's ministers delivered the "fast day sermons" that were traditional to Colonial America, calling for humility and repentance, but with a new focus: America was at war in defense of inalienable rights. "On that day," historian Moses Coit Tyler would observe, "from New Hampshire to Georgia, the pulpit became the organ of a new national consciousness . . . to Englishmen, to freemen and to Christians."[9]

In Chester County, Pennsylvania, Baptist minister David Jones titled his fast day sermon "A Defensive War in a Just Cause is Sinless." In the camp of the new Continental Army near Boston, the Reverend Ezra Sampson, a young Yale graduate, delivered a sermon so powerful that the soldiers declared him "Sampson by name and Samson by nature," referring to the Old Testament strongman. In Connecticut, a Loyalist minister named Samuel Andrews sermonized against the fast day with a text from the prophet Amos: "I hate, I despise your feast days. . . ." His congregation abandoned his church in droves, leaving the parson with nothing to do but plod around his backyard on an old white horse.[10]

The Continental Congress observed the official fast day by spending most of it in church. At Christ Church that morning, the delegates passed beneath a wall sculpture of King George II, which stood as a marble reminder of the Anglican Church's official status as Britain's national church. Despite that connection, it was the pastor of Christ Church, the Reverend Jacob Duché, who had led the First Continental Congress in its opening prayer.

Now, on the congressional fast day, he looked down from his people at the assembled delegates and boldly delivered a sermon titled "The American Vine." It was based on a text from Psalm 80, which referred to God's rescue of the Hebrew nation from ancient Egypt:

Thou hast brought a vine out of Egypt: thou hast cast out the heathen, and planted it. Thou preparedst room before it, and didst cause it to take deep root, and it filled the land. The hills were covered with the shadow of it, and the boughs thereof were like the goodly cedar. . . . O God of hosts: look down from heaven, and behold, and visit this vine; And the vineyard which thy right hand hath planted, and the branch that thou madest strong for thyself.[11]

To the delegates seated in the pews of Christ Church, the point of Duché's sermon had to be obvious: Would a new American nation take deep root and fill the land? And who was to blame for attempting to destroy the "American Vine"? Duché's sermon left no doubt as to where he felt blame should rest: "[It] is even, thou, Britain, that with merciless and unhallowed hands, wouldst cut down and destroy this branch of thine own vine, the very branch, which Providence hath made strong even for thyself!"

Duché had words of caution for the Congress, however, and Americans everywhere. In the face of "present chastisements," all Americans should humble themselves, repent, and trust God for the struggle that lay ahead.

Injured and oppressed as we are, unmeriting the harsh and rigorous treatment which we have received from such an unexpected quarter, let us, however, look up to a higher cause for the awful infliction; and whilst we are faithfully persevering in the defense of our temporal rights, let us humble ourselves before God, lay our hands upon our hearts, and seriously and

> *impartially inquire what returns we have made to Heaven for its past favors, and whether its present chastisements have not been drawn down upon us by a gross neglect of our past privileges.*[12]

That afternoon, the Congress attended another worship service. The delegates had scheduled two for the fast day—the Anglican service in the morning and a Presbyterian service in the afternoon at Philadelphia's Old Pine Street Church. The church's pastor, Dr. Francis Alison, a Scots-Irish immigrant, was a prominent American clergyman and educator. He had founded schools that would someday become the universities of Pennsylvania and Delaware, and he had mentored several members of Congress. Devoted to the authority of Scripture and the Higher Law, Alison ardently supported American independence. By attending two worship services—one Anglican and the other Presbyterian—the delegates put aside a long history of fear, mistrust, and denominational differences to unite in the fundamentals of a common faith.[13]

The pulpit pronouncements on behalf of American liberty and independence were not limited to the congressional day of prayer. Just as they had done during the Stamp Act crisis and when the Intolerable Acts were imposed, America's pastors waged a war of words in the aftermath of Lexington, Concord, and Bunker Hill. "Your Lordship can scarcely conceive," a dismayed Loyalist complained to a colleague, "what Fury the Discourses of some mad Preachers have created in this Country. . . ." In a new wave of sermons, American pastors likened the conflict between colonists and the Mother Country to the confrontation between David and Goliath. They compared King George to the tyrannical King Rehoboam, who forced the breakup of Israel in the Old Testament. They cited the prophet Samuel's admonitions against ungodly kingship, compared King George to the pharaoh of the Exodus, and quoted a warning from the book of Proverbs: "As a roaring lion and a raging bear, so is a wicked ruler over the poor people."[14]

Some compared Americans to the Jews of the Exodus. Just as the Hebrews of old were eventually brought into the Promised Land, predicted New York preacher Archibald Laidlie, God would someday make America "the happy place where not only civil Liberty, but true Religion should flourish in spite of all our enemies." Presbyterians resurrected calls for Bible-based resistance from two famous Scots: John Knox, who founded Scotland's Presbyterian Church, and clergyman Samuel Rutherford, whose writings were immensely influential in America. In his most famous work, *Lex Rex*, Rutherford had argued that even kings must submit to Higher Law. Many Reformed pastors cited the "just war" defense from the 1646 Westminster Confession of Faith, a statement crafted during the English civil wars by an assembly of Protestant theologians at the request of Parliament. If six conditions were met, it stated, participation in a "just" war was "lawful for Christians."[15]

With the outbreak of warfare, many Americans put away denominational differences in defense of liberty—even Anglicans. Although many of their ministers were reluctant Patriots and some fled to Britain, most Anglicans supported the American cause despite their membership in the national church. "Thus Baptists and Anglicans, backcountry Presbyterian farmers and tidewater gentleman planters, struck bargains and surmounted their differences," historian Patricia Bonomi would observe. Irishman Edmund Burke, one of America's few friends in Parliament, recognized the biblical foundation of American resistance, and its motivating influence. "The people are Protestants," he tried to tell Parliament, "and of that kind which is most adverse to all implicit submission of mind and opinion."[16]

Submission was not on the congressional agenda in Philadelphia; instead Congress was gaining strength. In September 1775, a delegation from Georgia joined the Congress, giving it full representation from all thirteen American colonies. In October, John Adams took the lead in pushing for the creation of an American navy, and Congress agreed, authorizing an initial four-ship navy and two battalions of marines. On November 9, news arrived from London that King George III not only had refused to consider Congress's Olive Branch Petition for reconciliation, he had issued a royal proclamation declaring Colonial America to be in open rebellion. The king had followed his proclamation by ordering *all* American ports closed in the same way he had closed the port of Boston. His order was backed by the British navy, which had already bombarded and burned several communities on the coast of New England.[17]

With reconciliation no longer an option, John Adams, Samuel Adams, Virginia's Richard Henry Lee, and others worked to shift the consensus of Congress toward independence. John Adams skillfully worked to orchestrate a vote on the issue, while Samuel Adams lobbied persuasively behind the scenes. In early 1776, they received influential assistance from an unexpected source—the son of a Quaker corset maker. His name was Thomas Paine. At thirty-nine, he had tried a variety of occupations, and had failed at all of them. Two years earlier, he had come from Britain to Philadelphia, where he worked as a part-time writer for one of Ben Franklin's publications. His obscurity ended in January 1776, when a booklet he wrote made him a household name in America and gave the cause of American independence a dramatic boost.[18]

It was called *Common Sense*, and it became the rage in Colonial America, selling more than a half million copies in record time. It rang with Old Testament allusions, likening the king to the "hardened, sullen-tempered Pharaoh of Egypt," and it built a Bible-based case for American independence. Thomas Paine was no Christian; he would eventually become a French-style radical and skeptic. His grasp of biblical theology was woeful, according to John Adams, who would eventually label Paine a "blackguard" for his harsh, irreverent skepticism. Paine understood the heart of the American people, however, and he crafted his arguments in *Common Sense* to appeal to the Bible-based thinking of eighteenth-century America. "The sun never shined on a cause of greater worth," the booklet declared; "for God's sake, let us come to a final separation. . . ." *Common Sense* popularized the cause of independence in a mighty way and bolstered support for it in the Continental Congress.[19]

As the impact of *Common Sense* was surging in the spring of 1776, Americans learned that King George not only intended to unleash all-out war on the United Colonies—he intended to do so with hired mercenaries. Twenty thousand German troops from the state of Hesse-Kassel had been recruited to help wage war on America. The Hessians, as they were called, had a fearsome reputation, both as hardened fighters and harsh occupiers. The king's decision revealed his true feelings for the American people, many colonists believed, and it reinforced the charge made by Thomas Paine's *Common Sense:* "He hath wickedly broken through every moral and human obligation, trampled nature and conscience beneath his feet, and by a steady and constitutional spirit of insolence and cruelty procured for himself a universal hatred."[20]

On May 17, 1776, Americans observed another day of "fasting, humiliation and prayer" officially called by the Continental Congress. It too passed Congress unanimously on a motion introduced by New Jersey delegate William Livingston, a prominent lawyer and political leader who had once served as a missionary to the Mohawk Indians. Congress again summoned the people to prayer and fasting by placing public notices in the newspapers. As before, Congress ordered no one to participate, but it recommended that Americans everywhere beseech God for his protection "through the merits and mediation of Jesus Christ."[21]

The lengthy congressional resolution concluded with a plea

that Almighty God "would be graciously pleased to bless all his people in these colonies with health and plenty, and grant that a spirit of incorruptible patriotism, and of pure undefiled religion, may universally prevail; and this continent be speedily restored to the blessings of peace and liberty, and enabled to transmit them inviolate to the latest posterity. And it is recommended to Christians of all denominations, to assemble for public worship, and abstain from servile labour on the said day."[22]

Americans put aside work and filled churches in city, town, and countryside to observe another congressional fast day and hear a new round of preaching. The delegates observed the day, a Friday, by again attending worship services in Philadelphia, where once more the streets were deserted and quiet. At some churches, independence supporters moved among departing worshippers and gathered signatures for a petition calling for a public meeting. A few days later, an estimated four thousand Philadelphians stood in a drizzle and cheered enthusiastically for American independence.[23]

Their mood was not shared by all in Congress: numerous delegates still held deep reservations about voting for independence. John and Samuel Adams had seen the doubts firsthand. A week before the day of prayer, John Adams had introduced a resolution calling for each American colony to proclaim self-government, which he hoped would advance the cause of independence. Debate had droned on all day. "Our petitions have not been heard, yet answered with fleets and armies," Sam Adams had argued at one point. "We cannot go upon stronger reasons than the King has thrown us out of his protection." Although the proposal finally passed, the debate had revealed deep divisions within the Congress.[24]

Then, ten days after the prayer day observance, on Monday, May 27, 1776, the mood in Congress began to shift. That morning, two resolutions were presented to Congress, both advocating independence. One was submitted by the North Carolina delegation. It had been passed by a convention in North Carolina back in April, and it authorized the North Carolina delegation to vote for a declaration of independence. The other one came from a convention in Virginia. It was called the Virginia Resolve, and it instructed Richard Henry Lee, the head of the Virginia delegation, to introduce a motion in the Continental Congress calling for a vote on independence.[25]

The push from North Carolina and Virginia gave new momentum to the cause of independence in Congress. His hope renewed, John Adams penned a quick note to Patrick Henry, who had gone home to help draft a Virginia constitution and serve as governor. "The decree is gone forth," Adams wrote, "and it cannot be recalled. . . ." On Friday, June 7, 1776, Virginia's Richard Henry Lee rose before the Congress. A black silk handkerchief was draped over his hand to hide the scars of an old hunting accident. Speaking clearly in the hushed chamber of the Pennsylvania State House, he presented a history-changing resolution: "That these United Colonies are, and of right ought to be, free and independent states, that they are absolved from all allegiance to the British Crown, and that all political connection between them and the State of Great Britain is, and ought to be, totally dissolved."[26]

CHAPTER 15

"Endowed by their Creator"

This was the decisive day, and they all knew it. On July 1, 1776, the Continental Congress assembled to vote for—or against—American independence. Three weeks earlier, Richard Henry Lee's independence resolution had been debated long into the night, but without a decision. Despite the determined efforts of John and Samuel Adams, some delegates had adamantly opposed breaking with Britain. After prolonged debate, the Congress had adjourned for the Lord's Day, then had resumed deliberation on Monday, June 10. Still no decision. Finally, South Carolina's Edward Rutledge had moved to postpone debate for three weeks, which would allow the delegations to receive more direction from the legislatures and conventions back home. The Congress had agreed, and had set the vote for July 1, 1776.[1]

In preparation for the vote, Congress had appointed a five-man committee to draft a proposed declaration of independence, in case it was needed. The committee members included John Adams, Benjamin Franklin, Robert Livingston of New York, Roger Sherman of Connecticut—and Thomas Jefferson. Jefferson was asked to author a draft of the document, which would then be proofed by the committee. The tall, lanky, thirty-three-year-old Virginian had been raised with the educated refinements of a Southern aristocrat. He was conversant in several languages, played the violin with accomplished skill, moved with grace on the ballroom floor, recited the classics with ease, and could "sit a good horse." A consummate student, he possessed an insatiable curiosity and—while an awkward public speaker—he was a gifted and experienced writer. "You can write ten times better than I do," Adams told him. Jefferson agreed to the task, and set about to meet the three-week deadline.[2]

He sequestered himself in the upstairs suite he had rented in a house on the outskirts of Philadelphia, where he believed the air circulated better. Rising every day before sunrise, he would habitually bathe his feet in a pan of cold water, then prop his portable writing desk on his lap, and—using a quill pen—fill large, folded sheets of thick paper with his precise handwriting. Typically, he would write awhile, stop and read over his work, strike through anything he disliked, insert revisions in tiny handwriting, and keep writing. He used no reference works, he would later say, although he did draw from his own recent work on Virginia's new constitution, and he obviously picked up some phrasing from fellow Virginian George Mason, whose proposal for the Virginia constitution was published in Philadelphia newspapers while Jefferson was at work.[3]

When the draft was finished, he took it to John Adams and Ben Franklin. Neither made many changes. Adams was Jefferson's mentor in Congress, and he knew his friend was sensitive about editing. Even so, Adams thought Jefferson's charges against the king read a little harsh—"too much like scolding, for so grave and solemn a document." Otherwise he was impressed with Jefferson's work. "I was delighted with its high tone and flights of oratory," he would later recall. When it was his turn to proof Jefferson's draft, Franklin did it from a sickbed—he was laid up at a friend's home with an attack of gout. He examined the document with the skill of a veteran editor—his *Poor Richard's Almanack* was one of the most successful journals in Colonial America. Jefferson's dramatic charge that the king's forces intended to "deluge us in blood" became simply "destroy us"—but Franklin also found little to change. As expected, the document was presented to Congress and tabled for consideration if needed after the independence vote.[4]

Three weeks later, as planned, Richard Henry Lee's resolution was again placed before the Continental Congress. It was July 1, 1776. "The morning is assigned for the greatest debate of all," John Adams observed. For months Adams had felt a sense of anxiety about the issue of "independency," as he called it. He believed there was a rising "torrent" of interest in the issue among the delegates, but, he wrote his wife,

> *the arbiter of events, the sovereign of the world, only knows which way the torrent will be turned. Judging by experience, by probabilities, and by all appearances, I conclude it will roll on to dominion and glory, though the circumstances and consequences may be bloody. In such great changes and commotions, individuals are but atoms. It is scarcely worthwhile to consider what the consequences will be to us. What will be the effects upon present and future millions, and millions of millions, is a question very interesting to benevolence, natural and Christian. God grant they may, and I firmly believe they will be happy.*[5]

When the question of "independency" finally came to the floor of Congress, deliberations continued for nine hours—from morning until twilight. The opposition was led by Pennsylvania delegate John Dickinson, one of the most famous and able orators in America. The Thirteen Colonies were not prepared for independence, he argued at length. America simply could not withstand British military might, he warned. Declaring independence at this time, he told the Congress, would be like sailing on a stormy sea "in a skiff made of paper." When he concluded, the chamber was silent and his arguments went unchallenged. Finally, John Adams felt compelled to speak.[6]

He arose from his seat, took the floor, and made an eloquent case for American independence. It was a persuasive argument, superbly presented, and it "sustained the debate," said one delegate. Within moments, however, Adams had to repeat his performance. Three new delegates from New Jersey entered the chamber, and they wanted to hear the speech. Adams arose and made the speech again—and this time, some said, it was even more effective. At one point, North Carolina's Joseph Hewes, a former Quaker who had long opposed independence, suddenly sat upright, raised his hands heavenward as if in submission, and cried aloud—"It is done! And I will abide by it!" Adams talked for about forty-five minutes, until the New Jersey delegates politely interrupted him—and pledged their delegation's vote for independence. After nine hours of speechmaking, it was finally time to vote.[7]

Nine of the thirteen delegations voted for independence, hence, the vote was not unanimous. Adams and the other independence supporters believed it *needed* to be. How could they proclaim themselves to be "united" states if they were not unified? For various reasons, Pennsylvania, New York, South Carolina, and Delaware held out. Then South Carolina's Edward Rutledge made a pivotal motion: Why not have a final vote the next day? John Adams immediately grasped Rutledge's strategy: with a little more time, the South Carolinians might tip toward independence—and other reluctant delegations might switch, too. Congress passed the motion and adjourned—with a final vote scheduled for July 2.[8]

In Philadelphia's taverns and coffee shops that night, the delegates continued the debate. Sam and John Adams knew that Pennsylvania's John Dickinson carried great sway with the indecisive delegates, and both politicked fervently to counter his influence. Dickinson was a champion of American liberties, but he conscientiously opposed independence, despite the pro-independence stand held by most of his constituents. Dickinson would not change his position, but overnight he nevertheless made a decision that would decisively alter the vote.[9]

When the Continental Congress reconvened on the morning of July 2, the vote count had changed. Pro-independence delegate Caesar Rodney of Delaware had been absent for the first vote, leaving Delaware with a split delegation. Urgently summoned back to Philadelphia, he rode through the night in a ferocious thunderstorm, changing mounts several times and pounding down muddy roads under lightning flashes. He made it. Just in time for the vote, he dramatically strode into the chamber wearing muddy boots—and tipped Delaware's vote in favor of independence. The New York delegation was committed to independence, too—and now, as Edward Rutledge had hinted, so was South Carolina. That left Pennsylvania: John Dickinson and Robert Morris could not bring themselves to personally break with Britain—but both intentionally failed to appear, allowing Pennsylvania to cast its vote for independence.[10]

Equally critical to the shift in sentiment, some said, was a moving speech delivered by one of the newly arrived New Jersey delegates—Dr. John Witherspoon, who was president of Princeton University. A Presbyterian minister who had immigrated from Scotland, Witherspoon was the first clergyman to serve in the Continental Congress. His eloquent and persuasive preaching on behalf of American liberty had propelled him to Congress—just in time to deliver an impassioned speech for independence. His influence on the Continental Congress, then and later, was powerful. Upon learning that Witherspoon had joined the Congress in time for the independence vote, a leading member of Parliament would reportedly comment, "There is no use crying about it. Cousin America has run off with a Presbyterian parson. . . ."[11]

Finally, the vote was taken. It was unanimous—no dissenting votes. Every delegation supported independence. The Thirteen Colonies were no more—and the United States of America was born. The Declaration of Independence would not be adopted by the Continental Congress for two more days, and that date—July 4—would become Independence Day. John Adams expected July 2—the day of the critical independence vote—to become America's birthday. "The second day of July, 1776, will be the most memorable epocha in the history of America," he predicted. Future generations should celebrate the day with "pomp and parade, with shows, games, sports, guns, bells, bonfires, and illuminations," he declared, "from one end of this continent to the other, from this time forward, forevermore." It should also be a time for thanksgiving to God, he wrote, "commemorated as the day of deliverance, by solemn acts of devotion to God Almighty."[12]

On the afternoon of July 2, Thomas Jefferson sat glumly at his seat in the congressional chamber. Delegates were discussing and editing his draft of the Declaration of Independence, and he was not happy. Although Jefferson would forever be known as the author of the history-making document, the delegates understood that the Declaration was not *his:* it was to be the work of the entire Congress. It was theirs to edit, amend, and finalize—and they did, making more than eighty changes. Most were minor, although Jefferson would later complain that his work had been "mutilated."[13]

Not only was Jefferson's draft edited by Congress, John Adams would later explain, its content had been molded by prolonged congressional debate even before Jefferson wrote it. "There is not an idea in it," Adams would later observe, "but what had been hackneyed in Congress for two years before." So, through their efforts before and after Jefferson skillfully rendered his draft, the delegates made the Declaration of Independence into a congressional creation. Through it, they made a clear case to the world that America's quest for independence was justified before God—and it was a case familiar and acceptable to Americans everywhere.[14]

Occasionally in the centuries to come, revisionists would attempt to redefine the Declaration of Independence as a radical, humanistic document devoid of the faith-based values on which eighteenth-century America was founded. At times, Jefferson and his writing would be likened to the radical humanism of the French Revolution, with its disdain for all things Christian. In reality, not only did the Declaration of Independence reflect the worldview of eighteenth-century America—and the prevailing philosophy of the Continental Congress—it also reflected Thomas Jefferson's general respect and acceptance of that worldview.[15]

Jefferson was no "Last Puritan" like Samuel Adams. Later in life, he would take a pair of scissors to the New Testament and snip out accounts of miraculous acts in order to create what he would call an authentic "extract" of the Gospels. As a child, he was raised as an Anglican and was tutored by two ministers. While he was a student at the College of William & Mary, however, an affair of the heart appears to have affected his faith. Enamored with a fetching young woman named Rebecca Burwell, he clumsily bumbled two marriage proposals—and was crushed when his intended married one of his best friends. Soon afterward he turned away from the faith of his youth and plunged into the works of secular English philosophers.[16]

Although he developed a conflicted personal theology, dabbling at times in Unitarianism and deism, his personal philosophy remained rooted in the Judeo-Christian worldview. He could be disparaging of clergymen—John Adams once reprimanded him on the floor of Congress for an irreverent comment—but he was quick to condemn critics of Christianity, whom he dismissed as "heathen moralists." Like his congressional colleague Benjamin Franklin, Jefferson did not acknowledge a personal salvation experience. But he continued to read the Bible as an adult and appears to have considered himself a Christian throughout his life. "I am a Christian," he privately wrote in 1803, during his presidency, "in the only sense in which He wished anyone to be, sincerely attached to His doctrines, in preference to all others."[17]

Evidence of what Jefferson believed at the time he drafted the Declaration may be surmised from his response to another congressional assignment. Perhaps to encourage the gifted Virginian as he moped over his "mutilated" draft of the Declaration, Congress honored Jefferson with an important new assignment. Jefferson, Franklin and John Adams were put on a committee to design a national seal for the United States. Franklin wanted an image on the seal that showed God parting the Red Sea to rescue the Israelites, accompanied by the motto, "Resistance to tyrants is obedience to God." Jefferson's proposal: an image depicting "the children of Israel in the wilderness led by a cloud by day and a pillar [of fire] by night." Although his suggestion was not adopted—perhaps because it would have been artistically complicated—it presumably revealed Jefferson's attitude toward America's biblical foundation. What secular-minded humanist would have advocated a biblical image for America's official national seal?[18]

As crafted by Jefferson and Congress, the Declaration of Independence was intended to be acceptable to the American people—it *had* to be if Congress expected them to live by it and die for it. "Nothing could have been more futile," historian Carl Becker would note, "than to attempt to justify a revolution on principles that nobody had heard of before." Congress had nothing to gain by calling for sacrifice in the name of radical, French-style humanism. "I did not consider it as any part of my charge to invent new ideas altogether," Jefferson would later explain, "and to offer no sentiment which had ever been expressed before." Instead, he crafted the Declaration of Independence to be what he called "an expression of the American mind."[19]

He knew his work had to be approved by a congressional committee and the full Congress, and then had to satisfy the American people—and it did. As written by Thomas Jefferson, and revised by the Continental Congress, the Declaration of Independence reaffirmed the values of the American people and reassured them that their cause was right before God and man. It was notable not for radical new proposals, but for its expression of the cherished belief system on which Colonial America had been established—the Judeo-Christian worldview.[20]

The Declaration of Independence not only reflected the prevailing worldview of Colonial American culture, but also the heritage of English law. As a well-educated American of his day, Jefferson had been exposed to a variety of sources on government—classical Greek and Roman works, Anglo-Saxon political traditions, the philosophers of the Renaissance and the Enlightenment. His writing, he once said, was even inspired by William Shakespeare, whom he praised for his command of "the full powers of the English language." Yet it was English legal tradition that Jefferson and the Congress followed in framing the Declaration of Independence.[21]

The minister-tutors of Jefferson's childhood and his college mentor, the respected attorney George Wythe, had schooled Jefferson in English legal tradition. During Jefferson's time at the College of William & Mary, required reading for the study of law included the works of the Puritan legal scholar Sir Edward Coke. Indeed, a basic text for law in Colonial America was Coke's 1628 *Institutes of the Laws of England*, which placed God-given inalienable rights above the authority of the monarchy. Jefferson believed, as did others of his day, that the foundation of English law was on the Higher Law of Scripture—which had inspired the Magna Carta of 1215 and English common law.[22]

Jefferson and his peers in Congress were also influenced by other English thinkers—especially John Locke's *Second Treatise of Government* and *The Reasonableness of Christianity*. The view of Natural Law commonly held by Jefferson's generation was based on Locke's view that the "Laws of Nature and of Nature's God" were God's general revelation to man, inscribed in the human heart. "That God has given a rule whereby men should govern themselves," Locke wrote, "I think there is nobody so brutish as to deny. He has a right to do it, we are his creature; he has goodness and wisdom to direct our actions to that which is best. . . ." Natural Law, Locke believed, was ultimately confirmed by God's revealed truth—the Higher Law of Scripture. "The holy Scripture is to me, and always will be, the constant guide of my assent," he wrote. "I shall immediately condemn and quit any opinion of mine, as soon as I am shown that it is contrary to any revelation in the holy scripture."[23]

Also influential among the lawmakers of Jefferson's day was the Scot philosopher Henry Home, also known as Lord Kames. Home's work was required reading for any law student and taught that a God-given sense of morality encouraged "an equal pursuit of the happiness of all." Most influential, perhaps, was an Oxford professor acclaimed as the eighteenth century's leading expert on English law—Sir William Blackstone. In his *Commentaries on the Laws of England*, Blackstone defined an entire set of criminal acts as actions that "offend God, by openly transgressing the precepts of religion, either natural or revealed." Life and liberty, taught Blackstone, were God-given "natural rights":

> *Those rights, then, which God and nature have established, and are therefore called natural rights, such as are life and liberty, need not the aid of human laws to be more effectually invested in every man than they are. . . . Natural liberty [is] a*

> *right inherent in us by birth, and one of the gifts of God to man at his creation.*[24]

The Declaration of Independence did indeed manifest "an expression of the American mind," as Jefferson intended—and it was laced with the language of faith, beginning with its preamble:

> *When in the Course of human events, it becomes necessary for one people to dissolve the political bands which have connected them with another, and to assume among the powers of the earth, the separate and equal station to which the Laws of Nature and of Nature's God entitle them, a decent respect to the opinions of mankind requires that they should declare the causes which impel them to the separation.*

The fact that the Declaration of Independence contained nothing new was one of its great strengths. It assured Americans that they were not placing themselves in harm's way for some novel political fad, but for the cherished truths they held most dear—the faith of their fathers.

> *We hold these truths to be self-evident, that all men are created equal, that they are endowed by their Creator with certain unalienable Rights, that among these are Life, Liberty and the pursuit of Happiness.*[25]

The "self-evident" truths proclaimed in the Declaration were the foundation of eighteenth-century American life. The American people universally believed that God was their Creator, and that he held everyone equally precious in his sight. They believed that life, liberty, and the "pursuit of happiness" were indeed God-given, "unalienable" rights that were "endowed" on humanity by God's grace. For generations, they had heard these truths preached in their churches, and Jefferson has originally described them as "sacred and undeniable" truths. Congress changed the phrase to "self-evident," making the point that these fundamental truths—the "unalienable" right to "life, liberty and the pursuit of happiness"—were not only God-given, but also universally known.[26]

Many believed that those self-evident, inalienable rights "endowed by their Creator" belonged to all people—including slaves in bondage. Thomas Jefferson, a slaveowner who disliked slavery, recognized the hypocrisy of defending the inalienable right of liberty in a land where slavery was legal. He and others had earlier tried to end the slave trade in Virginia, but their proposal had been vetoed by the king. In his original draft of the Declaration, Jefferson had denounced slavery, and he saw the Declaration of Independence as an opportunity to end the institution in America. Others agreed, including Benjamin Franklin—a former slave trader—and John Adams, who hated the institution. Most delegates, however, believed that Congress did not have the authority to deal with such a mammoth issue and that a prolonged debate on slavery would likely derail the drive for independence. Therefore, the issue was put aside to be resolved after independence was established—a decision many would later regret.[27]

Government existed, the Declaration stated, to protect the inalienable rights of its citizens, and it was intended to do so with the agreement of the people it served.

> *That to secure these rights, Governments are instituted among Men, deriving their just powers from the consent of the governed.*

It was an age-old principle, expressed a century and a half earlier on American shores in the Pilgrims' Mayflower Compact, which declared the colonists' intent to establish "just and equal laws . . . for the general good of the colony." Soon afterward, Puritan leader John Winthrop had proclaimed that "no commonwealth can be founded but by free consent." Far earlier, Reformation leaders such Martin Bucer—John Calvin's mentor—had declared that the Bible-based duty of government was to "preserve the people of God from evil and defend their safety and goods." The Declaration of Independence reflected those faith-based precedents and the biblical emphasis on the value of the individual.[28]

That whenever any Form of Government becomes destructive of these ends, it is the Right of the People to alter or to abolish it, and to institute new Government, laying its foundation on such principles and organizing its powers in such form, as to them shall seem most likely to effect their Safety and Happiness. Prudence, indeed, will dictate that Governments long established should not be changed for light and transient causes; and accordingly all experience hath shewn, that mankind are more disposed to suffer, while evils are sufferable, than to right themselves by abolishing the forms to which they are accustomed.

For generations, Americans had been instructed from the pulpit that all people had a biblical obligation to resist tyranny and restore godly rule. As the Reverend Jonathan Mayhew had proclaimed, "Having learnt from the Holy Scriptures that wise, brave and virtuous men were always friends to liberty . . . and 'where the Spirit of the Lord is there is Liberty'—this made me conclude that freedom was a great blessing." Therefore, if Great Britain was engaged in "Despotism," as the Declaration asserted, Americans believed resistance was biblically justified.[29]

But when a long train of abuses and usurpations, pursuing invariably the same Object evinces a design to reduce them under absolute Despotism, it is their right, it is their duty, to throw off such Government, and to provide new Guards for their future security.—Such has been the patient sufferance of these Colonies; and such is now the necessity which constrains them to alter their former Systems of Government. The history of the present King of Great Britain is a history of repeated injuries and usurpations, all having in direct object the establishment of an absolute Tyranny over these States. To prove this, let Facts be submitted to a candid world.

The Declaration then cited a lengthy list of abuses against George III. The king, it charged, had "refused his Assent to Laws, the most wholesome and necessary for the public good . . . dissolved Representative Houses repeatedly, for opposing with manly firmness his invasions on the rights of the people . . . obstructed the Administration of Justice . . . sent hither swarms of Officers to harass our people. . . ." He was also charged with "Quartering large bodies of armed troops among us . . . imposing Taxes on us without our Consent . . . taking away our Charters, abolishing our most valuable Laws, and altering fundamentally the Forms of our Governments . . . suspending our own Legislatures, and . . . waging War against us."[30]

To justify resistance to royal authority on biblical grounds, the delegates had to present the American people with evidence that the king had abused his God-given authority. "We are subject to men who rule over us," Reformation leader John Calvin had written, "but subject only in the Lord. If they command anything against Him, let us not pay the least need to it." Americans knew that Scripture allowed resistance to ungodly rule, but they needed to see the evidence of it—and Congress gave it to them. "We have Petitioned for Redress in the most humble terms," the Declaration explained. "Our repeated Petitions have been answered only by repeated injury." Rulers who usurped the Higher Law of God, Calvin had written, were "no longer worthy to be counted as princes." Accordingly, the Declaration concluded its charges against George III by describing him as "A Prince whose character is thus marked by every act which may define a Tyrant," and declaring him "unfit to be the ruler of a free people."[31]

The Declaration made no charge against Parliament and stated but two veiled references to it, noting that the king had "combined with others" to violate American liberties and that attempts had been made by Britain's "legislature" to "extend an unwarrantable jurisdiction over us." Why was Parliament not charged along with the king? It was because Congress believed the American colonies had been established with a biblical-style covenant or charter between king and colony, and Parliament had had no part in it. "The essence of this theory," historian Carl Becker would observe, "is that the colonies became parts of the empire by their own voluntary act, and remained parts of it solely by virtue of a compact subsisting between them and the king. Their rights were those of all men, of every free people; their obligations such as a free people might incur by professing allegiance to the personal head of the empire." Thus the Declaration addressed the British king alone.[32]

Near its conclusion, the Declaration did address the English people, reminding them that they and the American people shared a "common kindred," and noting that Americans—while willing to fight—generally wished to be "Friends" with the British people. Then, in its concluding sentences, the Declaration restated the importance Congress placed on being right before God in its actions: it made a final public appeal to "the Supreme Judge of the world" and beseeched him to recognize "the rectitude of our intentions." Only then—after providing the precedents of Higher Law, after citing biblically based justification, and after offering ample evidence of royal tyranny that demanded resistance—only then came the official declaration of American independence:

> *We, therefore, the Representatives of the united States of America, in General Congress, Assembled, appealing to the Supreme Judge of the world for the rectitude of our intentions, do, in the Name, and by Authority of the good People of these Colonies, solemnly publish and declare, That these United Colonies are, and of Right ought to be Free and Independent States; that they are Absolved from all Allegiance to the British Crown, and that all political connection between them and the State of Great Britain, is and ought to be totally dissolved; and that as Free and Independent States, they have full Power to levy War, conclude Peace, contract Alliances, establish Commerce, and to do all other Acts and Things which Independent States may of right do.*[33]

Finally, in language reminiscent of a benediction, the Declaration of Independence ended. The document's concluding words composed a vow by brave men in grave danger. Every delegate to the Continental Congress who voted for independence or signed the Declaration could have been deemed guilty of treason and punished by death.

> *And for the support of this Declaration, with a firm reliance on the protection of divine Providence, we mutually pledge to each other our Lives, our Fortunes and our sacred Honor.*

For the cause of liberty—that uniquely American faith-based freedom—America's founding fathers were willing to sacrifice their lives, their fortunes, and their sacred honor, and would do so with a "firm reliance" on "divine Providence." More than a few of them would lose their fortunes. Some would lose their lives—but the "sacred honor" they defended would remain intact. The founding document they risked all to create—the Declaration of Independence—would long endure as an American commitment to the self-evident truth "that all men are created equal, that they are endowed by their Creator with certain unalienable Rights, that among these are Life, Liberty and the pursuit of Happiness."[34]

On Thursday, July 4, 1776, the Continental Congress officially approved the Declaration of Independence. It was then printed, with copies sent to "each of the United States" for public reading. On July 8, it was read aloud to a crowd of several hundred outside what would become known as Independence Hall. When the reading ended, exuberant cheers echoed over the streets of Philadelphia. In New York, Commander-in-Chief General George Washington ordered it read to his assembled troops. In Williamsburg, Virginia, it was publicly read at three locations. In Boston, worshippers risked exposure to a smallpox epidemic to hear it read at a church service.[35]

In early August 1776, the delegates to the Continental Congress gathered to begin recording signatures on the Declaration, a process that would casually continue for months. It was an unceremonious event, hurried along because the black flies of summer were biting the delegates' stockinged legs. According to tradition, John Hancock signed his name in giant letters so, he said, King George could read it without his spectacles. Benjamin Franklin reportedly joked, "We must all hang together, or most assuredly we shall hang separately." American independence had been declared, but it still had to be secured on hard-fought fields of fire. Among the first to pen his signature on the Declaration of Independence was Samuel Adams—"the Last Puritan." Afterward, as he was leaving, a crowd outside begged him for an impromptu speech. As usual, Sam Adams obliged them.[36]

As he stood there before them, attired perhaps in his donated suit, his hands trembling from his palsy, what images raced through his mind? Did he recall the long debates, the backroom lobbying, the protest rallies and bonfires? Did he remember the smudged faces of "Indians" at the Boston Tea Party, the smoke rising from Lexington green, the caked mud on Caesar Rodney's boots as he hurried in to vote for independence? Did he think of the young Americans now marching into combat beneath flags adorned with the battle cry "Resistance to Tyrants is Obedience to God"? Or did he envision a fast day worship service, where members of Congress—like their countrymen everywhere—sat with bowed heads, silently beseeching the Lord God of the ages for his protection and blessings?[37]

Whatever memories flashed before him that day would remain unknown, but Samuel Adams did share his thoughts with the citizens outside Independence Hall. "We have this day," he told them, "restored the Sovereign to whom alone men ought to be obedient. He reigns in Heaven, and with a propitious eye beholds his subjects assuming that freedom . . . which he bestowed on them. From the rising to the setting sun, may His kingdom come."[38]

ACKNOWLEDGMENTS

"The finest traditions of a free people, like their liberties, can be maintained only by eternal vigilance and incessant labors." So observed twentieth-century American historian Dumas Malone, who was editor of *The Dictionary of American Biography*. "National heroes can be cast from their pedestals by unholy hands and the ideas that patriots lived by can be dishonored," he concluded. "Unlike stones, literary monuments have life within them and they often prove more enduring." I'm thankful to have been able to labor a bit on this "literary monument" to the Americans of the Colonial Era and the foundational faith with which they forged our nation. I hope Dumas Malone's words can be aptly applied to this work—that it has life within it and proves enduring.

No author writes a book alone, and that's especially true of historians. I'm grateful to many people who helped produce this book. My editor, Cindy Lambert, made a major contribution to this work, which benefited immensely from her insight, advice, and direction. Many thanks also to Karen Longino, managing editor at Howard Books, an imprint of Simon & Schuster, and the talented team of professionals in Nashville and New York who edited the manuscript, designed the book, and directed its marketing. I'm genuinely grateful for the contributions made to this work by Tom Pitoniak, Evelyn Bence, Jennifer Willingham, Greg Petree, and Susan Wilson.

From beginning to end, Lee Hough of Alive Communications was instrumental in this work. As a literary agent and friend, he provided invaluable wise counsel and much-needed good humor. The staff of the Independence National Historic Park Library and Archives in Philadelphia provided expert assistance and gracious hospitality—and I greatly appreciate it. Thanks too are due to the staff of Kimbel Library at Coastal Carolina University, the Library of Congress, the National Archives, the American Philosophical Society, the Historical Society of Pennsylvania, and the Library Company of Philadelphia.

As always, I'm deeply grateful for the encouragement I've received in this sometimes-daunting project from my friends and family. I value the good words and faithful prayers of my friends at Carolina Forest Community Church, Conway Christian School, and Grace Presbyterian Church. A lifetime of thanks is due my historian brother Ted Gragg, who kindled my love of history as a child. Thanks too to his wife, Connie, for tolerating decades of history hunting. My older cousins, Bob Melton and Charles Lunsford, made a mighty contribution to my fascination with American history by transforming anything historical into a great adventure. Their wives, Martha and Sandra, have been paragons of patience, and every author should have a booster like "Aunty" Delores. I'm also grateful for the consistent encouragement I receive from my "Outlaw In-laws"—Joe and Margaret Outlaw, Doug and Jackie Outlaw Rutt, John and Tina Outlaw, Jimmy and Gail Outlaw, and Newt and Deborah Outlaw.

My wonderful children deserve awards for good attitudes (and maybe for long suffering) as they were carted from one historic site to another throughout their childhood. Somehow they were always ready for one more trip (most of the time). My love and thanks for being my family to sons Skip and Matt, and to daughters and sons-in-law Penny and Jason, Joni and Tim, Elizabeth and Jon, Rachel and Jay, and Faith and Troy. My gift to them: a legacy of travel tales and endless home movies. Their gifts to me: Kylah and Sophia. A special debt of gratitude is due Elizabeth Lunsford Gragg—my mother—who long ago expertly packed a Ford Fairlane station wagon and directed a family tour of Revolutionary War sites that took me to Independence Hall for the first time. She and my father, L. W. ("Skip") Gragg, launched my lifelong love of history.

Most of all, I treasure my wife, Cindy, who never dreamed thirtysomething years ago that she would be "blessed" to visit *so* many historic places over the years. Although keenly aware of *that* passage in Ecclesiastes ("of making many books there is no end"), she has been a faithful prayer warrior and an irreplaceable supporter—especially with this work. She's also the love of my life.

Finally, I'm eternally grateful for the abiding truth of Romans 5:8, and deeply mindful of Sam Adams's observation: "Whether America shall long preserve her Freedom or not will depend on her Virtue."

Rod Gragg
Conway, South Carolina

NOTES

ABBREVIATIONS IN THE NOTES

DAB	*Dictionary of American Biography*. Allen Johnson and Dumas Malone, editors. New York: Charles Scribner's Sons, 1928–36.
DNB	*Dictionary of National Biography*. Leslie Stephens and Sidney Lee, editors. London: Oxford University Press, 1921.
JCC	*Journals of the Continental Congress, 1774–1789*. Worthington C. Ford, editor. Washington, D.C.: U.S. Government Printing Office, 1906.
LDC	*Letters of Delegates to Congress, 1774–1789*. Paul H. Smith, editor. Washington, D.C.: Library of Congress, 1976–2000.
WJA	Adams, John. *The Works of John Adams: Second President of the United States*. Charles Francis Adams, editor. Boston: Little, Brown, 1850–56.
WSA	Adams, Samuel. *The Writings of Samuel Adams*. Harry Alonzo Cushing, editor. New York: G. P. Putnam's Sons, 1908.
WTJ	Jefferson, Thomas. *The Writings of Thomas Jefferson*. Paul Leicester Ford, editor. New York: G. P. Putnam's Sons, 1904.

INTRODUCTION

1. DAB 1: 95–100.
2. William V. Wells, *The Life and Public Service of Samuel Adams*, Boston: Little and Brown, 1865: 3: 251–255.
3. WSA 4: 405–407.
4. Patricia U. Bonomi, *Under the Cope of Heaven: Religion, Society, and Politics in Colonial America*, New York: Oxford University Press, 1986: 209.
5. WSA 4: 405–407.
6. DAB 1: 99–100; WSA 4: 406–407.
7. Bonomi, *Under the Cope of Heaven:* 5, 211; James H. Hutson, *Forgotten Features of the Founding: The Recovery of Religious Themes in the Early American Republic*, Lanham: Lexington Books, 2003: 3–10; Benjamin Hart, *Faith & Freedom: The Christian Roots of American Liberty*, San Bernardino: Lewis & Stanley, 1988: 16–17.
8. WJA 1: 45; Hutson, *Forgotten Features of the Founding:* 3–10; Gary Amos and Richard Gardiner, *Never Before in History: America's Inspired Birth*, Dallas: Haughton, 1998: *v–vi*, 143, 146–147; Michael Healey, "Americans Don't Know Civics," *USA Today*, 21 November 2008; Naomi Wolf, "Don't Know Much About History," *Washington Post*, 25 November 2007.
9. Abraham I. Katsh, *The Biblical Heritage of American Democracy*, New York: KTAV, 1977: 116; Hart, *Faith & Freedom*: 28; Chris Matthews, "A Proud Bronx Attraction Continues to Struggle," *Mount Hope Monitor*, 5 April 2008; Amos and Gardiner, *Never Before in History: v–vi*.
10. "Topics in U.S. History," *Up Close and Personal*, 10 December 2008.
11. George Bancroft, *A History of the United States of America*, New York: D. Appleton, 1834: 2: 269, 401–405; Edward Channing, *History of the United States*, New York: Macmillan, 1908: 2: 440; Harry Norman Gardiner, "Jonathan Edwards," *Encyclopaedia Britannica*, edited by Hugh Chisolm, New York: Britannica, 1910: 9: 3–4; George Frederick Kunz, *The Hall of Fame*, New York: New York University Press, 1908: 7.
12. "Jonathan Edwards," Microsoft Encarta Online Encyclopedia, 2009.
13. Francis Schaeffer, *How Should We Then Live?: The Rise and Decline of Western Thought and Culture*, Wheaton: Crossway Books, 1985: 205–221; WSA 4: 124.

CHAPTER 1: "PLEAD OUR CAUSE, O LORD"

1. LDC 1: 26–33; JCC 1: 13–27; DAB 4: 632–633; Edmund Cody Burnett, *The Continental Congress*, New York: W. W. Norton, 1941, 38-40.
2. JCC 1: 25–26; John Adams, *The Works of John Adams: Second President of the United States*, edited by Charles Francis Adams, Boston: Little, Brown, 1856, 2: 368–373; James Munves, *Thomas Jefferson and the Declaration of Independence*, New York: Charles Scribner's Sons, 1978: 67–73; JCC 5: 491, 504–506.
3. George Neilson, "Drawing, Hanging and Quartering," *Notes & Queries*, 15

August 1891: 129–131; Christopher Hibbert, *Tower of London*, New York: Newsweek Books, 1971: 167; LDC 4: 329, 1: 50; JCC 1: 25–26; WJA 2: 368–373.

4. JCC 1: 25–27; LDC 1: 35, 75; DAB 4: 632–633; Hamilton Andrews Hill, *History of the Old South Church, 1669–1884*, Boston: Houghton, Mifflin, 1890: 131.
5. David Ramsay, *Ramsay's History of South Carolina*, Newberry, S.C.: W. J. Duffie, 1858: 269–270; Robert G. Ferris, *Signers of the Constitution: Historic Places Commemorating the Signing of the Constitution*, Washington, D.C.: U.S. Department of the Interior, 1976: 208–210.
6. DAB 10: 5–10; John Jay Institute for Faith, Society and Law, "John Jay," www.johnjayinstitute.org; DAB 11: 325–327, 16: 258–260; *The Book of Abigail and John: Selected Letters of the Adams Family 1762–1784*, edited by L. H. Butterfield, March Friedlaender and Mary Jo Kline, Cambridge: Harvard University Press, 1975: 76.
7. JCC 1: 13–27; LDC 1: 35, 75; WJA 2: 368–373; John Puls, *Samuel Adams: Father of the American Revolution*, New York: Palgrave McMillan, 2006: 14, 25; DAB 1: 95–101; Alan Heimert, *Religion and the American Mind: From the Great Awakening to the Revolution*, Cambridge: Harvard University Press, 1966: 359, 450; Hill, *History of the Old South Church* 2: 249–250.
8. JCC 1: 13–27; LDC 1: 35, 75; WJA 2: 368–373.
9. Edward D. Neil, "Rev. Jacob Duché: First Chaplain of Congress," *Pennsylvania Magazine of History and Biography* 2: 70–78; Francis V. Cabeen, "The Society of the Sons of Tammany of Philadelphia," *Pennsylvania Magazine of History and Biography* 25: 447; DAB 5: 476–477; LDC 1: 36.
10. LDC 1: 34–36; WJA 2: 368–373; Psalm 35.
11. LDC 1: 31, 34–36; WJA 2: 368–373; Psalm 35.
12. JCC 25: 551–552; WJA 2: 368–373; LDC 1: 31, 35–36, 45, 55; Bonomi, *Under the Cope of Heaven*: 3.
13. Katsh, *Biblical Heritage of American Democracy*: 133; Heimert, *Religion and the American Mind*: 295; Moses Coit Tyler, *The Literary History of the American Revolution 1763–1783*, New York: G. P. Putnam's Sons, 1897: 2: 284–286; JCC 2: 81.

CHAPTER 2: "NEW JERUSALEM"

1. John Smith, *Travels and Works of Captain John Smith, President of Virginia and Admiral of New England, 1580–1631*, edited by Edward Arber, Edinburgh: John Grant, 1910: 2: 385, 389, 958; DAB 9: 391–392; Samuel Eliot Morison, *The Oxford History of the American People*, New York: Oxford University Press, 1965: 86–87.
2. Smith, *Travels and Works of Captain John Smith* 2: 386, 958; DAB 9: 391–392; Frank E. Grizzard and D. Boyd Smith, *Jamestown Colony: A Political, Social and Cultural History*, Santa Barbara: ABC-Clio, 2007: xxiv.

3. Smith, *Travels and Works of Captain John Smith* 2: 386, 957; DAB 9: 391–392.
4. Grizzard and Smith, *Jamestown Colony:* 92–93; Smith, *Travels and Works of Captain John Smith* 2: 236; DAB 9: 391–392.
5. Clarence L. Ver Steeg, *The Formative Years 1607–1763*, New York: Hill and Wang, 1965: 21–24; Grizzard and Smith, *Jamestown Colony:* 56–57.
6. First Charter of Virginia, Avalon Project, Yale University, www.yale.edu/lawweb/avalon/states/va01.htm; Vernon L. Parrington, *The Colonial Mind 1620–1800*, New York: Harcourt, Brace and World, 1927: 16; Morison, *Oxford History of the American People:* 82–87; Grizard and Smith, *Jamestown Colony:* xx.
7. Ver Steeg, *Formative Years:* 21–24; Morison, *Oxford History of the American People* 86–87; *Encyclopedia of American History*, edited by Jeffrey B. Morris and Richard B. Morris, New York: HarperCollins, 1996: 30–31; George Percy, " 'A Trewe Relacyon'—Virginia from 1609–1612," *Tyler's Historical and Genealogical Magazine*, edited by Leon G. Tyler, 1922: 3: 267; *Travels and Works of Captain John Smith*: 498–499.
8. DAB 7: 190; Smith, *Travels and Works of Captain John Smith:* 474, 537, 502; 2 Thessalonians 3: 10; *Encyclopedia of American History:* 31; Morison, *Oxford History of the American People:* 84, 89.
9. Winton U. Solberg, *Redeem the Time: The Puritan Sabbath in Early America*, Cambridge: Harvard University Press, 1977: 86–89; DAB 5: 34–35; Alexander Brown, *The Genesis of the United States*, Boston: Houghton Mifflin, 1890: 1: 56–57; DAB 7: 190.
10. Bonomi, *Under the Cope of Heaven:* 16; *For the Colony in Virginea Britannia, Lawes Divine, Morall and Martiall*, London: Walter Burre, 1612: 9–10; DAB 5: 34–35; 7: 190.
11. DAB 5: 34–35; 7: 190; *Lawes Divine, Morall and Martiall:* 9–10; Morison, *Oxford History of the American People:* 84, 89.
12. Morison, *Oxford History of the American People:* 90–93; John Smith, *The Generall Historie of Virginia, New England and the Summer Isles*, New York: Macmillan, 1907: 1: 222; DAB 17: 295–296; *Encyclopedia of American History:* 31.
13. Brown, *Genesis of the United States* 2: 991–993, 1065; Grizzard and Smith, *Jamestown Colony:* 191–193; "Sir Edwin Sandys," *Encyclopedia Britannica* 11: 24: 144; DAB 16: 344–345; Bonomi, *Under the Cope of Heaven:* 16.
14. Grizzard and Smith, *Jamestown Colony:* xlv, 79–80; Brown, *Genesis of the United States* 2: 991–993; "Sir Edwin Sandys," 24: 144; DAB 16: 344–345; Bonomi, *Under the Cope of Heaven:* 16.
15. Walter Bagehot, *The English Constitution*, London: Paul, Trench and Trubner, 1902: vii-xi; Walter F. Hook, *Lives of the Archbishops of Canterbury*, London: Bentley and Son, 1884: 2: 758–760; Jesse Macy, *The English Constitution: A Commentary on Its Nature and Growth*, London: Macmillan and Company, 1897: 361–362; William Sharp McKechnie, *The Magna Carta: A Commentary on the Great Charter of King John*, New York: Burt Franklin, 1914: 186, 191; W. F. Finlason, *History of the English Law: From the Time of*

the Romans to the End of the Reign of Elizabeth, Philadelphia: M. Murphy, 1880: 1: 303.

16. Grizzard and Smith, *Jamestown Colony:* 78–79; Morison, *Oxford History of the American People:* 92; Gary Amos and Richard Gardiner, *Never Before in History*, Dallas: Haughton, 1998: 128–129; Bonomi, *Under the Cope of Heaven:* 16; Solberg, *Redeem the Time:* 89; Ver Steeg, *Formative Years:* 24; Brown, *Genesis of the United States* 2: 835; Records of the Virginia Company, 1606–26, Thomas Jefferson Papers, Manuscript Division, Library of Congress: 8: 3: 152; William Smith, *History of the First Discovery and Settlement of Virginia*, New York: Joseph Sabin, 1865: 33.
17. Morison, *Oxford History of the American People:* 92; Bonomi, *Under the Cope of Heaven:* 16; Amos and Gardiner, *Never Before in History:* 128–129; Solbert, *Redeem the Time:* 89; Ver Steeg, *Formative Years:* 24; Brown, *Genesis of the United States* 2: 835; Records of the Virginia Company, Thomas Jefferson Papers, 8: 3: 153; Smith, *History of the First Discovery and Settlement of Virginia:* 33; Grizzard and Smith, *Jamestown Colony:* 77.

CHAPTER 3: "ONE SMALL CANDLE"

1. Roland G. Usher, *The Pilgrims and Their History*, New York: Macmillan, 1918: 75; William Bradford, *Bradford's History "Of Plimoth Plantation" From the Original Manuscript*, Boston: Wright & Potter, 1899: 92, 94; Morison, *Oxford History of the American People* 1: 94–95; *Encyclopedia of American History:* 36.
2. Usher, *Pilgrims and Their History:* 75; Bradford, *Of Plimoth Plantation:* 92, 94; Morison, *Oxford History of the American People:* 1: 94–95.
3. Usher, *Pilgrims and Their History:* 72–76; Bradford, *Of Plimoth Plantation:* 92; Morison, *Oxford History of the American People:* 1: 93–95.
4. Bradford, *Of Plimoth Plantation:* 92; Usher, *Pilgrims and Their History:* 72–76; Morison, *Oxford History of the American People* 1: 93–95.
5. Usher, *Pilgrims and Their History:* 17–53; Morison, *Oxford History of the American People* 1: 94–95; *The Oxford Encyclopedia of the Reformation*, edited by Hans J. Hillerbrand, New York: Oxford University Press, 1996: 3: 31, 469–470; *The Oxford Dictionary of the Christian Church*, edited by F. L. Cross and E. A. Livingstone, Oxford: Oxford University Press, 1953: 135, 859–860; Nathaniel Morton, *New England's Memorial*, Boston: Congregational Board of Publication, 1855: 266; Bradford, *Of Plimoth Plantation:* 40.
6. Winifred Cockshott, *The Pilgrim Fathers: Their Church and Colony*, New York; G. P. Putnam's Sons, 1909: 144–145; Ozara S. Davis, *John Robinson: The Pilgrim Pastor*, New York: Pilgrim Press, 1903: 246–248; Morton, *New England's Memorial:* 16–18; James Thatcher, *History of the Town of Plymouth*, Boston: Marsh, Capen & Lyon, 1835: 261–262.
7. Davis, *John Robinson:* 246–248; Thatcher, *History of Plymouth:* 261–262; Cockshott, *Pilgrim Fathers:* 144.

8. Bradford, *Of Plimoth Plantation:* 90–96; Usher, *Pilgrims and their History:* 69, 73; Cockshott, *Pilgrim Fathers:* 177–181.
9. Bradford, *Of Plimoth Plantation:* 109; Cockshott, *Pilgrim Fathers:* 177–181; Thatcher, *History of Plymouth:* 261–262.
10. Cockshott, *Pilgrim Fathers:* 178; Bradford, *Of Plimoth Plantation:* 78–82, 109.
11. Morison, *Oxford History of the American People* 1: 94–95; Bradford, *Of Plimoth Plantation:* 78–82; "Mayflower Compact, 1620," Avalon Project, Yale University, www.yale.edu/laweb/avalon/amerdoc/mayflower.htm; William MacDonald, *Select Charters and Other Documents Illustrative of American History 1607–1775*, New York: Macmillan, 1899: 33–34.
12. Thomas Prince, *A Chronological History of New England*, Boston: Kneeland & Green, 1826: 169, 177–178; Katsh, *Biblical Heritage of American Democracy:* 26, 38, 94; Morison, *Oxford History of the American People* 1: 94; Benjamin Hart, Hart, *Faith & Freedom:* 235.
13. Bradford, *Of Plimoth Plantation:* 111, 116, 120, 162; Morison, *Oxford History of the American People* 1: 94–95; Usher, *Pilgrims and Their History:* 75, 83–89.
14. Bradford, *Of Plimouth Plantation:* 111, 116, 120, 162; Morison, *Oxford History of the American People* 1: 94–95; Usher, *Pilgrims and Their History:* 75, 83–89.
15. Bradford, *Of Plimouth Plantation:* 126–127; *Puritans and Puritanism in Europe and America: A Comprehensive Encyclopedia*, edited by Francis J. Bremer and Tom Webster, Santa Barbara: Clio, 2006: 642.
16. Exodus 23:16; Numbers 18:8–32; Leviticus 23:20–21; Deuteronomy 16:11–12; 2 Chronicles 8:12–12; Philippians 4:6; John D. Davis, *A Dictionary of the Bible*, Philadelphia: Westminster, 1917: 800–801, 856; John Brand, *Observations on Popular Antiquities*, London: Chatto & Windus, 1900: 189–190; *New Webster Dictionary of Liturgy*, edited by Paul Bradshaw, Louisville: John Knox Press, 2002: 233–234.
17. *Puritans and Puritanism:* 562; Austin Allibone, *A Critical Dictionary of English Literature and American Authors*, Philadelphia: Lippincott, 1899: 2: 2784.
18. *Cyclopedia of Biblical, Theological and Ecclesiastical Literature*, Edited by John McLintock and James Strong, New York; Harper and Brothers, 1891: 10: 301; Christine Kooi, *Liberty and Religion: Church and State in Reformation Leiden*, Boston: Brill, 2000: 34–37; Carried B. Adams, "Thanksgiving," *The Inland Educator: A Journal for the Progressive Teacher* (August 1895): 1: 248–249; *Puritans and Puritanism:* 642; George B. Cheever, *The Pilgrim Fathers*, London: Williams Collins, 1849: 231–232; Psalms 107:1–8.
19. *Mourt's Relation Or Journal of the Plantation at Plymouth*, edited by Henry Martyn Dexter, Boston: John Kimball Wiggin, 1865: 60, 133; Bradford, *Of Plimoth Plantation:* 535, 127; John Gorham Palfrey, *History of New England*, Boston: Little, Brown, 1858: 1: 213–214.
20. *Mourt's Relation:* 133; Bradford, *Of Plimoth Plantation:* 127; Usher, *Pilgrims and Their History:* 90, 93–94; Deuteronomy 16: 13–14; Frederick A. Noble, *The Pilgrims*, Boston: Pilgrim, 1907: 309; *Puritans and Puritanism:* 642.
21. *Bradford's History of Plymouth Plantation:* 153; *Mourt's Relation:* 133; Thatcher,

History of Plymouth: 59; Adams, "Thanksgiving," 1: 248–249; *Puritans and Puritanism:* 642.

22. *Puritans and Puritanism:* 642; Edward Winslow, *Good Newes from New England: A True Relations of Things Very Remarkable at the Plantation of Plimoth in New England*, London: William Bladen and John Bellamie, 1624: 29; Adams, "Thanksgiving," 1: 248–249; *Cyclopedia of Biblical, Theological and Ecclesiastical Literature* 10: 301; Thatcher, *History of Plymouth:* 153; *Mourt's Relation:* 133.
23. Bradford, *Of Plimoth Plantation:* 161–163.
24. Thatcher, *History of Plymouth:* 153; Bradford, *Of Plimoth Plantation: 161–163;* 2 Thessalonians 3:10.
25. Perry Miller and Thomas H. Johnson, *The Puritans: A Sourcebook of Their Writings*, New York: Harper & Row, 1963: 181; *Calvinism and the Political Order*, edited by George L. Hunt, Philadelphia: Westminster, 1965: 185; Thatcher, *History of Plymouth:* 81.
26. Clarence L. Ver Steeg, *The Formative Years 1607–1763*, New York: Hill & Wang, 1961: 27–28; Morton, *New England's Memorial:* 5; Thatcher, *History of Plymouth:* 81; Usher, *Pilgrims and Their History:* 290–291; Psalms 80:8–9.
27. Morton, *New England's Memorial:* 110 (italics added); Ver Steeg, *Formative Years:* 28; Miller and Johnson, *The Puritans:* 188.
28. Bradford, *Of Plimoth Plantation:* 332.

CHAPTER 4: "FAREWELL, DEAR ENGLAND"

1. Edward Johnson, *Wonder Working Providence: Sion's Saviour in New England*, Andover: Warren F. Draper, 1867: xxi; Francis Higginson, *New England's Plantation: A Short and True History of the Commodities and Discommodities of that Country*, London: Michael Sparke, 1680: 5; William C. Fowler, "Local Law in Massachusetts, Historically Considered," *The New England Historical and Genealogical Register* 25: 281; Green, *History of the English People* 3: 170–171; Daniel Neal, *The History of the Puritans or Protestant Non-Conformists*, Boston: Charles Ewer, 1817: 2: 232 Morison, *Oxford History of the American People* 1: 105–107.
2. Green, *History of the English People* 3: 170–171; Morison, *Oxford History of the American People:* 105–106.
3. *Puritans and Puritanism:* 419; Martin Luther, *The Works of Martin Luther*, edited by Adolph Spaeth, L. D. Reed and Henry Jacobs, Philadelphia: J. Holman: 1915: 29–38; Thomas Lindsey, *A History of the Reformation*, New York: Charles Scribner's Sons, 1906: 207; Brinton, Christopher and Wolff, *History of Western Civilization* 1: 203–209.
4. Elias B. Sanford, *A History of the Reformation*, Hartford: S. S. Scranton, 1917: 80; Brinton, Christopher and Wolff, *History of Western Civilization*, 1: 203–209; Lindsey, *History of the Reformation:* 207; Bill R. Austin, *Austin's Topical History of Christianity*, Wheaton: Tyndale House, 1983: 229–231; Jeremy C. Jackson, *No Other Foundation: The Church Through Twenty Centuries*, West-

chester: Cornerstone, 1980: 127–129; R. J. Knecht, *The Rise and Fall of Renaissance France 1483–1610*, Oxford: Blackwell, 2001: 366; *Cyclopaedia of Biblical Literature* 1: 626.

5. George Fisher, *The Reformation*, New York: Scribner & Armstrong, 1873: 324; *Oxford Dictionary of the Christian Church*, edited by Frank Leslie Cross, New York: Oxford University Press, 1974: 752–753, 1051.
6. Arthur G. Dickens, *The English Reformation*, University Park: Penn State University Press, 1991: 339–340; Sanford, *History of the Reformation:* 217; *Puritans and Puritanism:* 324.
7. Neal, *History of the Puritans*: 179–180; Green, *History of the English People* 4: 191; Dicken, *English Reformation:* 352–353.
8. Neal, *History of the Puritans*: 179–180; Green, *History of the English People* 4: 191; Dicken, *English Reformation:* 352–353.
9. Green, *History of the English People* 3: 18; John Calvin, *Calvin's Institutes*, edited by Donald K. McKim, Louisville: Westminster John Knox Press, 2000: 173; "Editor's Easy Chair," *Harper's New Monthly Magazine* 27: 712 James Mackintosh, *History of England*, London: Longman and Taylor: 1835: 4: 289.
10. John Gorham Palfrey, *History of New England*, Boston: Little and Brown, 1899: 1: 111–114; *Puritans and Puritanism:* 130, 320.
11. *Eerdmans' History of Christianity*, edited by Tim Dowler, Grand Rapids: William B. Eerdmans, 1973: 380–382, 388–389; Green, *History of the English People* 5: 61–67; *Austin's History of Christianity:* 280–283; Miller and Johnson, *The Puritans: A Sourcebook of Their Writings:* 6–7: *The Encyclopedia of Religion and Ethics*, edited by John Hastings, New York: Charles Scribner's Sons, 1919: 10: 507; Romans 13:12–14.
12. "James I," *Oxford Dictionary of the Christian Church:* 859–860; Brinton, Christopher and Wolff 1: 591–592, 2: 332–339; Ira Maurice Price, *The Ancestry of Our English Bible: An Account of Manuscripts, Texts and Versions of the Bible*, New York: Harper & Brothers, 1956: 250–251; *Puritans and Puritanism:* 354.
13. E. Parmalee Prentice, "The New Opportunity of the Small College," *Harper's New Monthly Magazine* 123: 133; Perry Miller, *Errand into the Wilderness*, Cambridge: Harvard University Press, 1956: 8, 113; Alexis de Tocqueville, *Democracy in America*, New York: Appleton: 1904: 17.
14. Perry Miller, *The American Puritans: Their Prose and Poetry*, New York: Columbia University Press, 1982: 88–89; Thomas J. Conant, *The Popular History of the Translations of the Holy Scriptures into the English Tongue*, New York: I. K. Funk, 1873: 238–239; F. C. Montague, *The History of England from the Accession of James I to the Restoration 1603–1660*, London: Longmans, Green, 1907: 11.
15. Jacob Abbott, *Makers of History: Charles I*, New York: Harper and Brothers, 1876: 113, 145; William Henry Stowell, *History of the Puritans in England*, London: Thomas Nelson, 1878: 255–256.
16. Green, *History of the English People* 3: 158–163; John Braun, "Surplice," *The Catholic Encyclopedia*, edited by Charles G. Herbermann, New York: Univer-

sity Knowledge Foundation, 1913: 14: 343–344; Palfrey, *History of New England* 1: 111–114; Perry Miller, *The New England Mind: From Colony to Province*, Cambridge: Harvard University Press, 1983: 3.

17. Green, *History of the English People* 3: 158–163; Palfrey, *History of New England* 1: 62–64; John Philips Kenyon, *A Dictionary of British History*, New York: Stein & Day, 1983: 197; John Campbell, *Lives of the Lord Chancellors and Keepers of the Great Seal of England*, Jersey City: Frederick Linn, 1880: 3: 206.
18. Green, *History of the English People* 3: 141–144; Abbott, *Makers of History: Charles I:* 113, 145; Stowell, *History of the Puritans in England:* 255–256.
19. Samuel R. Gardiner, *History of the Great Civil War, 1642–1649*, London: Longmans, Green, 1901: 4: 40–43, 85, 124–128, 300–322; Green, *History of the English People* 3: 328–330; "Cromwell, Oliver" *Encyclopedia Britannica* 5: 291–294.
20. *The Humble Request of His Majesties Loyall Subjects, the Governor and the Company Late Gone for New England*, London: John Bellamie, 1630: 2–6; Green, *History of the English People* 3: 169–170.
21. Green, *History of the English People* 3: 163, 170–171; Willis Mason West, *The Story of American Democracy*, Boston: Allyn and Bacon, 1922: 67; Morison, *Oxford History of the American People:* 105–107.
22. Green, *History of the English People* 3: 170; George McGregor Waller, *Puritanism in Early America*, Lexington: D. C. Heath, 1953: 25.

CHAPTER 5: "A CITY UPON A HILL"

1. John Winthrop, *Life and Letters of John Winthrop*, edited by Robert C. Winthrop, Boston: Little & Brown, 1869: 2: 19, 301–302; DAB 20: 408–409; Francis J. Bremer, *John Winthrop: America's Forgotten Founding Father*, New York: Oxford University Press, 2005: 187–188, 201.
2. Winthrop, *Life and Letters of John Winthrop* 2: 19–20; Matthew 5:14; *Puritans and Puritanism:* 505; Miller, *New England Mind:* 23–24.
3. Johnson, *Wonder Working Providence:* 38; Winthrop, *Life and Letters of John Winthrop* 2: 51, 60; *Puritans and Puritanism:* 281; Bremer, *John Winthrop:* 193.
4. George Bancroft, *History of the United States of America*, New York: D. Appleton and Company, 1890: 1: 280; Mackintosh, *History of England* 4: 289; Morison, *Oxford History of the American People:* 94–95, 105–106; *Oxford Encyclopedia of the Reformation* 3: 31, 469–470; *Oxford Dictionary of the Christian Church* 135, 859–860; DAB 20: 408–410; Ver Steeg, *Formative Years:* 37–38; Amos and Gardiner, *Never Before in History:* 17; "Model of Christian Charity by Gov. Winthrop," 3: 7: 46–48; Deuteronomy 30:19; Gabriel Sivan, *The Bible and Civilization*, Jerusalem: Keter, 1973: 236; Hart, *Faith & Freedom:* 84; Morison, *Oxford History of the American People* 1: 105–107.
5. Morison, *Oxford History of the American People* 1: 105–107; 1 Corinthians 10:31; 1 Thessalonians 4:11; 2 Timothy 3:17; 1 Corinthians 4:12; 2 Corinthians 9:8; Lyland Ryken, *Worldly Saints: The Puritans as They Really Were*, Grand

Rapids: Zondervan, 1991: 3, 24–25; Ver Steeg, *Formative Years:* 37–38; DAB 20: 408–410; Cotton Mather, *A Christian at His Calling*, Boston: n.p. 1701: 36.

6. Bancroft, *History of the United States* 1: 280, 320; Ver Steeg, *Formative Years:* 37–38.
7. DAB 20: 408–410; Morison, *Oxford History of the American People* 1: 105–107; Ver Steeg, *Formative Years:* 37–38; *Encyclopedia of American History:* 38–39; Miller, *Errand into the Wilderness:* 10.
8. Edward Channing, *A History of the United States*, New York: Macmillan & Co., 1921: 4: 431–433; Miller, *The Puritans:* 2–6; Ver Steeg, *Formative Years:* 75; Calvin, *Institutes of the Christian Religion* 1: 647; Morison, *Oxford History of the American People:* 105–107, 112–113, 117; Richard Sibbes, *The Complete Works of John Richard Sibbes*, edited by John Allen, Edinburgh: James Nichols, 1893: 6: 507; Ryken, *Worldly Saints:* 3, 24–25: Richard Baxter, *The Saints' Everlasting Rest*, New York: Lane and Scott, 1848: 330.
9. Channing, *History of the United States:* 431–433; Ryken, *Worldly Saints:* 3–7; Alan Taylor, *Writing Early American History*, Philadelphia: University of Pennsylvania Press, 2005: 38.
10. Ryken, *Worldly Saints:* 3–7; Ephesians 5:25; Proverbs 22:6; Deuteronomy 6:4–9; Green, *History of the British People* 5: 69–70.
11. Ryken, *Worldly Saints:* 3–7; Channing, *History of the United States:* 431–433; Romans 10:17; Perry Miller, *The New England Mind: The Seventeenth Century*, New York: Macmillan, 1939: 463; Henry E. Sawyer, "Public Schools in Connecticut," *Education: An International Magazine* 4: 36; Hart, *Faith & Freedom:* 108–109.
12. Sawyer, "Public Schools in Connecticut" 4: 36; Ellwood Cubberly, *Readings in the History of Education*, New York: Houghton Mifflin, 1920: 292; Hart, *Faith & Freedom:* 108–109.
13. Amos and Gardiner, *Never Before in History:* 73–74; *The New England Primer: A History of Its Origin and Development*, edited by Paul Leicester Ford, New York: Dodd, Mead: 1897: 16–19, 25–28.
14. Palfrey, *History of New England* 302: DAB 20: 408–409; Winthrop, *Life and Letters of John Winthrop:* 230.
15. Miller, *Errand to the Wilderness:* 39; Covenant of the Town of Salem, *Collections of the Massachusetts Historical Society*, Boston: Samuel Hall, 1798: 28; Miller and Johnson, *The Puritans:* 188.
16. Acts 6:1–5; Deuteronomy 1:13; 1 Samuel 13:13–14; 1 Kings 21:17; Covenant of the Town of Salem, *Collections of the Massachusetts Historical Society:* 28; Morison, *Oxford History of the American People* 1: 107–109; Ver Steeg, *Formative Years:* 39–41; Hart, *Faith & Freedom:* 83; Channing, *History of the United States* 1: 347–350; Acts 5:29.
17. Daniel W. Howe, *The Puritan Republic of Massachusetts Bay*, Indianapolis: Bowen-Merrill, 1879: 46–56; Ver Steeg, *Formative Years:* 39–41; Hart, *Faith & Freedom:* 83; Channing, *History of the United States* 1: 347–350; Morison, *Oxford History of the American People* 1: 107–109.

18. Bancroft, *History of the United States* 1: 322; Howe, *Puritan Republic:* 46–56; Charles W. Elliot, *The New England History*, New York; Charles Scribner, 1857: 2: 428.
19. Howe, *Puritan Republic:* 46–56, 202; DAB 19: 433–434; *The Bill of Rights and the States: The Colonial and Revolutionary Origins of American Liberties*, edited by Patrick T. Conley and John T. Kaminski, Madison: University of Wisconsin Press, 1996: 72–75.
20. DAB 9: 199–200; Amos and Gardiner, *Never Before in History:* 43–44; Morison, *Oxford History of the American People* 1: 109; Bancroft, *History of the United States* 1: 265; Deuteronomy 1:13.
21. *Classics of American Political and Constitutional Thought*, edited by Scott J. Hammond, Indianapolis: Hackett, 2007: 1: 8–9; James Brown Scott, *The United States: A Study in International Organization*, New York: Oxford University Press, 1926: 4.
22. John Warner Barber, *Connecticut Historical Collections*, New Haven: Durrie, Peck and Barber, 1836: 138; Charles H. Levermore, *The Republic of New Haven*, Baltimore: Johns Hopkins University, 1886: 17–21; Benjamin Trumbell, *A General History of the United States of America*, New York: Williams and Whiting, 1810: 1: 104; Walter E. Pratt Jr., "New Haven Colony's Fundamental Articles, 1639," *Religion and American Law: An Encyclopedia*, edited by Paul Finkelman, New York: Garland, 2000: 340; Hart, *Faith & Freedom:* 99–101; Edward Atwater, *History of the Colony of New Haven to Its Absorption into Connecticut*, Boston: Rand, Avery, 1881: 96–99; *America's Founding Charters: Primary Documents of Colonial and Revolutionary Era Governance*, edited by Jon Wakelyn, Westport: Greenwood Press, 2006: 1: 129–130; George Magoun, "The Source of American Education—Popular and Religious," *The New Englander and Yale Review*, New Haven: W. L. Kingsley, 1877: 36: 479.
23. Charles W. Tuttle, *Captain John Mason*, Boston: Prince Society, 1877: 419; Jeremy Belknap, *The History of New Hampshire*, Dover: Stevens, Ela and Wadleigh, 1831: 1: 454; Bancroft, *History of the United States* 2: 115–117.
24. Scott, *The United States:* 6–7; West, *Story of American Democracy:* 104–106: James Gregory, *Puritanism in the Old World and in the New*, New York: Fleming H. Revell, 1896: 297–298; *Records of the Colony or Jurisdiction of New Haven*, edited by Charles J. Hoadley, New Haven: Case, Lockwood, 1858: 562–563; Howe, *Puritan Republic:* 301–304.
25. Morison, *Oxford History of the American People* 1: 105–107; Ver Steeg, *Formative Years:* 37–38.
26. Morison, *Oxford History of the American People* 1: 105–107, 112; Ver Steeg, *Formative Years:* 37–38; De Tocqueville, *Democracy in America:* 30.

CHAPTER 6: "GOD'S MERCIFUL PROVIDENCE"

1. James D. Knowles, *Memoir of Roger Williams Founder of the State of Rhode Island*, Boston: Lincoln, Edmands, 1834: 31, 37–38; DAB 20: 287–289; James

Ernest, *Roger Williams: New England Firebrand*, New York: Macmillan, 1932: 1–22; Edwin Scott Gaustad, *Roger Williams*, New York: Oxford University Press, 2005: 5–8.

2. DAB 20: 287–289; Ernest, *Roger Williams:* 1–22; Gaustad, *Roger Williams:* 5–8.
3. DAB 20: 287–289; Vernon L. Parrington, *The Colonial Mind: 1620–1800*, New York: Harcourt, Brace & World: 1927: 64; Hart, *Faith & Freedom:* 113–118.
4. Perry Miller, *Roger Williams: His Contribution to the American Tradition*, Indianapolis: Bobbs-Merrill, 1953: 9; DAB 20: 287–289; Ernst, *Roger Williams:* 34, 46.
5. Miller, *Roger Williams*, 9; DAB 20: 287–289; Ernst, *Roger Williams:* 34, 46; Parrington, *Colonial Mind:* 63; Hart, *Faith & Freedom:* 114.
6. DAB 20: 287–289; Ver Steeg, *Formative Years:* 76–77; John Stephen Flynn, *The Influence of Puritanism on the Political and Religious Thought of the English*, New York: E. P. Dutton, 1920: 43; Hart, *Faith & Freedom:* 114–115.
7. DAB 20: 287; Ver Steeg, *Formative Years:* 47, 76–77; Marion Lena Starkey, *The Congregational Way: The Role of the Pilgrims and Their Heirs in Shaping America*, New York: Doubleday, 1966: 73; Hart, *Faith & Freedom:* 114–115.
8. DAB 20: 287; Charles M. Andrews, *Colonial Self-Government 1652–1689*, New York: Harper Brothers, 1904: 46; Ver Steeg, *Formative Years:* 47, 76–77; Hart, *Faith & Freedom:* 114–115.
9. DAB 20: 287; Andrews, *Colonial Self-Government:* 46; Ver Steeg, *Formative Years:* 47, 76–77; Hart, *Faith & Freedom:* 114–115.
10. DAB 20: 287; "Roger Williams: A Warning to Endicott," *A Library of American Literature: From the Earliest Settlement to the Present Time*, edited by Edmund Clarence Stedman and Ellen Mackay Hutchinson, New York: Charles Webster, 1889: 1: 250.
11. Ver Steeg, *Formative Years:* 48–49; DAB 20: 287–288; Gaustad, *Roger Williams:* 8; Morison, *Oxford History of the American People* 1: 109–110; Hart, *Faith & Freedom:* 114–115.
12. DAB 20: 287–288; Ver Steeg, *Formative Years:* 48–49; Hart, *Faith & Freedom:* 114–115; Jenkin Loyd Jones, "Civil and Religious Liberty" *Encyclopedia Americana*, 1904: 16: 48.
13. DAB 20: 287–288; *Rhode Island Historical Society Collections*, Providence: Knowles & Vose, 1843: 5: 30, 404; Jones, "Civil and Religious Liberty" 16: 48.
14. *Rhode Island Historical Society Collections* 5: 30; DAB 20: 287–289.
15. Ver Steeg, *Formative Years:* 48–49; Adelos Gorton, *The Life and Times of Samuel Gorton*, Philadelphia: George S. Ferguson, 1907: 35; *Encyclopedia of American History:* 40; Hart, *Faith & Freedom:* 116; DAB 20: 287–288; George Washington Greene, *A Short History of Rhode Island*, Providence: J. R. Reid, 1877: 291–300.
16. DAB 20: 287–289; Samuel Greene Arnold, *History of the State of Rhode Island*

and Providence Plantations, New York; Appleton, 1860: 2: 495; Roger Williams, *The Bloudy Tenent of Persecution for Cause and Conscience Discussed and Mr. Cotton's Letter Examined and Answered*, Whitefish: Kessinger, 2004: 1–2.

17. Gorton, *Life and Times of Samuel Gorton:* 35; DAB 20: 287–289; Hart, *Faith & Freedom:* 116; Morison, *Oxford History of the American People* 1: 109–110; Ver Steeg, *Formative Years:* 48–49; DAB 20: 289.
18. Hart, *Faith & Freedom:* 116; DAB 20: 287–288.
19. Jones, "Civil and Religious Liberty" 16: 48; DAB 20: 288; Hart, *Faith & Freedom:* 116.
20. DAB 20: 288; Hart, *Faith & Freedom:* 116; Jones, "Civil and Religious Liberty" 16: 48.

CHAPTER 7: "THE HOLY EXPERIMENT"

1. DAB 14: 434–435; Morison, *Oxford History of the American People* 1: 181–184; Hart, *Faith & Freedom:* 198–201.
2. Thomas Hodgkin, *George Fox*, Boston: Houghton, Mifflin, 1898: 19; Morison, *Oxford History of the American People* 1: 101–102; *Eerdman's History of Christianity:* 481–483; Hart, *Faith & Freedom:* 197–198.
3. Hodgkin, *George Fox:* 19; Morison, *Oxford History of the American People* 1: 101–102; *Eerdman's History of Christianity:* 481–483; Hart, *Faith & Freedom:* 197–198: Channing, *History of the United States* 2: 103–106.
4. *Eerdman's History of Christianity:* 481–483; Hart, *Faith & Freedom:* 198; Bonomi, *Under the Cope of Heaven:* 26–29; Morison, *Oxford History of the American People* 1: 101–102; Channing, *History of the United States* 2: 99.
5. *Eerdman's History of Christianity:* 481–482; Hart, *Faith & Freedom:* 198; Bonomi, *Under the Cope of Heaven:* 26–29; Morison, *Oxford History of the American People* 1: 101–102.
6. *Eerdman's History of Christianity:* 481–482; Hart, *Faith & Freedom:* 198; Bonomi, *Under the Cope of Heaven:* 26–29; Morison, *Oxford History of the American People* 1: 101–102.
7. *Eerdman's History of Christianity:* 481–482; Hart, *Faith & Freedom:* 198; Bonomi, *Under the Cope of Heaven:* 29; Morison, *Oxford History of the American People* 1: 101–102.
8. Bonomi, *Under the Cope of Heaven:* 29; Jonathan Sarna, *American Judaism: A History*, New Haven: Yale University Press, 2003: 1–7; Morison, *Oxford History of the American People* 1: 214, 240–241; Channing, *History of the United States* 2: 41–42; *Narratives of New Netherland*, edited by J. Franklin Jameson, New York; Charles Scribner's Sons, 1909: 448–449; George E. Howard, *An Introduction to the Local Constitutional History of the United States*, Baltimore: Johns Hopkins University Press, 1889: 1: 105–106; Edwin Gaustad and Leigh Schmidt, *The Religious History of America*, San Francisco: HarperCollins, 2002: 74–78; *Encyclopedia of Religious Freedom*, edited by Catherine Cookson, New York: Routledge, 2003: 301.

9. *Making the Nonprofit Sector in the United States*, edited by David Hammack, Bloomington: Indiana University Press, 2000: 39–41; Bonomi, *Under the Cope of Heaven:* 29; Howard, *Local Constitutional History* 1: 105–106; Matthew 7:12; *Encyclopedia of Religious Freedom:* 301.
10. Gaustad, *Religious History of America:* 78–81; *Encyclopedia of Religious Freedom: 300–302*; Channing, *History of the United States* 4: 45–47.
11. DAB 14: 433; *The Select Works of William Penn*, edited by Deborah Logan and Edward Armstrong, London: James Phillips, 1782: 1: 5–21; Samuel M. Janney, *The Life of William Penn*, Philadelphia: Lippencott, Grambo, 1852: 22–25; Rufus Jones, *The Quakers in the American Colonies*, London: Macmillan Company, 1923: 418–419.
12. Jones, *The Quakers in the American Colonies:* 418–419; DAB 14: 432–433; *Select Works of William Penn* 1: 5–21; Channing, *History of the United States* 2: 103–106.
13. DAB 14: 432–433; Isaac Sharples, "William Penn," *Encyclopedia Americana* 21: 513.
14. Sharples, "William Penn" 21: 513; Channing, *History of the United States* 2: 45–46, 102.
15. DAB 14: 433–434; *The History of New Jersey from its Earliest Settlement to the Present Time*, edited by W. H. Carpenter and T. S. Arthur, Philadelphia: Lippincott, 1856: 70–72; Bernard Schwartz, *The Great Rights of Mankind: A History of the American Bill of Rights*, Lanham, Maryland: Rowman & Littlefield, 1991: 44–47; *Select Charters and Other Documents of American History*, edited by William McDonald, New York: Macmillan and Company, 1899: 141.
16. DAB 14: 433–443; Schwartz, *Great Rights of Mankind:* 44–47; Samuel Smith, *History of the Colony of New Jersey*, Orangeburg, S.C.: Reprint Company, 1966: 80–81; Albert M. Friedenberg, "The Jews of New Jersey from the Earliest Times to 1850," *Publications of the American Jewish Historical Society*, Baltimore: Lord Baltimore Press, 1909: 17: 33–35.
17. DAB 14: 434–435; Morison, *Oxford History of the American People* 1: 181–184; Gaustad, *Religious History of America:* 72–78; Hart, *Faith & Freedom:* 198–201.
18. DAB 14: 433–443; Sharples, "William Penn" 21: 513; Channing, *History of the United States* 2: 106–109.
19. DAB 14: 434–435; William Penn, *No Cross, No Crown*, London: Society of Friends, 1896: 1: 51.
20. Ver Steeg, *Formative Years:* 116–118; Richard Vinen, *A History in Fragments: Europe in the 20th Century*, New York: De Capo, 2001: 15; Morison, *Oxford History of the American People* 1: 181–184; Hart, *Faith & Freedom:* 198–201: Matthew 5:44.
21. John A. Munroe, *History of Delaware*, Dover: University of Delaware Press, 2006: 42–46; Gaustad, *Religious History of America:* 74–78.
22. Munroe, *History of Delaware:* 42–46; *Federal and State Constitutions, Colonial Charters and Organic Laws of the United States*, edited by Benjamin Perley Poore, Washington: U.S. Government Printing Office, 1877: 1: 270–273.

23. Vinen, *History in Fragments:* 116–118; Morison, *Oxford History of the American People* 1: 181–184; Hart, *Faith & Freedom:* 198–201; DAB 14: 436.

CHAPTER 8: "FOR OUR SAVIOUR AND OUR SOVEREIGN"

1. DAB 3: 428–431; Thomas O'Gorman, *A History of the Roman Catholic Church in America*, New York: Christian Literature Company, 1894: 219.
2. DAB: 3: 428–431; *Narratives of Early Maryland 1633–1684*, edited by Clayton Coleman Hall, New York; Charles Scribner's Sons, 1910: 14–16; Charles Carton, *Charles I: The Personal Monarch*, New York: Routledge, 1995: 139.
3. DAB: 3: 428–431; O'Gorman, *History of the Roman Catholic Church in America:* 219–222.
4. C. Ernest Smith, *Religion Under the Barons of Baltimore*, Baltimore: Allen Lycett, 1899: 135; 141–145.
5. Smith, *Religion Under the Barons of Baltimore: 165–167*; *Narratives of Early Maryland:* 14; Philip Fisher, "Early Christian Missions Among the Indians of Maryland," *Maryland Historical Magazine* 1:4: 294–295.
6. Smith, *Religion Under the Barons of Baltimore:* 160; "Lord Baltimore's Instructions to Colonists," *The Calvert Papers*, edited John Stockbridge, Baltimore: Maryland Historical Society, 1889: 1: 131; *Narratives of Early Maryland:* 14–16.
7. *The English Statutes in Maryland*, edited by Bernard C. Steiner, Baltimore: Johns Hopkins University Press, 1903: 31; Smith, *Religion Under the Barons of Baltimore:* 167; *Narratives of Early Maryland:* 14–16; *Encyclopedia of Religious Freedom:* 267.
8. Smith, *Religion Under the Barons of Baltimore:* 167; *Narratives of Early Maryland:* 177; A. Leo Knott, "Maryland," *The Catholic Encyclopedia*, 1910: 9: 755–757.
9. William King, "Lord Baltimore and His Freedom in Granting Religious Toleration," *Records of the American Catholic Historical Society of Philadelphia*, Philadelphia: American Catholic Historical Society, 1921: 32: 303; Fisher, "Early Christian Missions Among the Indians": 302–304.
10. *Encyclopedia of Religious Freedom:* 267; King, "Lord Baltimore and His Freedom," 32: 301–307; *Select Charters of American History:* 54.
11. *Encyclopedia of Religious Freedom:* 267; King, "Lord Baltimore and His Freedom": 32: 301–307; *Select Charters of American History:* 54; *Archives of Maryland*, edited by Bernard C. Steiner, Baltimore: William Dulany, 1904: 115.
12. Smith, *Religion Under the Barons of Baltimore:* 315–318; O'Gorman, *A History of the Roman Catholic Church:* 221–225; James S. Buckingham, *America: Historical, Statistical and Descriptive*, New York: Harper Brothers, 1841: 1: 257.
13. DAB 9: 474–475; *Encyclopedia of Religious Freedom:* 267; Newton D. Mereness, *Maryland as a Proprietary Colony*, New York: Macmillan, 1901: 432–433. J. Thomas Scharf, *A History of Maryland from the Earliest Period to the Present Day*, Baltimore: John Piet, 1879: 1: 53.
14. DAB 3: 430; O'Gorman, *History of the Roman Catholic Church in America:*

226–227; Smith, *Religion Under the Barons of Baltimore:* 315–318; *Encyclopedia of Religious Freedom:* 267; Bernard Schwartz, *The Great Rights of Mankind: A History of the American Bill of Rights*, Lanham, Maryland: Rowman & Littlefield, 1991: 44–47; Samuel Smith, *History of the Colony of New Jersey*, Orangeburg, S.C.: Reprint Company, 1966: 80–81.

15. O'Gorman, *History of the Roman Catholic Church in America:* 226–227; Knott, "Maryland": 9: 757–758; *Encyclopedia of Religious Freedom:* 266–267; Matthew 7:12.
16. David Ramsey, *The History of South Carolina: From its First Settlement in 1670 to the Year 1808*, Charleston: David Longworth, 1809: 1: 87: *The South Carolina Encyclopedia*, edited by Walter Edgar, Columbia: University of South Carolina Press, 2006: 132.
17. *Federal and State Constitutions, Colonial Charters and Other Organic Laws* 5: 2742; Walter Edgar, *South Carolina: A History*, Columbia: University of South Carolina Press, 1998: 43.
18. *South Carolina Encyclopedia:* 216–217; 223–224; Henry R. Bourne, *The Life of John Locke*, New York: Harper Brothers, 1876: 1: 143–144: John Locke, *The Works of John Locke*, London: John Davidson, 1823: 1: xxv-xxvi; *Encyclopedia of Religion in American Politics*, edited by Jeffrey Schultz, John West, and Ian MacLean, Abington: Greenwood, 1998: 141–42; Amos and Gardiner, *Never Before in History:* 28–29.
19. Jeremy Waldron, *God, Locke and Equality: Christian Foundations in Locke's Political Thought*, New York: Cambridge University Press, 2002: 12; Bourne, *Life of John Locke*, 177–179; Amos and Gardiner, *Never Before in History* 28–29; *Works of John Locke* 4: 96, 7: 421.
20. Waldron, *God, Locke and Equality:* 12; Elwood Worcester, *The Religious Opinions of John Locke*, Geneva: Humphrey Press, 1889: 69; *Encyclopedia of Religion in American Politics:* 141–142; Amos and Gardiner, *Never Before in History:* 28–29, 177.
21. Worchester, *Religious Opinions of John Locke:* 69; Bourne, *Life of John Locke:* 241; *Statutes at Large of South Carolina*, edited by Thomas Cooper, Columbia: A. S. Johnson, 1886: 1: 43, 53–56; Locke, *Works of John Locke* 9: 196.
22. *South Carolina Encyclopedia:* 216; Edgar, *South Carolina:* 43; Clinton Rossiter, *1787: The Grand Convention*, New York: Macmillan, 1966: 51.
23. Samuel A. Ashe, *History of North Carolina*, Greensboro: Charles Van Noppen, 1908: 1: 178; Charles Jones, *The History of Georgia*, Boston: Houghton Mifflin, 1883: 2: 259; Morison, *Oxford History of the American People:* 214; Bonomi, *Under the Cope of Heaven:* 31–33, 50, 98, 200.
24. Morison, *Oxford History of the American People:* 130; Ver Steeg, *Formative Years:* 216–217; Bonomi, *Under the Cope of Heaven:* 15, 21–26, 31–37.
25. Bonomi, *Under the Cope of Heaven:* 46–52; Evarts B. Green, *The American Nation: A History*, New York: Harper Brothers, 1905, 6: 100–104; G. W. Acton, A. W. Ward and Stanley Prothero, *Cambridge Modern History of the United States*, Cambridge: Cambridge University Press, 1970: 7: 59.

26. Green, *History of England:* 4: 174; Bonomi, *Under the Cope of Heaven:* 15; Ver Steeg, *Formative Years:* 216.
27. Thorpe, *Federal and State Constitutions, Colonial Charters and Organic Laws* 1: 77, 1: 249–252, 1: 529, 1: 577, 2: 765, 3: 1677, 3: 1841, 5: 2753, 6: 3047–3070, 7: 3783; *Colonial Laws of New York From the Year 1664 to the Revolution*, Edited by Charles Z. Lincoln, William H. Johnson, and Ansul J. Northrup, Albany: J. B. Lyon, 1894: 1: xii, 20.
28. Peter G. Mode, *Sourcebook and Bibliographical Guide for American Church History*, Menasha: The Collegiate Press, 1921: 192: Bancroft, *History of the United States* 1: 210.

CHAPTER 9: "THE GREAT AWAKENING"

1. DAB 6: 30–33; Alexander Allen, *Jonathan Edwards*, Boston: Houghton Mifflin, 1890: 2–19; Joseph Tracy, *The Great Awakening: A History of the Revival of Religion in the Time of Edwards and Whitefield*, Boston: Charles Tappan, 1845: 214; Oliver William Means, *A Sketch of the Strict Congregational Church of Enfield Connecticut*, Boston; Harvard Seminary Press, 1899: 19.
2. DAB 6: 30–33; Allen, *Jonathan Edwards:* 2–19; Tracy, *Great Awakening:* 214; Means, *Sketch of the Congregational Church:* 19; Gardiner, "Jonathan Edwards" 9: 3–4.
3. DAB 6: 30–33; Harry N. Gardiner and Alexander Allen, *Jonathan Edwards: A Retrospect*, Boston: Houghton Mifflin, 1901: 11–12, 30; Allen, *Jonathan Edwards:* 2–19; Gardiner, "Jonathan Edwards" 9: 3–4.
4. Tracy, *Great Awakening:* 2–5; DAB 6: 30–33; Katsh, *Biblical Heritage of Democracy* 66; Allen, *Jonathan Edwards:* 180–182; Gardiner, "Jonathan Edwards" 9: 3.
5. Tracy, *Great Awakening:* 2–5; Allen, *Jonathan Edwards:* 180–182; Carl Bridenbaugh, *Cities in Revolt: Urban Life in America 1743–1776*, New York: Capricorn Books, 1964: 150–151; William Henry Foote, *Sketches of Virginia, Historical and Biographical*, Philadelphia: William S. Martien, 1850: 109; John Findling and Frank Thackery, *Events That Changed America in the Eighteenth Century*, Westport: Greenwood, 1998: 7.
6. Tracy, *Great Awakening:* 2–5; Foote, *Sketches of Virginia:* 109; Findling and Thackery, *Events That Changed America:* 7.
7. Tracy, *Great Awakening:* 5, 10; Allen, *Jonathan Edwards:* 180–183; DAB 6:30–33; Ephesians 2: 8–9.
8. James H. Smylie, *A Brief History of the Presbyterians*, Louisville: Geneva Press, 1996: 52–53; Romans 3:23; Romans 6:23; Romans 5:8–9; John 3:16; John 3:3; DAB 6: 30–33.
9. Cedric B. Cowling, *The Great Awakening and the American Revolution: Colonial Thought in the 18th Century*, Chicago: Rand McNally, 1971: 67–69, 71–74; DAB 6:32–33; Allen, *Jonathan Edwards:* 185. Smylie, *History of the Presbyterians:* 52–53; Morison, *Oxford History of the American People:* 210.

10. Cowling, *Great Awakening:* 67–69; Allen, *Jonathan Edwards:* 185; DAB 6: 32–33; Morison, *Oxford History of the American People:* 210; Ezra H. Byington, *The Puritan as a Colonist and Reformer*, Boston: Little and Brown, 1899: 293–294.
11. Jonathan Edwards, *Thoughts on the Revival of Religion in New England, 1740: To Which is Prefixed, "A Narrative of the Surprising Work of God in Northampton, Mass., 1736,"* New York: American Tract Society, 1845: 152.
12. Byington, *Puritan as Colonist and Reformer:* 293–294; DAB 6: 32–33; Allen, *Jonathan Edwards:* 185; Edwards, *Thoughts on the Revival of Religion in New England:* 152; Ezra Hoyt Byington, "Jonathan Edwards and the Great Awakening," *The Bibliotheca Sacra: A Religious and Sociological Quarterly*, edited by Frederick Wright and Swift Holbrook 55: 123; *Eerdman's History of Christianity:* 439.
13. Edwards, *Thoughts on the Surprising Revival:* 152; *Eerdman's History of Christianity:* 438; Morison, *Oxford History of the American People:* 210.
14. DAB 6: 36–37; Allen, *Jonathan Edwards:* 180–183; Mark A. Noll, *A History of Christianity in the United States and Canada*, Grand Rapids: William B. Eerdmans, 1992: 92; Gardiner, "Jonathan Edwards" 9: 3–4.
15. DAB 6: 36–37; Allen, *Jonathan Edwards:* 180–183; Noll, *History of Christianity in the United States and Canada:* 92; Byington, *Puritan as Colonist and Reformer:* 296–297.
16. Jonathan Edwards, *The Works of President Edwards*, New York: S. Converse, 1829: 7: 163–177; Jonathan Edwards, *Selected Sermons of Jonathan Edwards*, edited by H. Norman Gardiner, New York: Macmillan, 1904: 86–87.
17. Edwards, *Selected Sermons of Jonathan Edwards:* 86–87.
18. Edwards, *Works of President Edwards* 7: 163–177; Edwards, *Selected Sermons of Jonathan Edwards:* 86–87.
19. J. William T. Youngs. *The Congregationalists: A History*, Greenwood: Greenwood, 1998: 75–76; Means, *Sketch of the Strict Congregational Church of Enfield:* 19; Byington, *Puritan as Colonist and Reformer:* 296–297.
20. Cowling, *Great Awakening:* 67–69, 71–74; DAB 6:32–33; Allen, *Jonathan Edwards:* 185. Smylie, *History of the Presbyterians:* 52–53; Youngs, *The Congregationalists:* 76; Bonomi, *Under the Cope of Heaven:* 3–8; Tracy, *Great Awakening:* 417–423; Heimert, *Religion and the American Mind:* 15.

CHAPTER 10: "IT SEEM'D AS IF ALL THE WORLD WERE GROWING RELIGIOUS"

1. Benjamin Franklin, *The Autobiography of Benjamin Franklin*, New York: Henry Holt, 1916: 101–102; DAB 6: 587–588; Amos and Gardiner, *Never Before in History:* 54–56.
2. Franklin, *Autobiography:* 101–102; Byington, *Puritan as Colonist and Reformer* 298–300; DAB 20: 126.
3. DAB 20: 124–125; *Eerdman's History of Christianity:* 440.

4. DAB 20: 124–125; *Dictionary of National Biography*, edited by Leslie Stephens and Sidney Lee, London: Oxford University Press, 1921: 58: 641.
5. DAB 20: 124–125; Luke Tyerman, *The Life and Times of the Rev. John Wesley*, London: Hodder & Stoughton, 1876: 1: 104–106; George Whitefield, *The Works of the Reverend George Whitefield*, edited by John Gillies, London: Dilly, Kincaid & Creech, 1871: 1: 16, 297.
6. *Oxford Dictionary of National Biography*: 640–649; DAB 20: 124–129; *Eerdman's History of Christianity*: 440; Whitefield, *Works of Reverend George Whitefield* 1: 297.
7. *Eerdman's History of Christianity*: 440; DAB 20: 124–125; *Oxford Dictionary of National Biography*: 640–649; Bridenbaugh, *Cities in Revolt*: 151; James P. Gledstone, *George Whitefield: Field Preacher*, Boston: American Tract Society, 1901: 149–150.
8. DAB 20: 124–125; *Eerdman's History of Christianity*: 440; DAB 20: 124–125; *Oxford Dictionary of National Biography*: 640–649; George C. Clark, *Connecticut, Its People and Its Institutions*, New York: G. P. Putnam's Sons, 1914: 267–269: Gledstone, *George Whitefield*: 91; Franklin, *Autobiography of Benjamin Franklin*: 191, 197.
9. *Eerdman's History of Christianity*: 440; DAB 20: 124–125; *Oxford Dictionary of National Biography*: 640–649; Franklin, *Autobiography of Benjamin Franklin*: 197; Gledstone, *George Whitefield*: 91.
10. *Eerdman's History of Christianity*: 440; DAB 20: 124–129.
11. *Eerdman's History of Christianity*: 441; Cowling, *Great Awakening and the American Revolution*: 29, 67–74; Robert Mathisen, *Critical Issues in American Religious History: A Reader*, Waco: Baylor University Press, 2006: 90, 107–123; Heimert, *Religion and the American Mind*: 2–9.
12. Nathan Cole, "The Spiritual Travels of Nathan Cole," edited by Michael J. Crawford, *William and Mary Quarterly*, 33: 89–126; Clark, *Connecticut, Its People and Its Institutions*: 267–269. *A Documentary History of Religion in America to 1877*, edited by Edwin S. Gaustad and Mark A. Noll, Grand Rapids: Eerdmans, 2003: 164–165.
13. Gledstone, *George Whitefield*: 102; James A. Gronniosaw, *A Narrative of the Most Remarkable Particulars in the Life of James Albert Ukawasaw Gronniosaw, An African Prince*, Bath: S. Hazzard, 1770: 25.
14. *Eerdman's History of Christianity*: 441; Cowling, *Great Awakening and the American Revolution*: 29; Mathisen, *Critical Issues in American Religious History*: 107–123; Heimert, *Religion and the American Mind*: 2–9.
15. Franklin, *Autobiography*: 191, 197; Cowling, *Great Awakening and the American Revolution*: 67–69, 71–74; Green, *History of the English People* 5: 163; Charles Woodmason, *The Carolina Backcountry on the Eve of the Revolution: The Journal and Other Writings of Charles Woodmason, Anglican Itinerant*, edited by Richard J. Hooker, Chapel Hill: University of North Carolina Press, 1953: 52–56; Mathisen, *Critical Issues in American Religious History*: 107–123, 198; "William Tennent," *Appleton's Cyclopaedia of American Biography*, 1889: 6: 62.

16. Cowling, *Great Awakening and the American Revolution:* 67–69, 71–74; Green, *History of the English People* 5: 163; Woodmason, *Carolina Backcountry on the Eve of the Revolution:* 52–54.
17. Mathisen, *Critical Issues in American Religious History:* 107–123, 198; "William Tennent," *Appleton's Cyclopaedia of American Biography*, 1889: 6: 62.
18. Bonomi, *Under the Cope of Heaven:* 3–10; Heimert, *Religion and the American Mind:* 12–13; Solberg, *Redeem the Time:* 296–302; Woodmason, *Carolina Backcountry on the Eve of the Revolution:* 56.
19. Bonomi, *Under the Cope of Heaven:* 3–10; Heimert, *Religion and the American Mind:* 5–6, 12–13; Mark 2: 26–28; Solberg, *Redeem the Time:* 296–302, 310.
20. Heimert, *Religion and the American Mind:* 5–7; Bonomi, *Under the Cope of Heaven:* 166–168; Woodmason, *Carolina Backcountry on the Eve of the Revolution:* 101–102; Merle Curti, *The Growth of American Thought*, New York: Harper & Row, 1943: 26.
21. Heimert, *Religion and the American Mind:* 5–7, 50–51, 165; John 3:3–16; Acts 4:12; John 14:16; Romans 10:9–11; Romans 5:8–9; I Peter 1:22–24; Bonomi, *Under the Cope of Heaven:* 164–167.
22. Heimert, *Religion and the American Mind:* 5–7; Bonomi, *Under the Cope of Heaven:* 166–168; Woodmason, *Carolina Backcountry on the Eve of the Revolution:* 101–102; Curti, *Growth of American Thought:* 26.
23. Heimert, *Religion and the American Mind:* 5–11, 120, 557; Bonomi, *Under the Cope of Heaven:* 164–167; Samuel Johnson, *Samuel Johnson: His Career and Writings*, edited by Herbert and Carol Schneider, New York: Columbia University Press, 1929: 3: 231; *Events That Changed America in the 18th Century:* 4.
24. Bonomi, *Under the Cope of Heaven:* 163–167; Heimert, *Religion and the American Mind:* 120.
25. Bonomi, *Under the Cope of Heaven:* 139–145; Heimert, *Religion and the American Mind:* 2–3; Ver Steeg, *Formative Years:* 210–213; Cowling, *Great Awakening and the American Revolution:* 67–74; Katsh, *The Biblical Heritage of American Democracy:* 127–130; Mathisen, *Critical Issues in American Religious History:* 111: Ver Steeg, *Formative Years*: 210–213; Heimert, *Religion and the American Mind:* 2–5.
26. Cowling, *Great Awakening and the American Revolution:* 67–74; Mathisen, *Critical Issues in American Religious History:* 111; Ver Steeg, *Formative Years:* 210–213; Heimert, *Religion and the American Mind:* 2–5; Curti, *Growth of American Thought:* 10–29; Daniel Dorchester, *Christianity in the United States: From the First Settlement Down to the Present Time*, New York: Hunt & Eaton, 1895: 102.
27. Heimert, *Religion and the American Mind:* 2–5; Curti, *Growth of American Thought:* 10–29; Katsh, *The Biblical Heritage of American Democracy:* 127–130; DAB 20: 129.
28. Thomas S. Kidd, *The Great Awakening: The Roots of Evangelical Christianity in Colonial America*, New Haven: Yale University Press, 2007: 180; Bonomi, *Under the Cope of Heaven:* 156–159; Heimert, *Religion and the American Mind:*

20–21; Keith L. Griffin, *Revolution and Religion: The American Revolutionary War and the Reformed Clergy*, New York: Paragon House, 1994: 28; James Douglas, *New England and New France: Contrasts and Parallels in Colonial History*, New York: G. P. Putnam's Sons, 1913: 298.

29. DAB 6:37; DAB 20: 129; Gledstone, *George Whitefield:* 339–340.

CHAPTER 11: "WHERE THE SPIRIT OF THE LORD IS, THERE IS LIBERTY"

1. DAB 8: 554–555; Moses Coit Tyler, *Patrick Henry*, Boston: Houghton Mifflin, 1897: 61–63; 72.
2. Thomas B. Macaulay, *Lord Macaulay's Essays*, London: George Routledge and Sons, 1892: 846; DAB 8: 554–555; Tyler, *Patrick Henry:* 61–63; 72.
3. Middlekauff, *Glorious Cause:* 75–83; Claude H. Van Tyne, *The American Nation: A History*, New York: Harper & Brothers, 1905: 9: 10–15.
4. Robert Rogers, *Diary of the Siege of Detroit in the War with Pontiac*. Edited by Franklin B. Hough, Albany: J. Munsell, 1860: 125–135; Van Tyne, *American Nation* 9: 9.
5. Brinton, Christopher and Wolfe, *History of Civilization* 2: 74–75.
6. Mumby, *George III:* 91; Brinton, Christopher and Wolfe, *History of Civilization* 2: 74–75; Fred Anderson, *Crucible of War: The Seven Years' War and the Face of Empire in British North America, 1754–1766*. New York: Alfred H. Knopf, 2000: 566.
7. Brinton, Christopher and Wolfe, *History of Civilization* 2: 74–75; Anderson, *Crucible of War:* 563, 648.
8. Green, *History of the English People* 5: 218.
9. Mumby, *George III:* 91; Briton, Christopher and Wolfe, *History of Civilization* 2: 74–75; Benjamin Franklin, *Memoirs of Benjamin Franklin*, edited by William Templeton Franklin, New York: Derby & Jackson, 1859: 2:79.
10. DAB 8: 554–555; Tyler, *Patrick Henry:* 61–63; 72.
11. DAB 8: 554–555; Tyler, *Patrick Henry:* 9.
12. DAB 8: 554–555; Tyler, *Patrick Henry:* 69.
13. DAB 8: 554–555; Tyler, *Patrick Henry:* 61; Henry Mayer, *A Son of Thunder: Patrick Henry and the American Republic*, New York: Grove, 2001: 81–83.
14. Benson J. Lossing, *The American Historical Record*, Philadelphia: John E. Potter, 1874: 3: 153; DAB 8: 544–555; Tyler, *Patrick Henry:* 69.
15. Norine Dickinson Campbell, *Patrick Henry: Patriot and Statesman*, Old Greenwich: Devin-Adair, 1969: 2–3, 17–19; Tyler, *Patrick Henry:* 14–15.
16. William Wirt Henry, *Patrick Henry: Life, Correspondence and Speeches*, New York: Charles Scribner's Sons, 1891: 2: 15; Frank Samuel Child, *The Colonial Parson of New England*, New York: Baker & Taylor, 1896: 208–210; DAB 8: 555–557.
17. Catherine L. Albanese, *Sons of the Fathers: The Civil Religion of the American Revolution*, Philadelphia: Temple University Press, 1976: 38; DAB 8: 555–557.

18. David W. Hall, *The Genevan Reformation and the American Founding*, Lanham: Lexington Books, 2003: 364–367; Heimert, *Religion and the American Mind:* 328; John Gillies, *Historical Collections Relating to Remarkable Periods of the Success of the Gospel*, London: James Nesbit, 1845: 503; Mayer, *Son of Thunder:* 364–367.
19. Heimert, *Religion and the American Mind:* 328; Samuel Davies, *The Curse of Cowardice: A Sermon Preached to the Militia of Hanover County, Virginia, at a General Muster, May 8, 1758*, London: Buckland, Ward & Field, 1758: 1–30.
20. Derek H. Davis, *Religion and the Continental Congress 1774–1789*, New York: Oxford University Press, 2000: 66; Hall, *Genevan Reformation and the American Founding:* 364–367; Middlekauff, *Glorious Cause:* 75–83.
21. Bonomi, *Under the Cope of Heaven:* 87–95, 123–126; Hall, *Genevan Reformation and the American Founding:* 392; Heimert, *Religion and the American Mind:* 346; Claude H. Van Tyne, "Influence of the Clergy and of Religious and Sectarian Forces on the American Revolution," *American Historical Review*, 9: 1: 64.
22. John Wingate Thornton, *The Pulpit of the American Revolution*, Boston: Gould & Lincoln, 1860: 86; Heimert, *Religion and the American Mind:* 253–255, 290.
23. Thornton, *Pulpit of the Revolution:* 43; Alice Mary Baldwin, *The New England Clergy and the American Revolution*, New York: Ungar Publishing, 1928: 87; Heimert, *Religion and the American Mind:* 244; Jaques Courvoisier, *Zwingli: A Reformed Theologian*, Berkeley: University of California Press, 1963: 83.
24. Henry, *Patrick Henry* 2: 519, 570; Tyler, *Patrick Henry:* 56, 393; Henry, *Patrick Henry* 2: 519.
25. William Wirt, *Sketches of the Life and Character of Patrick Henry*, New York: Derby & Jackson, 1860: 402; Henry, *Patrick Henry* 2: 519.
26. Mayer, *Son of Thunder:* 86; Anderson, *Crucible of War:* 663; Carl Bridenbaugh, *Seat of Empire: The Political Roles of 18th Century Williamsburg*, Williamsburg: Colonial Williamsburg Foundation, 1958: 61.
27. Tyler, *Patrick Henry:* 73–74; Middlekauff, *Glorious Cause:* 81–85.
28. *Liberty Documents: With Contemporary Exposition and Critical Comments Drawn from Various Writers*, edited by Albert Bushnell Hard and Mabel Hill, New York: Longmans & Green, 1903: 155; Tyler, *Patrick Henry:* 82; Middlekauff, *Glorious Cause:* 253.
29. Bonomi, *Under the Cope of Heaven:* 186–188; Hall, *Genevan Reformation and the American Founding:* 386–389; Heimert, *Religion and the American Mind:* 356–358.
30. Gilles, *Memoirs of George Whitefield:* 184; Frank Lambert, *Pedlar in Divinity: George Whitefield and the Trans-Atlantic Revival*, Princeton: Princeton University Press, 2002: 222–224; *Liberty Documents: With Contemporary Exposition and Critical Comments Drawn from Various Writers*, edited by Albert Bushnell Hard and Mabel Hill, New York: Longmans & Green, 1903: 76: Heimert, *Religion and the American Mind:* 357.
31. Charles W. Akers, *Called Unto Liberty: A Life of Jonathan Mayhew 1720–1766*,

Cambridge: Harvard University Press, 1964: 213–216; Heimert, *Religion and the American Mind:* 276; Middlekauff, *Glorious Cause:* 75–83.

CHAPTER 12: "AN APPEAL TO GOD AND THE WORLD"

1. Ellen Chase, *The Beginnings of the American Revolution*, New York: Baker and Taylor Company, 1910: 1: 321–326; George R. Hewes, *A Retrospect of the Boston Tea Party*, New York: S. S. Bliss, 1834: 38–41; *American History Told by Contemporaries: Building of the Republic*, edited by Albert Bushnell Hart, New York: Macmillan, 1910: 2: 431–432.
2. Benjamin Woods Labaree, *The Boston Tea Party*, New York: Oxford University Press, 1964: 144; Hewes, *Retrospect of the Boston Tea Party:* 38–41; *American History by Contemporaries* 2: 431–432; Chase, *Beginnings of the American Revolution* 1: 321–326.
3. Malone, *Declaration of Independence:* 9–10, 175; Middlekauff, *Glorious Cause:* 166–169, 183–184; Becker, *Eve of Revolution:* 114.
4. Middlekauff, *Glorious Cause:* 159; Becker, *Eve of Revolution:* 122–124.
5. Bancroft, *History of the United States* 3: 323; Middlekauff, *Glorious Cause:* 163–165.
6. Becker, *Eve of Revolution:* 127–128; Middlekauff, *Glorious Cause:* 210–214.
7. Bancroft, *History of the United States* 3: 414; Middlekauff, *Glorious Cause:* 219–221.
8. Chase, *Beginnings of the American Revolution* 1: 287–288; Becker, *Eve of Revolution:* 198–199.
9. Hewes, *Retrospect of the Boston Tea Party:* 37–39; Chase, *Beginnings of the American Revolution:* 316.
10. DAB 1: 96–97; DNB 7: 1069–1071; Ellis Gray, "The Father of the Revolution," *Harper's New Monthly Magazine* (1876) 53: 188; Samuel Fallows, *Samuel Adams: A Character Sketch*, Chicago: University Association, 1898: 102–103.
11. James K. Hosmer, *Samuel Adams*, Boston: Houghton Mifflin, 1913: 302–309; DAB 1: 95–97; Gray, "Father of the Revolution": 187; Fallows, *Samuel Adams:* 103; William V. Wells, *The Life and Public Service of Samuel Adams*, Boston: Little & Brown, 1865: 2: 18; James K. Hosmer, *The Life of Thomas Hutchinson, Royal Governor of the Province of Massachusetts Bay*, Boston: Houghton, Mifflin, 1896: 215.
12. Hosmer, *Samuel Adams:* 302–309; WSA 2: 351; DAB 1: 95–97.
13. Gray, "Father of the Revolution": 53, 188; Fallows, *Samuel Adams:* 102–103; Harry Clinton Green, *The Pioneer Mothers of America*, New York: G. P. Putnam's Sons, 1912: DAB 1: 95–97; Fallows, *Samuel Adams:* 103.
14. DAB 1: 96–97; Gray, "The Father of the Revolution": 53: 188; Fallows, *Samuel Adams:* 102–103; Chase, *Beginnings of the American Revolution:* 287.
15. Gray, "Father of the Revolution": 53, 188–189; DAB 1: 95–97; WSA: 4: 356–358; John T. Morse, *John Adams*, Boston: Houghton Mifflin, 1888: 10; Wells, *Life and Public Service of Samuel Adams:* 2: 18.

16. DAB 1: 95–99; James Graham, *History of the United States of North America*, Boston: Little & Brown, 1845: 4: 254; WJA 6: 414; Gray, "Father of the Revolution": 53: 188.
17. Graham, *History of the United States of North America* 4: 253–254; DAB 1: 95–99; Bancroft, *History of the United States* 6: 194; WJA 1: 673–674; Wells, *Life and Public Service of Samuel Adams* 1: 118; Hosmer, *Samuel Adams:* 307–310; WSA 4: 352; Acts 5:29; David E. Shi, *The Simple Life: Plain Living and High Thinking in American Culture*, Athens: University of Georgia Press, 2007: 59.
18. Hosmer, *Samuel Adams:* 302–309; DAB 1: 95–97; Gray, "Father of the Revolution": 187; Fallows, *Samuel Adams:* 103.
19. DAB 1: 95–97; Gray, "Father of the Revolution": 187; Wells, *Life and Public Service of Samuel Adams* 2: 419.
20. WSA 4: 356.
21. John William Fortesque, *The Correspondence of King George the Third from 1760 through December 1783*, New York: Macmillan, 1927: 3: 59; Chase, *Beginnings of the Revolution* 1: 346.
22. Middlekauf, *Glorious Cause:* 157–159, 221–223; Brinton, Christopher and Wolff, *History of Civilization* 2: 76; Mumby, *George III and the American Revolution:* 320–321.
23. Middlekauf, *Glorious Cause:* 157–159, 221–223; Brinton, Christopher and Wolff, *History of Civilization* 2: 76; Mumby, *George III:* 320–321.
24. Wells, *Life and Public Service of Samuel Adams* 2: 158; Chase, *Beginnings of the Revolution* 1: 352.
25. Holmes, *Annals of America* 2: 186; Bonomi, *Under the Cope of Heaven:* 187–208; Heimert, *Religion and the American Mind:* 157–158, 385–389; George Elliot Howard, *Preliminaries of the American Revolution*, 1763–1775, New York: Harper & Brothers, 1905: 284–286.
26. Kevin J. Hayes, *The Road to Monticello: The Life and Times of Thomas Jefferson*, New York: Oxford University Press, 2008: 151–155; Thomas Jefferson, *The Writings of Thomas Jefferson*, edited by Paul Leicester Ford, New York: G. P. Putnam's Sons, 1892: 1: 8–11; Tyler, *Patrick Henry:* 86.
27. Jefferson, *Writings of Thomas Jefferson* 1: 8; Hayes, *Road to Monticello:* 152–155; Mayer, *Son of Thunder:* 188; George Ticknor Curtis, *Constitutional History of the United States*, New York: Harper & Brothers, 1889: 1: 7.
28. Jefferson, *Writings of Thomas Jefferson* 1: 8–11; Hayes, *Road to Monticello:* 152–155; Bancroft, *History of the United States* 7: 53; "Letters from William and Mary College, 1798–1801," *The Virginia Magazine of History and Biography* (April 1921) 29: 162–163.
29. Bancroft, *History of the United States* 7: 53; Chase, *Beginnings of the Revolution* 1: 357, 381; *Revolution of the People:* 128; Mayer, *Son of Thunder:* 188–191: Bruce A. Ragsdale, *A Planter's Republic: The Search for Economic Independence in Revolutionary Virginia*, Lanham: Rowman and Littlefield, 1996: 181–183.

30. Middlekauf, *The Glorious Cause:* 233–234; *Encyclopedia of American History:* 92–93; Mayer, *Son of Thunder:* 188–191; John Fiske, *The American Revolution*, Boston: Houghton Mifflin, 1919: 103–104; Wells, *Life and Public Service of Samuel Adams* 2: 176; WSA 3: 111–112.

CHAPTER 13: "THE LOVE OF LIBERTY IS INTERWOVEN IN THE SOUL OF MAN"

1. WJA 2: 358; Page Smith, *John Adams*, Garden City: Doubleday, 1962: 1: 162–168.
2. David McCullough, *John Adams*, New York: Simon & Schuster, 2001: 19, 81, 648; DAB 1: 81, 96–97; Gray, "Father of the Revolution": 53, 188.
3. DAB 1: 81; McCullough, *John Adams* 19, 81, 648; Daniel Munro Wilson, *The "Chappel of Ease" and Church of Statesmen*, Cambridge: John Wilson & Sons, 1890: 59; Smith, *John Adams* 1: 2–5; James Darsey, *Prophetic Tradition and Radical Rhetoric in America*, New York: NYU Press, 1999: 47–48.
4. DAB 1: 73–74, 81; Smith, *John Adams* 1: 62; McCullough, *John Adams* 83; WJA 2: 6–7, 23; WJA 10: 104–105; WJA 3: 421.
5. DAB 1: 73–74; WJA 2: 6–7, 23; WJA 3: 421; WJA 10: 104–105.
6. WJA 10: 105; WJA 2: 6–7, 22–23.
7. WJA 1: 75; McCullough, *John Adams* 19; WJA 2: 22.
8. WJA 10: 45; Francis Schaeffer, *A Christian Manifesto*, Wheaton: Crossway, 1981: 128–129; Perry Miller, *Nature's Nation*, Cambridge: Belknap Press, 1962: 110.
9. Curti, *Growth of American Thought:* 198; Bonomi, *Under the Cope of Heaven:* 5.
10. WJA 10: 45; JCC 1: 25–26.
11. WJA 10: 45; JCC 1: 25–26.
12. Curti, *Growth of American Thought:* 198; Gary T. Amos, *Defending the Declaration: How the Bible and Christianity Influenced the Writing of the Declaration of Independence*, Brentwood: Wolgemuth & Hyatt, 1989: 76–77; Bonomi, *Under the Cope of Heaven:* 189, 217; Katsh, *Biblical Heritage of Democracy:* 116; Schaeffer, *Christian Manifesto:* 127–129; Romans 1:20; Acts 5:29; Esther 4:14.
13. JCC 1: 25–26; WJA 10: 45; Psalm 35: 1–4.
14. WJA 6: 413; WSA 4: 349; Adams, *Book of Abigail and John:* 95; Bonomi, *Under the Cope of Heaven:* 209–212.
15. Frank Lambert, *The Founding Fathers and the Face of Religion in America*, Princeton: Princeton University Press, 2003: 263; DAB 11: 325–326.
16. Noll and Harlow, *Religion and American Politics:* 49; Amos, *Never Before in History:* 13, 22–23; George L. Hunt, *Calvinism and the Political Order*, Philadelphia: Westminster, 1965: 72–75; Samuel Rutherford, *Lex Rex or The Law and the Prince*, Edinburgh: Ogle, Oliver & Boyd, 1843: 82–83; Griffin, *Revolution and Religion:* 19; *Encyclopedia of the Reformed Faith*, edited by Donald McKim and David Wright, Louisville: Westminster–John Knox, 1992: 278; Heimert, *Religion and the American Mind:* 461.

17. Edwin Scott Gaustad and Mark Noll, *A Documentary History of Religion in America to 1877*, Grand Rapids: William B. Eerdmans, 1982: 221–222; Heimert, *Religion and the American Mind:* 395–396, 400; Miller, *American Puritans:* 83.
18. Griffin, *Revolution and Religion:* 29, 65; Jacob Isadore Mombert, *An Authentic History of Lancaster County, in the State of Pennsylvania*, Lancaster: Elias Barr, 1869: 247; *Papers of the American Society of Church History*, edited by Frederick William Loetscher, New York: G. P. Putnam's Sons, 1921: 6: 602; Heimert, *Religion and the American Mind:* 395–396, 555; *The Revolution of the People: Thoughts and Documents on the Revolutionary Process in North America 1774–1776*, edited by Herman Wellenreuther, Gottingen: Universitatsverlag Gottingen, 2006: 110–111.
19. John Chester Miller, *Origins of the American Revolution*, Stanford: Stanford University Press, 1943: 186; John Adolphus, *The History of England from the Accession of King George III to the Conclusion of Peace*, London: Cadel & Davis, 1802: 2: 108; Heimert, *Religion and the American Mind:* 398–400.
20. JCC: 1: 64–74; Smith, *John Adams* 1: 180–184; Pauline Maier, *American Scripture: Making the Declaration of Independence*, New York: Alfred A. Knopf, 1997: 3–5.
21. Davis, *Religion and the Continental Congress:* 71; Marston, *King and Congress:* 43–45; JCC 1:33.
22. Maier, *American Scripture:* 3–5; Middlekauf, *Glorious Cause:* 234–238; JCC 1: 64–67; JCC 1: 82–100.
23. JCC 1: 91–100.
24. Mumby, *George III:* 323–345, 357–358; Middlekauf, *Glorious Cause:* 262–265; Marston, *King and Congress:* 45–48; Brenaman, *A History of Virginia Conventions*, Richmond: J. L. Hill, 1902: 13; Frederick W. Sims, "Patrick Henry 1736–1799," *Library of Southern Literature*, edited by Edwin Alderman, Atlanta: Martin and Hoyt, 1907: 6: 2355.
25. Middlekauff, *Glorious Cause:* 268–272; Mumby, *George III:* 396–401; Fiske, *American Revolution:* 125–129; Trevelyan, *American Revolution* 1: 286–289; Malone, *Declaration of Independence:* 42–44.
26. Fiske, *American Revolution:* 125–129; Trevelyan, *American Revolution* 1: 286–289; Middlekauf, *Glorious Cause:* 268–272; *Spirit of Seventy-Six: The Story of the American Revolution as Told by Participants*, edited by Henry Steele Commager and Richard B. Morris, New York: DeCapa Publishing, 1975: 70–89.
27. Trevelyan, *American Revolution* 1: 286–289; Middlekauf, *Glorious Cause:* 268–272.
28. Paul Revere, "Letter of Paul Revere to Dr. Belknap," *Proceedings of the Massachusetts Historical Society*, edited by George Dexter, Boston: Wilson and Son, 1879: 371–374; Fiske, *American Revolution:* 125; Mumby, *George III:* 346; Smith, *John Adams* 1: 197; Adams, *Letters of John Adams:* 38; Hosmer, *Samuel Adams:* 330; John and Abigail Adams, *Adams Family Correspondence, December 1761–May 1776*, Cambridge: Harvard University Press, 1963: 192; *Historical*

Collections of Virginia, edited by Henry Howe, Charleston: William Babcock, 1852: 109.

CHAPTER 14: "THOU HAST BROUGHT A VINE OUT OF EGYPT"

1. JCC 2: 87–88, 192; Christ Church Vestry Minutes, 15 June 1775, Second Continental Congress File, Library and Archives, Independence National Historic Park; *Extracts from the Diary of Christopher Marshall*, edited by William Duane, New York: Ayer, 1969: 32; Benjamin Dorr, *A Historical Account of Christ Church, Philadelphia*, New York: Swords and Standford, 1841: 26–27.
2. JCC 2: 11–13; McCullough, *John Adams:* 110–111; Gilbert Chinard, *Thomas Jefferson: Apostle of Americanism*, Boston: Little and Brown, 1929: 5, 14–16; Charlene Mires, *Independence Hall in American Memory*, Philadelphia: University of Pennsylvania Press, 2002: 147; Leviticus 25:10.
3. JCC 2: 11–13; Malone, *Declaration of Independence:* 239–21; *Encyclopedia of American History:* 96–97.
4. JCC 2: 83–84, 91–93; Douglas Southall Freeman, *George Washington: A Biography*, New York: Charles Scribner's Sons, 1951: 3: 543; *Encyclopedia of American History:* 97.
5. Middlekauff, *Glorious Cause:* 274–278; Freeman, *George Washington:* 3: 458.
6. Marston, *King and Congress:* 59–60; *Encyclopedia of American History:* 99; JCC 2: 140–157.
7. *Encyclopedia of American History:* 99, JCC 2: 140–157.
8. JCC 2: 81, 87–88; Adams, *Book of Abigail and John:* 89–90.
9. *Extracts from the Diary of Christopher Marshall:* 32; Bonomi, *Under the Cope of Heaven:* 275–278; JCC 2: 88: Moses Coit Tyler, *The Literary History of the American Revolution*, New York: G. P. Putnam's Sons, 1897: 2: 284–285.
10. JCC 2: 192; DAB 5: 476–477; Wellenreuther, Gehrke and Strange, *Revolution of the People:* 110–112; Tyler, *Literary History of the American Revolution* 2: 284–286; David Jones, "A Defensive War in a Just Cause is Sinless," Philadelphia: Henry Miller, 1775: 1–2; George M. Curtis, "Meriden and Wallingford in Colonial and Revolutionary Days," *Papers of the New Haven Colony Historical Society*, New Haven: Tuttle, Morehouse and Taylor, 1908: 7: 313, 318.
11. JCC 2: 192; DAB 5: 476–477; James Darsey, *Prophetic Tradition and Radical Rhetoric in America*, New York: NYU Press, 1999: 47–48; Benjamin Dorr, *The American Vine*, Philadelphia: Collins, 1861: 6–11.
12. Darsey, *Prophetic Tradition and Radical Rhetoric:* 47–48; Dorr, *American Vine:* 6–11; DAB 5: 476–477.
13. JCC 2: 192; Adams, *Book of Abigail and John:* 89–90; DAB 1: 181–182; *Extracts from the Diary of Christopher Marshall:* 32.
14. Bonomi, *Under the Cope of Heaven:* 183–187, 214; Harry S. Stout, *The New England Soul: Preaching and Religious Culture in Colonial New England*, New York: Oxford University Press, 1986: 278; *Ecclesiastical Records of the State of New York*

4: 3907; John Wingate Thornton, *The Pulpit of the Revolution*, Boston: Lothrop, 1876: 227; Griffin, *Revolution and Religion:* 76; Proverbs 28:15.

15. Amos, *Never Before in History:* 13, 22–23; Hunt, *Calvinism and the Political Order:* 72–75; Rutherford, *Lex Rex:* 82–83; Griffin, *Revolution and Religion:* 19; *Encyclopedia of the Reformed Faith:* 278.
16. Bonomi, *Under the Cope of Heaven:* 183–187; Heimert, *Religion and the American Mind:* 400; Miller, *Nature's Nation:* 110; J. C. D. Clark, *The Language of Liberty: 1660–1832*, Cambridge: Cambridge University Press, 1994: 301.
17. JCC 2: 192–194; Malone, *Declaration of Independence:* 239–241; *Encyclopedia of American History:* 100; McCullough, *John Adams:* 85–87.
18. DAB 14: 159–160, 166; McCullough, *John Adams:* 108–109; 3: 423.
19. WJA 2: 508; Thomas Paine, *The Complete Writings of Thomas Paine*, edited by Philip S. Foner, New York: Citadel, 1969: 1: 41; Middlekauff, *Glorious Cause:* 317–319.
20. Maier, *American Scripture:* 32–33; Middlekauf, *Glorious Cause:* 318–319; Marston, *King and Congress:* 62; McCullough, *John Adams:* 96–97; Thomas Paine, *Common Sense*, Charleston: Forgotten Books, 2007: 55.
21. JCC 4: 208–209; DAB 11: 325–326.
22. JCC 4: 208–209.
23. Henry M. Ward, *The War for Independence and the Transformation of American Society*, London: Taylor & Francis, 1999: 15; David F. Hawke, *Midst of a Revolution*, Philadelphia: University of Pennsylvania Press, 1961: 133–136.
24. McCullough, *John Adams:* 118–119; Wells, *Life and Public Services of Samuel Adams* 2: 401; WJA 2: 490.
25. JCC 4: 397; JCC 5: 425–426; Thomas Jefferson, *The Papers of Thomas Jefferson*, edited by Julian T. Boyd, Princeton: Princeton University Press, 1950: 1: 298–309.
26. DAB 6: 117–120; WJA 9: 387; McCullough, *John Adams: 185;* Maier, *American Scripture:* 41–45; JCC 5: 425.

CHAPTER 15: "ENDOWED BY THEIR CREATOR"

1. JCC 5: 504–505, 510; WJA 10: 418, 420; Malone, *Story of the Declaration of Independence:* 210–211; McCullough, *John Adams:* 126.
2. JCC 5: 425–426; WJA 2: 314; Chinard, *Thomas Jefferson:* 8–9, 16–21; DAB 5: 18–19; WTJ 11: 393, 461; McCullough, *John Adams:* 119.
3. WJA 2: 8; DAB 10: 19; Munves, *Thomas Jefferson and the Declaration of Independence:* 1–8; Chinard, *Thomas Jefferson:* 69–78; Maier, *American Scripture:* 48, 174; Malone, *Declaration of Independence:* 70–71.
4. Chinard, *Thomas Jefferson:* 119, 131, 142, 152, 492, 593; WJA 2: 514; Munves, *Thomas Jefferson and the Declaration of Independence:* 26; DAB 10: 19; McCullough, *John Adams:* 131–132.
5. JCC 5: 504; WJA 1: 199, 9: 414; Munves, *Thomas Jefferson and the Declaration of Independence:* 26.

6. JCC 5: 504, 507; LDC 4: 352; DAB 5: 300; McCullough, *John Adams:* 126.
7. JCC 5: 504, 507; WJA 3: 58; McCullough, *John Adams:* 269; Malone, *Declaration of Independence:* 222–223.
8. JCC 5: 504, 507; WJA 3: 58; Maier, *American Scriptures:* 45; McCullough, *John Adams:* 127–128; Malone, *Declaration of Independence:* 51–52.
9. WJA 3: 58; DAB 5: 300; McCullough, *John Adams:* 127–128.
10. JCC 5: 506–507; LDC 4: 352; Smith, *John Adams:* 1: 267–268; McCullough, *John Adams:* 126–128; Malone, *Declaration of Independence:* 210.
11. DAB 20: 437; John Watson, *The Scot of the Eighteenth Century: His Religion and His Life*, London: Hodder and Stoughton, 1907: 15; James Lyburn, *The Scotch Irish*, Chapel Hill: University of North Carolina Press, 1962: 305.
12. JCC 5: 507; McCullough, *John Adams:* 128–129; Maier, *American Scripture:* 45; WJA 1: 232, 2: 513–514.
13. WTJ 1: 187–188, 266–269, 342–343, 345–346; WTJ 1: 314–315, 10: 187–188, 266–267, 341–342, 345–346; John Hazelton, *The Declaration of Independence: Its History*, New York: Dodd-Mead, 1906: 145; Maier, *American Scripture:* 148–149.
14. WJA 2: 514; WTJ 7: 304, 407; Carl L. Becker, *The Declaration of Independence*, New York: Harcourt, Brace, 1922: 19.
15. David Koepsell, "The United States Is Not a Christian Nation," *Secular Humanist Bulletin* 21: 2 (Summer 2005); Becker, *Declaration of Independence:* 74–75; WJA 2: 514; WTJ 7: 304, 407.
16. Chinard, *Thomas Jefferson:* 8–9, 16–21; DAB 5: 18–19; WTJ 11: 393.
17. WJA 4: 479; Chinard, *Thomas Jefferson:* 526–529; DAB 5: 18–19; Maier, *American Scripture:* 130–131, 159; Chinard, *Thomas Jefferson:* 86.
18. JCC 5: 517–518; John Wells, *Wells' National Handbook: Embracing Numerous Invaluable Documents Connected with the Political History of America*, New York: John G. Wells, 1857: 73; Davis, *Religion and the Continental Congress:* 138–139.
19. WJA 4: 479; Becker, *Declaration of Independence:* 25; WTJ 7: 305.
20. WJA 10: 45; WTJ 7: 305; Becker, *Declaration of Independence:* 26.
21. Thomas Jefferson, *The Works of Thomas Jefferson*, edited by Paul Leicester Ford, New York: Putnam's Sons, 1904: 11: 425; WTJ 7: 305; WJA 10: 45.
22. Chinard, *Thomas Jefferson:* 526–529; DAB 5: 18–19; Imogene E. Brown, *American Aristides: A Biography of George Wythe*, Rutherford: Farleigh Dickinson Press, 1981: 87; Amos, *Never Before in History:* 70; Edward Coke, *A Systematic Arrangement of Lord Coke's First Institute of the Laws of England*, edited by John Henry Thomas, London: R. H. Small, 1827: 466.
23. Waldron, *God, Locke and Equality:* 12; Locke, *The Works of John Locke* 2: 98; Worcester, *Religious Opinions of John Locke:* 69; John Locke, *An Essay Concerning Human Understanding and a Treatise on the Conduct of the Understanding*, Philadelphia: James Kay, 1852: 238; John Locke, *The Reasonableness of Christianity: As Delivered in the Scriptures*, edited by John C. Higgins-Biddle, New York: Oxford University Press, 1999: xx; Amos, *Never Before in History:* 128–130.

24. *British Moralists: Selections from Writers Principally of the Eighteenth Century*, edited by L. A. Selbe-Bigge, Oxford: Clarendon, 1897: 2: 314; William Blackstone, *Commentaries on the Laws of England*, edited by William Carey Jones, San Francisco: Bancroft-Whitney, 1916: 2: 2209; Blackstone, *Commentaries on the Laws of England* 1: 210.
25. JCC 5: 510–515; WTJ 7: 304, 407; Becker, *Declaration of Independence:* 32–33.
26. JCC 4: 497–498; JCC 5: 510–515; WJA 10:45; Munves, *Thomas Jefferson and the Declaration of Independence:* 45–50; Maier, *American Scripture:* 145–150.
27. Chinard, *Thomas Jefferson:* 131; Walter Isaacson, *Benjamin Franklin: An American Life*, New York: Simon & Schuster, 2003: 464; *Dictionary of Afro-American Slavery*, edited by Randall M. Miller and John David Smith, New York: Greenwood, 1988: 123–124, 470–471, 522–524, 528–532, 780–781; McCullough, *John Adams:* 131–134; Maier, *American Scripture:* 146–147, 197–200.
28. JCC 5: 510–515; MacDonald, *Select Charters and Other Documents:* 33–34; *The Puritans in America: A Narrative Anthology*, edited by Alan Heimert and Andrew Delbanco, Cambridge: Harvard University Press, 1985: 165; Arthur P. Monahan, *From Personal Duties Toward Personal Rights: Late Medieval and Early Modern Political Thought*, Georgetown: McGill-Queen's University Press, 1994: 214.
29. JCC 5: 510–515; Thornton, *Pulpit of the Revolution:* 43; Baldwin, *New England Clergy and the American Revolution:* 87; Heimert, *Religion and the American Mind:* 244.
30. JCC 5: 510–515; Maier, *American Scripture:* 145–150.
31. JCC 5: 510–515; Calvin, *Institutes of the Christian Religion* 4: 22, 32; Amos, *Never Before in History:* 13, 22–23; Hunt, *Calvinism and the Political Order:* 72–75; Rutherford, *Lex Rex:* 82–83; Griffin, *Revolution and Religion*: 19; *Encyclopedia of the Reformed Faith:* 278.
32. JCC 5: 510–515; Amos, *Never Before in History:* 140–141; Becker, *Declaration of Independence:* 22.
33. JCC 5: 510–515; Amos, *Never Before in History:* 140–141.
34. JCC 5: 510–515; *A Rising People:* 80–96; Benson J. Lossing, *Signers of the Declaration of Independence*, New York: George F. Cooledge, 1848: 47–49, 63–76, 87–89, 112–116, 130–132, 141–143, 178–179, 188–190, 201–203, 205–207, 212–226, 229–231; DAB 6: 523–524.
35. JCC 5: 515–516; LDC 2: 7–8; Hawke, *Midst of a Revolution:* 181; Maier, *American Scripture:* 156–157; *A Rising People:* 72–76; Malone, *Declaration of Independence:* 82–83; McCullough, *John Adams:* 137; Middlekauff, *Glorious Cause:* 328.
36. George Read to "Dear Sir," 22 August 1813, Second Continental Congress File; Wills, *Inventing America:* 339–344; "Delegates to Congress," Second Continental Congress File; McCullough, *John Adams:* 138; Malone, *Declaration of Independence:* 190–192; *Speeches and Addresses by the Most Eminent Orators of America*, edited by Frank Moore, New York: D. Appleton & Co., 1857:

324; George V. Bohman, *A Study in Pre-Revolutionary American Political Oratory*, Madison: University of Wisconsin Press, 1934: 2: 419.

37. *Speeches and Addresses:* 324; Bohman, *Study in Pre-Revolutionary American Political Oratory* 2: 419.
38. *Speeches and Addresses:* 324; Bohman, *Study in Pre-Revolutionary American Political Oratory* 2: 419.

BIBLIOGRAPHY

Abbott, Jacob. *Makers of History: Charles I.* New York: Harper & Brothers, Publishers, 1876.

Acton, A. W., G. W. Ward and Stanley Prothero. *Cambridge Modern History of the United States.* Cambridge: Cambridge University Press, 1970.

Adams, John. *The Letters of John Adams.* Charles Francis Adams, editor. Boston, Little, Brown and Company, 1841.

———. *The Works of John Adams: Second President of the United States.* Charles Francis Adams, editor. Boston: Little, Brown and Company, 1850.

Adams, John and Abigail. *The Book of Abigail and John: Selected Letters of the Adams Family, 1762–1784.* L. H. Butterfield, March Friedlaender, and Mary Jo Kline, editors. Cambridge: Harvard University Press, 1975.

Adams, Samuel. *The Writings of Samuel Adams.* Harry Alonzo Cushing, editor. New York: G. P. Putnam's, 1980.

Akers, Charles W. *Called Unto Liberty: A Life of Jonathan Mayhew, 1720–1766.* Cambridge: Harvard University Press, 1964.

Allen, Alexander. *Jonathan Edwards.* Boston: Houghton Mifflin, 1890.

Allen, John. *An Oration, Upon the Beauties of Liberty, or, The Essential Rights of the Americans.* Wilmington: James Adams, 1775.

American History Told by Contemporaries: Building of the Republic. Albert Bushnell Hart, editor. New York: Macmillan Company, 1910.

American Literature: From the Earliest Settlement to the Present Time. Edmund C. Stedman and Ellen M. Hutchinson, editors. New York: Jenkins & McCowan, 1888.

America's Founding Charters: Primary Documents of Colonial and Revolutionary Era Governance. Jon Wakelyn, editor. Westport: Greenwood Press, 2006.

Amos, Gary, and Richard Gardiner. *Never Before in History: America's Inspired Birth*. Dallas: Haughton Publishing Company, 1998.

Anderson, Christopher. *The Annals of the English Bible*. London: William Pickering, 1845.

Anderson, Fred. *Crucible of War: The Seven Years' War and the Face of Empire in British North America, 1754–1766*. New York: Alfred H. Knopf, 2000.

Andrews, Charles M. *Colonial Self-Government 1652–1689*. New York: Harper Brother Publishers, 1904.

Appleton's Cyclopaedia of American Biography. New York: D. Appleton & Company, 1889.

Archives of Maryland. Bernard C. Steiner, editor. Baltimore: William Dulany, 1904.

Arnold, Samuel Greene. *History of the State of Rhode Island and Providence Plantations*. New York; Appleton and Company, 1860.

Ashe, Samuel A. *History of North Carolina*. Greensboro: Charles Van Noppen, 1908.

Atwater, Edward. *History of the Colony of New Haven to its Absorption into Connecticut*. Boston: Rand, Avery, 1881.

Austin, Bill. *Austin's Topical History of Christianity*. Wheaton: Tyndale House, 1983.

Bacon, Edwin M. *The Connecticut River and the Valley of the Connecticut*. New York: G. P. Putnam's Sons, 1907.

Bagehot, Walter. *The English Constitution*. London: Paul, Trench & Trubner, 1902.

Baldwin, Alice Mary. *The New England Clergy and the American Revolution*. New York: Ungar Publishing, 1928.

Bancroft, George. *History of the Colonization of America*. New York: Julius Hart, 1886.

Barber, John Warner. *Connecticut Historical Collections*. New Haven: Durrie, Peck & Barber, 1836.

Baxter, Richard. *The Saints' Everlasting Rest*. New York: Lane & Scott, 1848.

Beach, Stewart. *John Adams: The Fateful Years, 1764–1776*. New York: Dodd-Mead, 1965.

Becker, Carl L. *The Declaration of Independence*. New York: Harcourt, Brace and Company, 1922.

Belknap, Jeremy. *The History of New Hampshire*. Dover: Stevens, Ela & Wadleigh, 1831.

Bellamy, Joseph. *The Works of Joseph Bellamy*. Tyron Edwards, editor. Boston: Doctrinal Tract & Books Society, 1853.

Boham, George V. *A Study in Pre-Revolutionary American Political Oratory*. Madison: University of Wisconsin, 1934.

Bonomi, Patricia U. *Under the Cope of Heaven: Religion, Society, and Politics in Colonial America*. New York: Oxford University Press, 1986.

Book of Days: A Miscellany of Popular Antiquities. R. Chambers, editor. Detroit: Gale Research, 1967.

Bourne, Henry R. *The Life of John Locke*. New York: Harper Brothers, 1876.

Bradford, William. *Bradford's History "Of Plimoth Plantation" from the Original Manuscript*. Boston: Wright & Potter, 1899.

———. *Bradford's History of Plymouth Plantation 1606–1646*. William T. Davis, editor. New York: Charles Scribner's, 1908.

Brand, John. *Observations on Popular Antiquities*. London: Chatto & Windus, 1900.

Braun, John. "Surplice." In *The Catholic Encyclopedia*, edited by Charles G. Herbermann. New York: University Knowledge Foundation, 1913.

Bremer, Francis J. *John Winthrop: America's Forgotten Founding Father*. New York: Oxford University Press, 2005.

Brenaman, J. N. *A History of Virginia Conventions*. Richmond: J. L. Hill, 1902.

Bridenbaugh, Carl. *Cities in Revolt: Urban Life in America 1743–1776*. New York: Capricorn Books, 1964.

———. *Mitre and Sceptre: Transatlantic Faith, Ideas, Personalities and Politics, 1689–1775*. New York: Oxford University Press, 1962.

———. *Seat of Empire: The Political Roles of 18th Century Williamsburg*. Williamsburg: Colonial Williamsburg Foundation, 1958.

Brinton, Crane, John B. Christopher and Robert Lee Wolfe. *A History of Civilization*. Englewood Cliffs, New Jersey: Prentice-Hall, 1955.

British Moralists: Selections from Writers Principally of the Eighteenth Century. L. A. Selbe-Bigge, editor. Oxford: Clarendon Press, 1897.

Brown, Alexander. *The Genesis of the United States*. Boston: Houghton Mifflin Company, 1890.

Brown, Imogene E. *American Aristides: A Biography of George Wythe*. Rutherford: Farleigh Dickinson Press, 1981.

Bruce, F. F. *The Books and the Parchments*. Westwood: Fleming H. Revell, 1963.

Buckingham, James S. *America: Historical, Statistical and Descriptive*. New York: Harper Brothers, 1841.

Burnett, Edmund Cody. *The Continental Congress*. New York: W. W. Norton, 1941.

Butler, Jon. *Awash in a Sea of Faith: Christianizing the American People*. Cambridge: Harvard University Press, 1990.

Byington, Ezra Hoyt. "Jonathan Edwards and the Great Awakening." *The Bibliotheca Sacra: A Religious and Sociological Quarterly*. Frederick Wright and Swift Holbrook, editors. Vol. 55.

———. *The Puritan as a Colonist and Reformer*. Boston: Little and Brown, 1899.

———. *The Puritans in England and New England*. Boston: Roberts Brothers, 1897.

Cabeen, Francis V. "The Society of the Sons of Tammany of Philadelphia," *Pennsylvania Magazine of History and Biography*, Vol. 25. Philadelphia: Historical Society of Pennsylvania, 1901.

The Calvert Papers. John Stockbridge, editor. Baltimore: Maryland Historical Society, 1889.

Calvin, John. *Calvin's Institutes*. Donald K. McKim, editor. Louisville: Westminster–John Knox, 2000.

———. *Institutes of the Christian Religion*. John Allen, editor. Philadelphia: Presbyterian Board of Publication, 1844.

Calvinism and the Political Order. George L. Hunt, editor. Philadelphia: Westminster Press, 1965.

Campbell, John. *Lives of the Lord Chancellors and Keepers of the Great Seal of England.* Jersey City: Frederick Linn, 1880.

Campbell, Norine Dickinson. *Patrick Henry: Patriot and Statesman.* Old Greenwich: Devin-Adair, 1969.

Carey, Patrick W. *Catholics in America: A History.* Westport: Praeger, 2004.

Carton, Charles. *Charles I: The Personal Monarch.* New York: Routledge Publishing, 1995.

The Catholic Encyclopedia. George Herbermann, editor. New York; Encyclopedia Press, 1910.

Channing, Edward. *A History of the United States.* New York: Macmillan, 1921.

Chase, Ellen. *The Beginnings of the American Revolution.* New York: Baker and Taylor, 1910.

Cheever, George B. *The Pilgrim Fathers.* London: Williams Collins, 1849.

Child, Frank Samuel. *The Colonial Parson of New England: A Picture.* New York: Baker & Taylor, 1896.

Childsey, Donald Barr. *The World of Samuel Adams.* Nashville: Thomas Nelson, 1974.

Chinard, Gilbert. *Thomas Jefferson: Apostle of Americanism.* Boston: Little & Brown, 1929.

Clark, George C. *Connecticut, Its People and Its Institutions.* New York: G. P. Putnam's Sons, 1914.

Classics of American Political and Constitutional Thought. Scott J. Hammond, editor. Indianapolis: Hackett Publishing, 2007.

Cockshott, Winifred. *The Pilgrim Fathers: Their Church and Colony.* New York; G. P. Putnam's Sons, 1909.

Coke, Edward. *A Systematic Arrangement of Lord Coke's First Institute of the Laws of England.* John Henry Thomas, editor. London: R. H. Small, 1827.

Cole, Nathan. "The Spiritual Travels of Nathan Cole." Michael J. Crawford, editor. *William and Mary Quarterly*, Vol. 33.

The Colonial Laws of New York from the Year 1664 to the Revolution. Charles Z. Lincoln, William H. Johnson, and Ansul J. Northrup, editors. Albany: J. B. Lyon, 1894.

Conant, Thomas J. *The Popular History of the Translations of the Holy Scriptures into the English Tongue.* New York: I. K. Funk, 1873.

Courvoisier, Jaques. *Zwingli: A Reformed Theologian.* Berkeley: University of California Press, 1963.

"Covenant of the Town of Salem." *Collections of the Massachusetts Historical Society.* Boston: Samuel Hall, 1798.

Cowling, Cedric B. *The Great Awakening and the American Revolution: Colonial Thought in the 18th Century.* Chicago: Rand McNally, 1971.

Cubberly, Ellwood. *Readings in the History of Education.* New York: Houghton Mifflin, 1920.

Curti, Merle. *The Growth of American Thought.* New York: Harper & Row, 1943.

Curtis, George M. "Meriden and Wallingford in Colonial and Revolutionary Days." *Papers of the New Haven Colony Historical Society.* New Haven: Tuttle, Morehouse and Taylor, 1908.

Curtis, George Ticknor. *Constitutional History of the United States.* New York: Harper & Brothers, 1889.

Curwen, Samuel. *Journals and Letters of the Late Samuel Curwen, Judge of Admiralty, An American Refugee in England, 1775–1784.* Waterbury: Bronson Press, 2007.

Cyclopaedia of American Literature. Edward and George Duyckinck, editors. New York: Charles Scribner, 1856.

Cyclopaedia of Biblical, Theological and Ecclesiastical Literature. John McLintock and James Strong, editors. New York; Harper and Brothers, 1891.

Darsey, James. *Prophetic Tradition and Radical Rhetoric in America.* New York: NYU Press, 1999.

David, Saul. "The Disorder Responsible for George III's 'Madness' Also Affected Many of His Descendants." London *Sunday Telegraph*, 19 July 1998.

Davies, Samuel. *The Curse of Cowardice: A Sermon Preached to the Militia of Hanover County, Virginia, at a General Muster, May 8, 1758.* London: Buckland, Ward & Field, 1758.

———. *The Sermons of the Rev. Samuel Davies.* Philadelphia: Presbyterian Board of Publication, 1864.

———. *Sermons on Important Subjects.* New York: Robert Carter and Brothers, 1854.

Davis, Derek H. *Religion and the Continental Congress 1774–1789.* New York: Oxford University Press, 2000.

Davis, John D. *A Dictionary of the Bible.* Philadelphia: Westminster Press, 1917.

Davis, Ozara S. *John Robinson: The Pilgrim Pastor.* New York: Pilgrim Press, 1903.

Demaus, R. *William Tyndale: A Biography.* London: Religious Tract Society, 1886.

Dictionary of Afro-American Slavery. Randall M. Miller and John David Smith, editors. New York: Greenwood Press, 1988.

Dictionary of American Biography. Allen Johnson and Dumas Malone, editors. New York: Charles Scribner's Sons, 1928–1936.

Dictionary of National Biography. Leslie Stephens and Sidney Lee, editors. London: Oxford University Press, 1921.

A Documentary History of Religion in America to 1877. Edwin S. Gaustad and Mark A. Noll, editors. Grand Rapids: William B. Eerdmans, 2003.

Dorchester, Daniel. *Christianity in the United States: From the First Settlement Down to the Present Time.* New York: Hunt & Eaton, 1895.

Dorr, Benjamin. *A Historical Account of Christ Church, Philadelphia.* New York: Swords and Standford, 1841.

———. *The American Vine.* Philadelphia: Collins Printer, 1861.

Douglas, James. *New England and New France: Contrasts and Parallels in Colonial History.* New York: G. P. Putnam's Sons, 1913.

Ecclesiastical Records of the State of New York. E. T. Corwin, editor. Albany: J. B. Lyon, 1905.

Edgar, Walter. *South Carolina: A History*. Columbia: University of South Carolina Press, 1998.

"Editor's Easy Chair." *Harper's New Monthly Magazine*, Volume 27.

Edwards, Jonathan. *Selected Sermons of Jonathan Edwards*. H. Norman Gardiner, editor. New York: Macmillan, 1904.

———. *Thoughts on the Revival of Religion in New England, 1740: To Which is Prefixed, "A Narrative of the Surprising Work of God in Northampton, Mass., 1736."* New York: American Tract Society, 1845.

———. *The Works of President Edwards*. New York: S. Converse, 1829.

Eerdman's History of Christianity. Tim Dowley, editor. Grand Rapids: William B. Eerdmans Publishing Company, 1977.

Egle, William. "Joseph Montgomery." *The Pennsylvania Magazine of History and Biography*, 1870.

Emerson, Everett. *American Literature: The Revolutionary Years, 1764–1789*. Madison: University of Wisconsin Press, 1977.

Encyclopedia of American History. Jeffrey B. Morris and Richard B. Morris, editors. New York: HarperCollins, 1996.

Encyclopedia Britannica. Hugh Chisholm, editor. Cambridge: University of Cambridge, 1911.

Encyclopedia of the Reformed Faith. Donald McKim and David Wright, editors. Louisville: Westminster–John Knox, 1992.

Encyclopedia of Religion and Ethics. John Hastings, editor. New York: Charles Scribner's Sons, 1919.

Encyclopedia of Religion in American Politics. Jeffrey Schultz, John West and Ian MacLean, editors. Abington: Greenwood, 1998.

Encyclopedia of Religious Freedom. Catherine Cookson, editor. New York: Routledge Publishing, 2003.

The English Statutes in Maryland. Bernard C. Steiner, editor. Baltimore: Johns Hopkins University Press, 1903.

Ernest, James. *Roger Williams: New England Firebrand*. New York: Macmillan, 1932.

Extracts from the Diary of Christopher Marshall. William Duane, editor. New York: Ayer, 1969.

A Faithful Account of the Processions and Ceremonies Observed in the Coronations of the Kings and Queens of England. Richard Thomson, editor. London: John Major, 1820.

Fallows, Samuel. *Samuel Adams: A Character Sketch*. Chicago: University Association, 1898.

Federal and State Constitutions, Colonial Charters and Organic Laws of the United States. Benjamin Perley Poore, editor. Washington: U.S. Government Printing Office, 1877.

Ferris, Robert G. *Signers of the Constitution: Historic Places Commemorating the*

Signing of the Constitution. Washington, D.C.: U.S. Department of the Interior, 1976.

Findling, John and Frank Thackery. *Events That Changed America in the Eighteenth Century*. Westport: Greenwood Publishing, 1998.

Finkelstein, Norman H. *American Jewish History*. New York: Jewish Publication Society, 2007.

Finlason, W. F. *History of the English Law: From the Time of the Romans to the End of the Reign of Elizabeth*. Philadelphia: M. Murphy, 1880.

"First Charter of Virginia, April 10, 1606." Avalon Project, Yale University School of Law. www.yale.edu/lawweb/avalon/states/va01.htm.

Fisher, George. *The Reformation*. New York: Scribner & Armstrong, 1873.

Fisher, Philip. "Early Christian Missions Among the Indians of Maryland," *Maryland Historical Magazine*, Vol. 1 (March 1906).

Fiske, John. *The American Revolution*. Boston: Houghton Mifflin, 1919.

Flynn, John Stephen. *The Influence of Puritanism on the Political and Religious Thought of the English*. New York: E. P. Dutton, 1920.

Foote, William Henry. *Sketches of Virginia, Historical and Biographical*. Philadelphia: William S. Martien, 1850.

For the Colony in Virginea Britannia, Lawes Divine, Morall and Martiall. London: Walter Burre, 1612.

Ford, Daniel J. *In the Name of God, Amen: Rediscovering Biblical and Historical Covenants*. St. Louis: Lex Rex, 2003.

Fortesque, John William. *The Correspondence of King George the Third from 1760 through December 1783*. New York: Macmillan, 1927.

Fowler, William C. "Local Law in Massachusetts, Historically Considered." *The New England Historical and Genealogical Register*, Vol. 5.

Franklin, Benjamin. *The Autobiography of Benjamin Franklin*. New York: Henry Holt, 1916.

———. *Memoirs of Benjamin Franklin*. William Templeton Franklin, editor. New York: Derby & Jackson, 1859.

Freeman, Douglas Southall. *George Washington: A Biography*. New York: Charles Scribner's Sons, 1951.

Friedenberg, Albert M. "The Jews of New Jersey from the Earliest Times to 1850." *Publications of the American Jewish Historical Society*. Baltimore: Lord Baltimore, 1909.

Frothingham, Richard. *History of the Siege of Boston*. Boston: Little & Brown, 1873.

"Fundamental Agreement, or Original Constitution of the Colony of New Haven, June 4, 1639," The Avalon Project Website. Yale University School of Law. www.yale.edu/lawweb/avalon/avalon.htm.

"Fundamental Constitution of Carolina." *Statutes at Large of South Carolina*. Thomas Cooper, editor. Columbia: A. S. Johnson, 1886.

"Fundamental Orders of Connecticut." *The Federal and State Constitutions, Colonial Charters, and Other Organic Laws of the States, Territories and Colonies Now or*

Heretofore Forming the United States of America. Benjamin P. Poore, editor. Washington: U.S. Government Printing Office, 1877.

Galloway, Charles B. *Christianity and the American Commonwealth.* Nashville: Methodist Episcopal Publishing House, 1898.

Gardiner, Harry N. and Alexander Allen. *Jonathan Edwards: A Retrospect.* Boston: Houghton Mifflin, 1901.

Gardiner, Samuel R. *History of the Great Civil War, 1642–1649.* London: Longmans, Green, 1901.

Gaustad, Edwin S. *Roger Williams.* New York: Oxford University Press, 2005.

Gaustad, Edwin, and Leigh Schmidt. *The Religious History of America.* San Francisco: HarperCollins, 2002.

Geisler, Norman L. and William E. Nix. *A General Introduction to the Bible.* Chicago: Moody, 1986.

Gillies, John. *Historical Collections Relating to Remarkable Periods of the Success of the Gospel.* London: James Nesbit, 1845.

———. *Memoirs of George Whitefield.* Hartford: Hunt & Son, 1853.

Gledstone, James P. *George Whitefield: Field Preacher.* Boston: American Tract Society, 1901.

Gorton, Adelos. *The Life and Times of Samuel Gorton.* Philadelphia: George S. Ferguson, 1907.

Graham, James. *History of the United States of North America.* Boston: Little & Brown, 1845.

Grant, Neil. *Kings & Queens.* Glasgow: HarperCollins, 1996.

Gray, Ellis. "The Father of the Revolution." *Harper's New Monthly Magazine.* Vol. 3, June–November 1876.

Green, Evarts B. *The American Nation: A History.* New York: Harper Brothers, 1905.

Green, Harry Clinton. *The Pioneer Mothers of America.* New York: G. P. Putnam's Sons, 1912.

Green, John Richard. *England.* New York: Peter Collier, 1898.

———. *History of the English People.* London: Macmillan, 1885.

Greene, George Washington. *A Short History of Rhode Island.* Providence: J. R. Reid, 1877.

Gregory, James. *Puritanism in the Old World and in the New.* New York: Fleming H. Revell, 1896.

Griffin, Keith L. *Revolution and Religion: The American Revolutionary War and the Reformed Clergy.* New York: Paragon, 1994.

Griffin, Martin Ignatius. *Catholics and the American Revolution.* Cambridge: Harvard University Press, 1902.

Griffith, Lucille Blanche. *The Virginia House of Burgesses.* Tuscaloosa: University of Alabama Press, 1970.

Grizzard, Frank E. and D. Boyd Smith, *Jamestown Colony: A Political, Social and Cultural History.* Santa Barbara: ABC-Clio, 2007.

Gronniosaw, James A. *A Narrative of the Most Remarkable Particulars in the Life of*

James Albert Ukawasaw Gronniosaw, An African Prince. Bath: S. Hazzard, 1770.

Hall, David W. *The Genevan Reformation and the American Founding*. Lanham: Lexington Books, 2003.

Hart, Benjamin. *Faith & Freedom: The Roots of Liberty in America*. La Vergne: Spring Arbor, 1988.

Hawke, David F. *Midst of a Revolution*. Philadelphia: University of Pennsylvania Press, 1961.

Hayes, Kevin J. *The Road to Monticello: The Life and Times of Thomas Jefferson*. New York: Oxford University Press, 2008.

Healey, Michael. "Americans Don't Know Civics." *USA Today*. 21 November 2008.

Heimert, Alan. *Religion and the American Mind: From the Great Awakening to the Revolution*. Cambridge: Harvard University Press, 1966.

Henry, William Wirt. *Patrick Henry: Life, Correspondence and Speeches*. New York: Charles Scribner's Sons, 1891.

Hewes, George R. *A Retrospect of the Boston Tea Party*. New York: S. S. Bliss, 1834.

Hibbert, Christopher. *George III: A Personal History*. New York: Basic Books, 1998.

———. *Tower of London*. New York: Newsweek Books, 1971.

Higginson, Francis. *New Englands Plantation: A Short and True History of the Commodities and Discommodities of that Country*. London: Michael Sparke, 1680.

Hill, Hamilton Andrew. *History of the Old South Church, 1669–1884*. Boston: Houghton Mifflin, 1890.

History of New Jersey from its Earliest Settlement to the Present Time. W. H. Carpenter and T. S. Arthur, editors. Philadelphia: Lippincott, 1856.

Hodgkin, Thomas. *George Fox*. Boston: Houghton, Mifflin, 1898.

Holifield, E. Brooks. *God's Ambassadors: A History of the Christian Clergy in America*. Eerdmans Publishing, 2007.

Holmes, Abiel. *The Annals of America*. Cambridge: Hilliard & Brown, 1829.

The Holy Bible: Containing the Old and New Testaments; Translated Out of the Original Tongues. Authorized Version. New York: American Bible Society, 1865.

Hook, Walter F. *Lives of the Archbishops of Canterbury*. London: Bentley & Son, 1884.

Hosmer, James K. *The Life of Thomas Hutchinson, Royal Governor of the Province of Massachusetts Bay*. Boston: Houghton Mifflin, 1896.

———. *Samuel Adams*. Boston: Houghton Mifflin, 1913.

Howard, George Elliot. *Preliminaries of the American Revolution, 1763–1775*. New York: Harper & Brothers, 1905.

The Humble Request of His Majesties Loyall Subjects, the Governor and the Company Late Gone for New England. London: John Bellamie, 1630.

Hunt, George L. *Calvinism and the Political Order*. Philadelphia: Westminster, 1965.

Hutson, James H. *Forgotten Features of the Founding: The Recovery of Religious Themes in the Early American Republic*. Lanham: Lexington Books, 2003.

Janney, Samuel M. *The Life of William Penn.* Philadelphia: Lippencott, Grambo, 1852.

Jefferson, Thomas. *The Papers of Thomas Jefferson.* Julian T. Boyd, editor. Princeton: Princeton University Press, 1950.

———. *The Works of Thomas Jefferson.* Paul L. Ford, editor. New York: G. P. Putnam's Sons, 1905.

———. *The Writings of Thomas Jefferson.* Paul L. Ford, editor. New York: G. P. Putnam's Sons, 1892.

Jenyns, Soame. *View of the Internal Evidence of the Christian Religion.* London: J. Dodsley, 1776.

"John Jay." John Jay Institute for Faith, Society and Law website. www.johnjay institute.org.

Johnson, Edward. *Wonder Working Providence: Sion's Saviour in New England.* Andover: Warren F. Draper, 1867.

Johnson, Samuel. *Samuel Johnson: His Career and Writings.* Herbert and Carol Schneider, editors. New York: Columbia University Press, 1929.

"Jonathan Edwards." Microsoft Encarta Online Encyclopedia, 2009.

Jones, Charles. *The History of Georgia.* Boston: Houghton Mifflin, 1883.

Jones, Jenkin Loyd. "Civil and Religious Liberty." *Encyclopedia America,* 1904.

Jones, Rufus. *The Quakers in the American Colonies.* London: Macmillan, 1923.

Journals of the Continental Congress, 1774–1789. Worthington C. Ford, editor. Washington: U.S. Government Printing Office, 1906.

Katsh, Abraham Isaac. *The Biblical Heritage of Democracy.* Jersey City: KTAV, 1977.

Kelley, Robert Lloyd. *Transatlantic Persuasion: The Liberal-Democratic Mind in the Age of Gladstone.* New York: Alfred A. Knopf, 1969.

Kelly, Douglas F. *The Emergence of Liberty in the Modern World.* Phillipsburg: Presbyterian and Reformed, 1992.

Kenyon, John Philips. *A Dictionary of British History.* New York: Stein and Day, 1983.

Keopsell, David. "The United States is Not a Christian Nation." *Secular Humanist Bulletin,* Vol. 21, No. 2 (Summer 2005).

Kidd, Thomas S. *The Great Awakening: The Roots of Evangelical Christianity in Colonial America.* New Haven: Yale University Press, 2007.

King, William. "Lord Baltimore and His Freedom in Granting Religious Toleration." *Records of the American Catholic Historical Society of Philadelphia.* Philadelphia: American Catholic Historical Society, 1921.

Knowles, James D. *Memoir of Roger Williams Founder of the State of Rhode Island.* Boston: Lincoln, Edmands, 1834.

Kooi, Christine. *Liberty and Religion: Church and State in Reformation Leiden.* Boston: Brill Publishing, 2000.

Kunz, George Frederick. *The Hall of Fame.* New York: New York University Press, 1908.

Labaree, Benjamin Woods. *The Boston Tea Party.* New York: Oxford University Press, 1964.

Lambert, Frank. *The Founding Fathers and the Face of Religion in America.* Princeton: Princeton University Press, 2003.

———. *Pedlar in Divinity: George Whitefield and the Trans-Atlantic Revival.* Princeton: Princeton University Press, 2002.

"Letters from William and Mary College, 1798–1801." *The Virginia Magazine of History and Biography.* Vol. 29.

Letters of Delegates to Congress, 1774–1789. Paul H. Smith, editor. Washington: Library of Congress, 1976–2000.

Letters of Members of the Continental Congress, Edmund C. Burnett, editor. Washington, D.C.: Carnegie Institute, 1921–1936.

Levermore, Charles H. *The Republic of New Haven.* Johns Hopkins University, 1886.

Liberty Documents. Albert Bushnell Hart and Mabel Hill, editors. New York: Longmans, Green, 1903.

Lindsey, Thomas. *A History of the Reformation.* New York: Charles Scribner's Sons, 1906.

Locke, John. *The Reasonableness of Christianity: As Delivered in the Scriptures.* John C. Higgins-Biddle, editor. New York: Oxford University Press, 1999.

———. *The Works of John Locke.* London: C. & J. Rivington, 1823.

Lossing, Benson J. *The American Historical Record.* Philadelphia: John E. Potter, 1874.

———. *Signers of the Declaration of Independence.* New York: George F. Cooledge, 1848.

Luther, Martin. *The Works of Martin Luther.* Adolph Spaeth, L. D. Reed and Henry Jacobs, editors. Philadelphia: J. Holman, 1915.

Lyburn, James. *The Scotch Irish.* Chapel Hill: University of North Carolina Press, 1962.

Macaulay, Thomas B. *Lord Macaulay's Essays.* London: George Routledge, 1892.

Mackintosh, James. *History of England.* London: Longman & Taylor, 1835.

Macy, Jesse. *The English Constitution: A Commentary on Its Nature and Growth.* London: Macmillan, 1897.

Magoun, George. "The Source of American Education—Popular and Religious." *The New Englander and Yale Review.* Vol. 36. New Haven: W. L. Kingsley, 1877.

Mahaffey, Jerome. *Preaching Politics: The Religious Rhetoric of George Whitefield and the Founding of a New Nation.* Waco: Baylor University Press, 2007.

Maier, Pauline. *American Scripture: Making the Declaration of Independence.* New York: Alfred A. Knopf, 1997.

Making the Nonprofit Sector in the United States. David Hammack, editor. Bloomington: University of Indiana Press, 2000.

Malone, Dumas. *The Story of the Declaration of Independence.* New York: Oxford University Press, 1954.

Marston, Jerrilyn Green. *King and Congress: The Transfer of Political Legitimacy, 1774–1776.* Princeton: Princeton University Press, 1987.

Mather, Cotton. *A Christian at His Calling*. Boston: B. Green & J. Allen, 1701.

Mathinsen, Robert. *Critical Issues in American Religious History: A Reader.* Waco: Baylor University Press, 2006.

Matthews, Chris. "A Proud Bronx Attraction Continues to Struggle." *Mount Hope Monitor.* 5 April 2008.

Mayer, Henry. *A Son of Thunder: Patrick Henry and the American Republic.* New York: Grove Press, 2001.

"Mayflower Compact, 1620." Avalon Project Website, Yale University School of Law. http://www.yale.edu/lawweb/avalon/amerdoc/mayflower.htm.

Mayhew, Jonathan. *A Discourse Concerning Unlimited Submission and Non-Resistance to the Higher Powers.* Boston: D. Fowle, 1750.

McCullough, David. *John Adams.* New York: Simon & Schuster, 2001.

McKechnie, William Sharp. *The Magna Carta: A Commentary on the Great Charter of King John.* New York: Burt Franklin, 1914.

Means, Oliver William. *A Sketch of the Strict Congregational Church of Enfield, Connecticut.* Boston: Harvard Seminary, 1899.

Melville, Lewis. *Farmer George.* London: Pittman & Sons, 1907.

Mereness, Newton D. *Maryland as a Proprietary Colony.* New York: Macmillan, 1901.

Middlekauf, Robert. *The Glorious Cause: The American Revolution 1763–1789.* New York: Oxford University Press, 1982.

Miller, John Chester. *Origins of the American Revolution.* London: Oxford University Press, 1962.

Miller, Perry. *The American Puritans: Their Prose and Poetry.* New York: Columbia University Press, 1982.

———. *Errand into the Wilderness.* Cambridge: Harvard University Press, 1956.

———. *Nature's Nation,* Cambridge: Belknap Press, 1962.

———. *The New England Mind: From Colony to Province.* Cambridge: Harvard University Press, 1983.

———. *The New England Mind: The Seventeenth Century.* New York: Macmillan, 1939.

———. *Roger Williams: His Contribution to the American Tradition.* Indianapolis: Bobbs-Merrill, 1953.

Miller, Perry and Thomas H. Johnson. *The Puritans: A Sourcebook of Their Writings.* New York: Harper & Row, 1963.

Mires, Charlene. *Independence Hall in American Memory.* Philadelphia: University of Pennsylvania Press, 2002.

Mode, Peter G. *Sourcebook and Bibliographical Guide for American Church History.* Menasha: The Collegiate Press, 1921.

Mombert, Jacob Isadore. *An Authentic History of Lancaster County, in the State of Pennsylvania.* Lancaster: Elias Barr, 1869.

Monahan, Arthur P. *From Personal Duties Toward Personal Rights: Late Medieval and Early Modern Political Thought.* Georgetown: McGill-Queen's University Press, 1994.

Moore, Frank. *Patriot Preachers of the American Revolution.* New York: Charles T. Evans, 1852.

Morison, Samuel Eliot. *The Oxford History of the American People.* New York: Oxford University Press, 1965.

Morse, John T. *John Adams.* Boston: Houghton Mifflin, 1888.

Morton, Nathaniel. *New England's Memorial.* Boston: Congregational Board of Publication, 1855.

Mourt's Relation Or Journal of the Plantation at Plymouth. Henry Martyn Dexter, editor. Boston: John Kimball Wiggin, 1865.

Mumby, Frank Arthur. *George III and the American Revolution.* London, Constable and Co., 1924.

Munroe, John A. *History of Delaware.* Dover: University of Delaware Press, 2006.

Munves, James. *Thomas Jefferson and the Declaration of Independence.* New York: Charles Scribner's Sons, 1978.

Music in American Society, 1776–1976. George McCue, editor. Milano: Hoepli Editore, 1976.

Narratives of Early Maryland, 1633–1684. Clayton Coleman Hall, editor. New York: Charles Scribner's Sons, 1910.

Neal, Daniel. *The History of the Puritans or Protestant Non-Conformists.* Boston: Charles Ewer, 1817.

Neil, Edward D. "Rev. Jacob Duché: First Chaplain of Congress," *The Pennsylvania Magazine of History and Biography,* 2. Philadelphia: Historical Society of Philadelphia, 1878.

Neilson, George. "Drawing, Hanging and Quartering." *Notes and Queries.* 15 August 1891.

New Dictionary of British History. S. H. Steinberg, editor. New York: St. Martin's, 1963.

The New England Primer: A History of Its Origin and Development. Paul Leicester Ford, editor. New York: Dodd, Mead, 1897.

New Webster Dictionary of Liturgy. Paul Bradshaw, editor. Louisville: John Knox, 2002.

Newling, Dan. "Did George III's Powdered Wig Send Him Mad?" London *Daily Mail,* 15 July 2004.

Noble, Frederick A. *The Pilgrims.* Boston: Pilgrim, 1907.

Noll, Mark A. *A History of Christianity in the United States and Canada.* Grand Rapids: William B. Eerdmans, 1992.

Noll, Mark A. and Luke E. Harlow. *Religion and American Politics: From the Colonial Period to the Present.* New York: Oxford University Press, 2007.

O'Gorman, Thomas. *A History of the Roman Catholic Church in America.* New York: Christian Literature, 1894.

Oxford Dictionary of the Christian Church. F. L. Cross, editor. New York: Oxford University Press, 1997.

Oxford Encyclopedia of the Reformation. Hans J. Hillerbrand, editor. New York: Oxford University Press, 1996.

Palfrey, John Gorham. *History of New England.* Boston: Little, Brown, 1899.

Papers of the American Society of Church History. Frederick William Loetscher, editor. New York: G. P. Putnam's Sons, 1921.

Parmalee, Prentice E. "The New Opportunity of the Small College." *Harper's New Monthly Magazine,* Vol. 123.

Parrington, Vernon L. *The Colonial Mind, 1620–1800.* New York: Harcourt, Brace and World, 1927.

Penn, William. *No Cross, No Crown.* London: Society of Friends, 1896.

———. *The Select Works of William Penn.* Deborah Logan and Edward Armstrong, editors. London: James Phillips, 1782.

Percy, George. "'A Trewe Relacyon'—Virginia from 1609–1612," *Tyler's Historical and Genealogical Magazine.* Leon G. Tyler, editor, 1922.

"The Pilgrim Fathers." *The Westminster and Foreign Quarterly Review.* London: Trubner, 1871.

Pratt, Walter E. "New Haven Colony's Fundamental Articles, 1639." *Religion and American Law: An Encyclopedia.* Paul Finkelman, editor. New York: Garland, 2000.

Price, Ira Maurice. *The Ancestry of Our English Bible: An Account of Manuscripts, Texts and Versions of the Bible.* New York: Harper & Brothers Publishers, 1956.

Prince, Thomas. *A Chronological History of New England.* Boston: Kneeland & Green, 1826.

Principles and Acts of the Revolution in America. Hezekiah Niles, editor. New York: A. S. Barnes, 1876.

The Pulpit of the American Revolution: Political Sermons of the Period of 1776. John W. Thornton, editor. Boston: D. Lothrop, 1876.

Puls, John. *Samuel Adams: Father of the American Revolution.* New York: Palgrave McMillan, 2006.

Puritans and Puritanism in Europe and America: A Comprehensive Encyclopedia. Francis J. Bremer and Tom Webster, editors. Santa Barbara: Clio, 2006.

The Puritans in America: A Narrative Anthology. Alan Heimert and Andrew Delbanco, editors. Cambridge: Harvard University Press, 1985.

Ragsdale, Bruce A. *A Planter's Republic: The Search for Economic Independence in Revolutionary Virginia.* Lanham: Rowman and Littlefield, 1996.

Ramsay, David. *The History of South Carolina: From Its First Settlement in 1670 to the Year 1808.* Newberry: W. J. Duffie, 1858.

Records of the Colony or Jurisdiction of New Haven. Charles J. Hoadley, editor. New Haven: Case, Lockwood, 1858.

"Records of the Virginia Company." Thomas Jefferson Papers. Washington, D.C.: Manuscript Division, Library of Congress.

Reichley, James. *Faith in Politics.* Washington: Brookings Institution, 2002.

Revere, Paul. "Letter of Paul Revere to Dr. Belknap." *Proceedings of the Massachusetts Historical Society,* George Dexter, editor. Boston: Wilson and Son, 1879.

The Revolution of the People: Thoughts and Documents on the Revolutionary Process in North America, 1774–1776. Herman Wellenreuther, editor. Göttingen: Universitatsverlag Göttingen, 2006.

Rhode Island Historical Society Collections. Providence: Knowles and Vose, 1843.

Richards, Larry. *The Dictionary of Basic Bible Truths.* Grand Rapids: Zondervan Publishing, 1987.

A Rising People: The Founding of the United States, 1765–1789. Philadelphia: American Philosophical Society, 1976.

Rogers, Robert. *Diary of the Siege of Detroit in the War with Pontiac.* Franklin B. Hough, editor. Albany: J. Munsell, 1860.

Rossiter, Clinton. *1787: The Grand Convention.* New York: Macmillan, 1966.

———. *Seedtime of the Republic: The Origin of the American Tradition of Political Liberty.* New York: Harcourt Brace Jovanovich, 1953.

Rowland, Kate Mason. *The Life of George Mason, 1725–1792.* New York: G. P. Putnam's Sons, 1892.

Rutherford, Samuel. *Lex Rex or The Law and the Prince.* Edinburgh: Ogle, Oliver & Boyd, 1843.

Ryken, Lyland. *Worldly Saints: The Puritans as they Really Were.* Grand Rapids: Zondervan, 1991.

Sarna, Jonathan. *American Judaism: A History.* New Haven: Yale University Press, 2003.

Sawyer, Henry E. "Public Schools in Connecticut." *Education: An International Magazine,* Vol. 4.

"Scala Santa Chapel: Under Soot and Grime, a Visual Treasure." Catholic News Service, 15 June 2007.

Schaeffer, Francis. *A Christian Manifesto.* Wheaton: Crossway, 1981.

———. *How Should We Then Live?: The Rise and Decline of Western Thought and Culture.* Wheaton: Crossway, 1985.

Scharf, J. Thomas. *A History of Maryland from the Earliest Period to the Present Day.* Baltimore: John Piet, 1879.

Schwartz, Bernard. *The Great Rights of Mankind: A History of the American Bill of Rights.* Lanham, Maryland: Rowman & Littlefield, 1991.

Scott, James Brown. *The United States: A Study in International Organization.* New York: Oxford University Press, 1926.

Second Continental Congress File. Library and Archives. Independence National Historic Park.

Select Charters and Other Documents of American History. William McDonald, editor. New York: Macmillan, 1899.

Shaff, Philip. *History of the Christian Church.* New York: Charles Scribner's Sons, 1910.

Sharples, Isaac. "William Penn." *Encyclopedia Americana,* 1919.

Shi, David E. *The Simple Life: Plain Living and High Thinking in American Culture.* Athens: University of Georgia Press, 2007.

Sibbes, Richard. *The Complete Works of John Richard Sibbes.* John Allen, editor. Edinburgh: James Nichols, 1893.

Sims, Frederick W. "Patrick Henry 1736–1799." *Library of Southern Literature.* Edwin Alderman, editor. Atlanta: Martin and Hoyt, 1907.

Sivan, Gabriel. *The Bible and Civilization.* Jerusalem: Keter, 1973.

Smith, C. Ernest. *Religion Under the Barons of Baltimore.* Baltimore: Allen Lycett, 1899.

Smith, Helen Ainslee. *The Thirteen Colonies.* New York: G. P. Putnam's Sons, 1901.

Smith, John. *The Generall Historie of Virginia, New England and the Summer Isles.* New York: Macmillan, 1907.

Smith, John. *Travels and Works of Captain John Smith, President of Virginia and Admiral of New England, 1580-1631,* Edward Arber, editor. Edinburgh: John Grant, 1910.

Smith, Samuel. *History of the Colony of New Jersey.* Orangeburg, S.C.: Reprint Company, 1966.

Smith, William. *History of the First Discovery and Settlement of Virginia.* New York: Joseph Sabin, 1865.

Smylie, James H. *A Brief History of the Presbyterians.* Louisville: Geneva Press, 1996.

Solberg, Winton U. *Redeem the Time: The Puritan Sabbath in Early America.* Cambridge: Harvard University Press, 1977.

The South Carolina Encyclopedia. Walter Edgar, editor. Columbia: University of South Carolina Press, 2006.

Speeches and Addresses by the Most Eminent Orators of America. Frank Moore, editor. New York: D. Appleton, 1857.

Spirit of Seventy-Six: The Story of the American Revolution as Told by Participants. Henry Steele Commager and Richard B. Morris, editors. New York: De Capa, 1975.

Spurgeon, Charles. "Scala Santa." *Sword and Trowel.* January, 1874.

Starkey, Marion Lena. *The Congregational Way: The Role of the Pilgrims and Their Heirs in Shaping America.* New York: Doubleday, 1966.

Statutes at Large of South Carolina. Thomas Cooper, editor. Columbia: A. S. Johnson, 1886.

Stout, Harry S. *The New England Soul: Preaching and Religious Culture in Colonial New England.* New York: Oxford University Press, 1986.

Stowell, William Henry. *History of the Puritans in England.* London: Thomas Nelson, 1878.

Thackeray, William Makepeace. *The Four Georges: Sketches of Manners, Morals, Court and Town Life.* London: John Long, 1905.

Thornton, John Wingate. *The Pulpit of the American Revolution.* Boston: Gould & Lincoln, 1860.

Thorpe, Francis Newton. *The Federal and State Constitutions, Colonial Charters, and Other Organic Laws of the States, Territories and Colonies Now or Heretofore Forming the United States of America.* Washington: U.S. Government Printing Office, 1877.

Tocqueville de, Alexis. *Democracy in America.* New York: Appleton & Company, 1904.

"Topics in U.S. History." *Up Close and Personal.* 10 December 2008.

Tracy, Joseph. *The Great Awakening: A History of the Revival of Religion in the Time of Edwards and Whitefield.* Boston: Charles Tappan, 1845.

Travels and Works of Captain John Smith, President of Virginia and Admiral of New England, 1580–1631, Edward Arber, editor. Edinburgh: John Grant, 1910.

Trevelyan, George Otto. *The American Revolution.* New York: Longmans, Green, 1915.

Trumbell, Benjamin. *A General History of the United States of America.* New York: Williams and Whiting, 1810.

Tuttle, Charles W. *Captain John Mason.* Boston: Prince Society, 1877.

Tyler, Moses Coit. *The Literary History of the American Revolution, 1763–1783.* New York: G. P. Putnam's Sons, 1897.

———. *Patrick Henry.* Boston: Houghton Mifflin, 1897.

Usher, Roland G. *The Pilgrims and Their History.* New York: Macmillan, 1918.

Van Tyne, Claude H. *The American Nation: A History.* New York: Harper & Brothers, 1905.

———. "Influence of the Clergy and of Religious and Sectarian Forces on the American Revolution," *American Historical Review*, Vol. 9, No. 1, October 1913.

Ver Steeg, Clarence L. *The Formative Years 1607–1763.* New York: Hill and Wang, 1965.

Vinen, Richard. *A History in Fragments: Europe in the 20th Century.* New York: De Capo Press, 2001.

Waldron, Jeremy. *God, Locke and Equality: Christian Foundations in Locke's Political Thought.* New York: Cambridge University Press, 2002.

Waller, George McGregor. *Puritanism in Early America.* Lexington: D. C. Heath, 1953.

Ward, Henry M. *The War for Independence and the Transformation of American Society.* London: Taylor & Francis, 1999.

Watson, John. *The Scot of the Eighteenth Century: His Religion and His Life.* London: Hodder and Stoughton, 1907.

Wegener, G. S. *6,000 Years of the Bible.* New York: Harper & Brothers, 1963.

Wells, John. *Wells' National Handbook: Embracing Numerous Invaluable Documents Connected with the Political History of America.* New York: John G. Wells, 1857.

Wells, William V. *The Life and Public Service of Samuel Adams.* Boston: Little & Brown, 1865.

West, Willis Mason. *The Story of American Democracy.* Boston: Allyn and Bacon, 1922.

Whitefield, George. *The Works of the Reverend George Whitefield.* John Gillies, editor. London: Dilly, Kincaid & Creech, 1871.

Williams, Roger. *The Bloudy Tenent of Persecution for Cause and Conscience Discussed and Mr. Cotton's Letter Examined and Answered.* Whitefish: Kessinger Publishing, 2004.

———. "Roger Williams: A Warning to Endicott." *A Library of American Literature: From the Earliest Settlement to the Present Time.* Edmund Clarence

Stedman and Ellen Mackay Hutchinson, editors. New York: Charles Webster, 1889.

Wineke, William R. "Modern Medicine Studies the Madness of King George." *Wisconsin State Journal*, 15 April 1996.

Winslow, Edward. *Good News from New England: A True Relations of Things Very Remarkable at the Plantation of Plymouth in New England.* London: William Bladen and John Bellamie, 1624.

Winthrop, John. *Life and Letters of John Winthrop.* Robert C. Winthrop, editor. Boston: Little & Brown, 1869.

———. "Model of Christian Charity by Gov. Winthrop." *Collections of the Massachusetts Historical Society.* Boston: Little & Brown, 1838.

Wirt, William. *Sketches of the Life and Character of Patrick Henry.* New York: McElrath and Bangs, 1832.

Wolf, Naomi. "Don't Know Much About History." *Washington Post*, 25 November 2007.

Woodmason, Charles. *The Carolina Backcountry on the Eve of the Revolution: The Journal and Other Writings of Charles Woodmason, Anglican Itinerant.* Richard J. Hooker, editor. Chapel Hill: University of North Carolina Press, 1953.

Worcester, Elwood. *The Religious Opinions of John Locke.* Geneva: Humphrey Press, 1889.

Young, Alexander. *Chronicles of the Pilgrim Fathers.* Boston: Charles C. Little and James Brown, 1844.

Youngs, J. William. *The Congregationalists: A History.* Greenwood: Greenwood, 1998.

INDEX

READING GROUP GUIDE

This reading group guide for *Forged in Faith* includes an introduction, discussion questions, and ideas for enhancing your book club. The suggested questions are intended to help your reading group find new and interesting angles and topics for your discussion. We hope that these ideas will enrich your conversation and increase your enjoyment of the book.

INTRODUCTION

In a series of vignettes featuring a who's who of America's Founding Fathers, Rod Gragg sets out to illustrate the influence Judeo-Christian values had on the forging of our nation. From the founding of Jamestown in 1607 up until the signing of the Declaration of Independence in 1776, Gragg weaves biographical profiles with historical narrative, expertly giving the reader a bird's-eye view of the developing colonies before swooping closer and leading us through the great moments in American history.

Forged in Faith allows readers to look at a familiar story through a new lens. Readers get to know Samuel Adams as the "Last Puritan," a moniker given to him because of his strict faith, experience William Penn's "Holy Experiment" that ends up becoming the state of Pennsylvania, and decide whether they would have been a "New Light" or "Old Light" during The Great Awakening of the mid-eighteenth century. Gragg is an able and eager guide through the annals of history, retracing the acts of faith and moments of humility demonstrating that America was, in fact, *Forged in Faith*.

TOPICS AND QUESTIONS FOR DISCUSSION

1. In the introduction, Gragg writes, "As the American national consensus shifts from a traditional, God-centered worldview to a secular, man-centered philosophy, perspectives and priorities change" (p. 6). Do you agree that America is currently shifting to a secular philosophy rather than God-centered worldview? What are some examples that this shift is occurring?

2. Do you think the first of America's colonies, Jamestown, lived up to its billing as the New Jerusalem? In what ways did Sir Thomas Gates and Sir Thomas Dale help the sustained success of Virginia?

3. "If any does not work, neither should he eat" (p. 34). In the Plymouth settlement, we see an example of a biblical maxim being used in early government. Do you think that all Bible-based laws used in early America were inherently moral?

4. How has the connotation of the word *pilgrim* changed since the early seventeenth-century settlers first arrived in America? Do you think of them as "the embodiment of all that was best in humankind," as Professor Clarence Ver Steeg suggests would have been the popular view prior to the twentieth century (p. 52)?

5. According to Gragg in chapter 6, under the guidance of Roger Williams, Rhode Island became the first American colony to offer its people full religious liberty. This simply meant that there would be no government-endorsed religious denomination. Why do you think it took nearly forty years for this to happen in a nation founded by religious separatists?

6. William Penn also adopted the notion of religious freedom in his colony of Pennsylvania, partly to allow a place for his fellow Quakers to thrive. Soon, however, Gragg notes that they were outnumbered and became a religious minority. Is there danger in allowing freedom of religion in a developing country where there are multiple branches of one theology? If there was any doubt that their own branch of the faith would have remained predominant, do you think religious freedom would have been promoted so readily?

7. Do you see the creation of America as a reaction against the Church of England or as a unification of like-minded believers following their calling? Would a land of religious freedom eventually have become a reality even without dissent?

8. In chapter 8, Gragg shows excerpts from documents from each of the thirteen colonies, and notes that all were constructed on the pillars of faith and freedom. Do you think it would have been possible for one of the colonies to ignore the notion of faith and still have survived?

9. During the Great Awakening, the theologically liberal Christians became known as the Old Lights and the more conservative "new birth" Christians as the New Lights. Discuss the differences between the Old Lights and New Lights. Why did the split occur? Can you still see any lingering effects of this differentiation today?

10. What do you make of Sam Adams's assertion that "We must obey God rather than men" (p. 141)? Was it arrogant or humble? Do you think the British also felt that they were obeying God?

11. In contrast to his cousin Sam, John Adams's faith came accompanied with an "independence of thought" (p. 150), according to biographer David McCullough. Both were evident in his politics. What relationship do you think faith and independent thinking should have? Even though our historical documents were forged in faith, were they also influenced by political realities?

12. Thomas Jefferson was perhaps the Founding Father most conflicted in his faith, as demonstrated by his creation of the Jeffersonian Bible and his dabbles in Unitarianism and deism. Ultimately, however, he condemned critics of Christianity. If Jefferson had ultimately rejected Christianity, do you think he still would have played a big role in the shaping of American history?

ENHANCE YOUR BOOK CLUB

1. There are a number of historic sermons quoted in the book. Sermons make up a large part of the extant literature we have from that time in American history, and tell us a lot about the values and priorities of the people in the congregations. Look up a few of these sermons and read them aloud in your book club. They are available on the web, or in many compendiums of early American literature. There are also great books devoted to the subject, such as *American Sermons* edited by Michael Warner. Some sermons referenced in the book include: "An Oration on the Beauties of Liberties" by John Allen, "Sinners in the Hands of an Angry God" by Jonathan Edwards, and "The American Vine" by Jacob Duche.

2. The first Great Awakening in American history helped lay the foundation of the political and religious climate for many of our laws, but it was not the only period of religious transformation in America dubbed a Great Awakening. There have been three others since, the second occurring from 1790 to 1840, the third from 1850 to 1900, and the fourth from roughly 1960 to 1980. You can learn about these other periods in American religious history in books, such as *Awash in a Sea of Faith: Christianizing the American People* by Jon Butler.

Do you think America is currently going through a fifth Great Awakening?

How would we know if we were? How do the different Great Awakenings compare to each other?

3. In chapter 15, Gragg writes about what must have been a great moment in American history: when Thomas Jefferson, Benjamin Franklin, and John Adams were tasked with designing a national seal for the United States. We all know what the result was, but who knew that Franklin favored an image of Moses parting the Red Sea or that Jefferson championed "the children of Israel in the wilderness led by a cloud by day and a pillar [of fire] by night" (p. 184)?

Break into groups within your book club and come up with your own designs for America's national seal. Try to put yourself into the mind-set of Franklin, Adams, and Jefferson and the American ethos at the time. Would it have religious undertones, perhaps depicting a scene from the Bible? What would your national motto be?